21ST CENTU

INDEPENDENT LIVING AND CCRCs

Survival, Success & Profitability Strategies for Not-for-Profit Sponsors and For-Profit Owner/Operators

Jim Moore

Independent Living and CCRCs
Survival, Success & Profitability Strategies for Not-For-Profit Sponsors and For-Profit Owner/Operators

First Printing, August, 2009

Westridge Publishing www.westridgepublishing.com
Fort Worth, Texas

 $60.00

Library of Congress Card Number: 2007942432

ISBN: 978-1-893405-03-5

ALSO BY JIM MOORE

Senior Housing – Co-Author
A Development & Management Handbook

Assisted Living – 1996
Pure & Simple Development and Operating Strategies

Assisted Living 2000
Practical Strategies for the Next Millennium . . . How to Survive and Succeed in This Large, But Complex Market

Senior Housing & Assisted Living
The Contemporary Long Term Care Monthly Column Series – 1991 to 2001

Assisted Living Strategies for Changing Markets - 2001
How For-Profits and Not-For-Profits Can Still Prosper While Serving Seniors

Senior Living Special Issue Briefs
- ***Management Companies & Fees – 2005, 2006, 2009***
- ***How to Successfully Challenge Common Misconceptions About the Cost of Independent Living – 2007***

Finance Talk Columns
- ***McKnight's Assisted Living***

Syndicated State Association Monthly Newsletters

Monthly Broadcast Email Newsletters for Not-For-Profit Sponsors and For-Profit Owner/Operators

TABLE OF CONTENTS

SECTION TWO - Design and Development Issues and Strategies

SECTION THREE - Capital Improvement Strategies

SECTION FOUR - Capital Costs, Operating Expenses and Operations Strategies

SECTION FIVE - Senior Consumer Finances

SECTION SIX - Pricing Strategies

SECTION SEVEN – A Look Into The Future

Appendices

Index

LIST OF FIGURES

SECTION ONE - Strategic Overview and Market Positioning

FIGURE

SECTION TWO - Design and Development Issues and Strategies

SECTION THREE - Capital Improvement Strategies

SECTION FOUR - Capital Costs, Operating Expenses and Financial Strategies

SECTION FIVE - Senior Consumer Finances

SECTION SIX – Pricing Strategies

SECTION SEVEN – A Look Into The Future

Appendices

INTRODUCTION – STRATEGIC OVERVIEW

As this book goes to press in July, 2009, we are experiencing the most significant economic recession since the Great Depression of 1929. While the senior living industry fundamentals are basically sound (supply-demand balance, etc.), the current recession is experiencing 7+ percent unemployment, a credit crisis, depressed home sales, significant consumer savings/investment portfolio losses and low consumer confidence.

The economic recession recovery time could be extensive. There will be a number of external economic factors that will continue to impact the current senior living market. The existing high unemployment rate will likely prevail for several quarters. Normal employment levels will likely take substantial time to fully recover. Many companies may not – in the intermediate run – return to their previous employment levels even after a reasonable economic recovery. Consumer spending and the availability of consumer and business credit will likely involve more cautious and conservative lender decisions in the future. This could have a modest, but not serious impact on the demand for senior housing in the short-run.

As a result, there will be some *delayed demand* and absorption for senior living units. However, this delayed demand should result in a relatively strong upside once the housing market stabilizes, the credit markets become more liquid and investment portfolios recover from current losses.

What does all this mean? Well for one thing, the margin for performance error is narrowing considerably. However, the opportunity for realizing significant organic growth and upside potential within the existing properties is huge. Striking a delicate balance in dealing with all of these variables is what this book is all about.

This book consists of 50 chapters. Yet, no single book can cover everything you need to know about CCRCs and independent living. I've tried to address the most relevant issues facing our industry both today and over at least the next five years. You will receive leading edge information in industry trends, strategies, tactics, benchmarks and rules of thumb along with future market place impacts. I present pure and simple winning strategies and money making ideas – communicated with sophisticated simplicity. Real world problems are identified and cost-effective, practical solutions are provided.

Throughout this book, I have essentially profiled a typical 150 unit independent living community and a CCRC; using detailed industry comparables, benchmarks and financial ratios that are believed representative of existing projects in approximately 75 percent of the U.S. markets in the 2009 time frame. Financial metrics and benchmarks are presented in 2009 dollars and using the prevailing capitalization and interest rates of this time period.

In all my books, the chapters and table of contents are structured and sequenced as a series of stand-alone, relevant senior living issues and strategies. I've written each chapter so that you can benefit from "random access". By that I mean you can scan the detailed table of contents and jump to the particular chapter addressing the issue of interest to you on any given day. I've also tried to strike a delicate balance between leading edge ideas and theories combined with proven experience and trends observed consistently in the marketplace. Each chapter ends with a sobering, but necessary *"Call to Action."*

These observations are the culmination of a 35 year odyssey where I've worked in over 750 markets in 49 states and over 40 international locations. I've travelled over 6.5 million air miles frequently working on an average of two to three senior housing markets a week. As I become an "age and income-qualified senior," I still love what I do. During my work, I've lived briefly in over 130 senior living communities in an attempt to get as close as possible to the residents and the front-line staff; observing the day-to-day operations while visiting the local competition.

A word of caution – each individual project in each market is unique; the quantitative examples used in this book should be used with caution and for guidance purposes; they must be appropriately adjusted for each individual, unique situation.

As is the case in my previous senior living books, I've tried to focus the content for two important audiences. For the experienced senior housing professional and their staff, this book can be useful as a checklist of appropriate strategies and initiatives. However, for those who are new to our industry, it can act as a strategic planning handbook – in many cases offering a step-by-step process. I wish you much success in your endeavors to better serve seniors and their families.

ACKNOWLEDGMENTS

This book reflects the consolidated experience and input of literally thousands of professionals, industry colleagues and senior consumers. In this ***Independent Living and CCRC*** book, and as an industry consultant, one of my roles was to act as a facilitator; translating their collective knowledge and experience into a usable format. I felt it necessary and appropriate to repeat the following statement in each of my books. I am deeply indebted to the professional staffs at hundreds of senior living communities that have taken valuable time from their very busy schedules to allow me to both help them and to expand my base of knowledge and experience. I have tremendous respect for these professionals who provide endless love, care and patience to their residents; much of it accomplished in a time sensitive, stressful environment.

Hundreds of clients, sponsors and owner/operators allowed me into their communities and boardrooms to exchange strategic ideas. Industry colleagues openly shared their ideas, experiences and strategies.

As with past books, my professional team at MDS played a significant role in creating this book. Each professional - in their own way - kept me focused and on target. I would especially like to thank Jane Barker for proofing and editing, Jeff Moore and Roy Barker for extensive fact-checking and technical consultation. Kim Jimenez performed manuscript editing and proofing; she also heads our book publishing company, *Westridge Publishing,* which is a wholly-owned subsidiary of Moore Diversified Services, Inc.

I'm especially indebted to Sue Bregenzer, who as MDS' Business Manager, has always found the time to provide enormous assistance in coordinating my columns for the past 25 years and producing the manuscript for this book during one of the busiest periods of our company's 38-year history.

Finally, my long days and busy travel schedule were made much easier because of the understanding, support and patience of my wife Gerry.

SECTION ONE

Strategic Overview

And

Market Positioning

CHAPTER 1

INDEPENDENT LIVING & CCRCs RECEIVE RENEWED FOCUS

The Sleeping Giants are Clearly Waking Up

In the late 1990s, some industry observers wondered whether Continuing Care Retirement Communities (CCRCs) would become the dinosaurs of senior living or the primary focus of just not-for-profit sponsors. CCRCs – typically campuses offering independent living, assisted living and, frequently, skilled nursing have been around for a long time. When the senior living industry hype quickly spread from Main Street to Wall Street and back to Main Street in the late 1990's, CCRCs had taken a back seat to the proliferation of assisted living. CCRCs had to prove themselves worthy of growing market share all over again.

Today, trends indicate that CCRCs and independent living communities are clearly alive and well. Let's look at their strong points.

1. CCRCs are experiencing a mature life cycle and are staying ahead of the learning curve. Experience is a major advantage for CCRCs and independent living. That's because they have had more time to respond to and master a number of major industry challenges; essentially moving up the industry learning curve. Assisted living is still in the middle stages of its life cycle. For example, assisted living operators are struggling to extend the average length of stay of their residents by providing increasing levels of specialized care, stabilizing operations and realizing acceptable operating profit margins. Many assisted living operators were surprised when they realized that annual resident turnover approached 50 percent or more. Independent living typically experiences an average annual turnover of 15 to 23 percent. Full scope CCRCs extend the stay of their residents by providing assistance in living services in independent living residences, dedicated assisted living sections, skilled nursing and, in some instances, formal home health services. Hence, the average length of stay in a CCRC is much longer and marketing stability is higher.

2. Independent living with assisted living "neighborhoods" and CCRCs are market-responsive – focusing on the consumer's complete continuum of needs. Some industry analysts categorize independent living as being desire-driven, while assisted living is clearly need-driven. While there may be some basis for this broad characterization, detailed resident interviews, focus groups and current resident profiles indicate that many seniors who move into independent living do so only after experiencing a health related life event that results in a "wake-up call."

In fact, CCRCs may be even more appealing to seniors who are planning more than one step ahead. For example, while most freestanding assisted living facilities must refer residents elsewhere when they need permanent skilled nursing care, full scope CCRCs can usually accommodate such residents over their entire remaining life. Many seniors, their spouses and their families like the idea that they won't have to move again, even if they eventually need 24-hour skilled nursing care.

3. CCRCs offer control of a comprehensive referral pipeline. Freestanding assisted living operators are realizing that their traditional referral patterns can be unpredictable and can change dramatically due to external circumstances beyond their control. Many are working hard at strategic initiatives in an attempt to control at least a portion of their referral pipeline. A well managed, comprehensive CCRC campus controls most of its own referral pipeline, since many residents eventually transition from independent to assisted living; with some residents actually transferring to on-campus skilled nursing or special purpose Alzheimer's/dementia living arrangements.

4. CCRC entry fee pricing is expanding and becoming more market-responsive. Where else in the world can a sponsor or owner/operator get an interest free loan of several hundred thousand dollars per unit? Properly structured, entry fee pricing can be a win/win situation for both the consumer and the sponsor. Entry fees can also reduce the concern of higher, ongoing monthly service fees. Chapter 42 addresses this important issue in detail.

5. The life care concept is growing. Properly structured life care can bring sound financial planning and peace of mind to the senior consumer. But it can be a risky business for the sponsor and owner/operator who does not have an actuarially sound pricing and financial plan.

With advantages like these, the fundamental position of CCRCs should remain strong. As this book goes to press in August, 2009, stabilized occupancies for independent living and CCRCs are 5 to 8 percent higher (90 percent or greater) than industry averages for stabilized assisted living communities (approximately 86 percent). In fact, many independent living and continuing care retirement communities report essentially 100 percent occupancy on a revenue basis, since they turn vacated units around for new owner occupancy within 30 days while retaining the original resident's initial entry fee deposit if they move on to assisted living or nursing.

Call to Action

Taking these facts and trends literally, one might ask, "***Can it get any better than this?***" The answer is clearly yes. However, there are a number of challenges and opportunities on the horizon and, for independent living and CCRCs, the future is clearly not what it used to be! That's what this book is all about. It was written to specifically assist sponsors and operators to benefit from these opportunities while addressing some significant challenges.

CHAPTER 2

CHALLENGES AND OPPORTUNITIES

The Future of Independent Living and CCRCs is Not What it Used To Be

The successful CCRCs of the future will not be sleeping giants, they will be vibrant, *progressive communities of choice.* These communities will succeed by effectively serving seniors while redefining the state-of-the-art of senior living. Read on – I hope this book will assist you in providing the community of choice in your market area!

Ten Challenging Issues and Trends

I have identified 10 challenging trends that independent living and CCRC sponsors and owner/operators will face with increasing frequency in the future. These 10 challenges are outlined in Figure 2-1. Throughout this book you will find practical and creative ways to address each challenge. Refer to this book on any given day as you attempt to define and attack a particular challenge. Start by using Figure 2-1 as a punch list of issues you must resolve in order to become a market-responsive community of choice.

FIGURE 2-1
TEN CHALLENGING TRENDS FACING INDEPENDENT LIVING COMMUNITIES AND CCRC SPONSORS AND OPERATORS TODAY

1. **Many campuses have yet to effectively complete the continuum – some have:**
    - Independent living only
    - Independent living and assisted living but also plan to add nursing
    - Not yet specifically addressed Alzheimer's/dementia
2. **Aging physical plants:**
    - Some of today's designs are not state-of-the-art or fully market-responsive
    - Physical plant retrofit and improvement is a mandatory initiative for many campuses
    - Deferred maintenance will require capital investment plans to be reset and expanded
3. **Residents aging in place:**
    - The negative effects of providing excessive assistance in living (AIL) to residents in independent living units
    - Average entry age is increasing and converging with the average age of the entire resident population
    - Many independent living communities are turning into a "naturally occurring assisted living community"
4. **Cost structures have drifted out of control resulting in marginal to unacceptable operating profit margins.**
5. **Current pricing frequently needs to be sharpened or completely revamped.**
6. **Life care contracts developed as strategies of the past may not be actuarially sound or market-responsive in the future.**
7. **New innovative competitors may be responding better to:**
    - Product
    - Price
    - Services
    - Value
    - Choice
8. **Sales and marketing must transition from "order taking" (acceptable in the past) to carefully planned and executed proactive sales and marketing strategies.**
9. **The psychographics and "birthmarks" of today's prospect for senior living have changed considerably.**
10. **Communities must pursue a strategy of becoming a *community of choice* – rather than just another price-sensitive *commodity.***

Moore Diversified Services, Inc.

Occupancy, Re-Sale and Cash Flow Dynamics

Full continuum CCRCs have traditionally been within the domain of the not-for-profit business sector. But, in recent years, many for-profit owner/operators have developed a number of comprehensive CCRCs. Some involve the ultimate life care commitment, which is characterized as Type 'A' life care. This pricing structure essentially allows the resident to continue to pay independent living-type monthly costs regardless of whether the person eventually resides in independent living, assisted living or the nursing facility on the CCRC campus. Type 'A' life care relies heavily on the significant one-time initial entry fee charged to fund this pre-paid health benefit.

For CCRCs, this entry fee poses a tough balancing act between managing price sensitivity and occupancy. The relatively high and largely refundable upfront entrance fees charged by many CCRCs have been characterized by some as an ideal and unique source of interest-free loans. These funds are typically used to build cash reserves, fund pre-paid health benefits and to reduce large portions of new construction loans. In addition, some sponsors and owner/operators depend heavily on the cash flow from ongoing entrance fees to fund a portion of the normal operating expenses. By the way, this is not a good policy. It's true that this cash flow source is ongoing in that it involves the net cash gain of unit turnover. But the monthly cash actually realized can experience wide variations.

Here's how it works: After a unit is re-sold, a portion of the new entry fee cash is used to fulfill a refund obligation to the previous resident or the deceased resident's estate. This means that when a resident either dies or moves off the campus, the entry fees can have relatively high refundability obligations as a contractual requirement.

The unit is typically re-sold at a higher entry fee than the initial sale; frequently resulting in a substantial net cash gain on the sale even after refunds to the resident or their estate. Some operators have become very accustomed to these positive cash flow trends. In fact, some actually ***depend*** upon resident turnover to make their monthly income statement work. This all works well as long as two things happen:

1. The turnover exists (which is largely predictable)
2. The unit is quickly re-sold

The re-sale of entry fees will become a bigger issue, especially as markets become more complex and sales and marketing challenges increase. The financial impact of a vacant independent living unit within a CCRC can be very significant. There is, for example, the vacant unit's opportunity cost from lost monthly service fees that impact the operating statement and operating profit margins. Refer to Chapter 31 for more details. And there could also be a significant amount of lost or delayed cash flow from the net gain on entry fee re-sale due to slowing occupancy and the depressed housing market. Delayed re-sales can also strain the patience of those waiting for you to fulfill your contractual refund obligation.

In general, the senior living industry - and CCRCs, in particular - are entering a changing competitive arena. Active adult housing and service-free senior apartments are surprising many with their success when competing for senior living market share. Some senior consumers have learned that they can delay the traditional entry into a CCRC continuum – bypassing independent living and accessing freestanding assisted living – when their needs intensify. This is becoming a predominant trend that must certainly be tracked very carefully in the future.

High stabilized occupancies are critical for all types of senior living communities, especially CCRCs. That's because most of the incremental bottom line profit flows when occupancies exceed 90 percent. With CCRCs, operating cash flow is enhanced further by the significant cash derived from the timely re-sale of vacated units. Conversely, units that stay vacant for an excessive amount of time can represent a significant cash drain.

Senior living has always been characterized by informed observers as a very complex business model involving health care (sometimes health care <u>insurance</u>), hospitality, food service, housekeeping, social services and real estate, etc. CCRCs have significant positive and negative cash flow swings which further complicate this business model. Properly operated and marketed, CCRCs reflect an excellent senior living product, service and business model.

The Need for Innovative and Market-Responsive CCRC Pricing

Five Key Unrealized Opportunities

Figure 2-2 provides a "punch list" for success. You'll note that I urge you to review the past with 20/20 hindsight but, look to the future with a more entrepreneurial vision. Again, there are specific chapters in the book that will provide guidance for practical future strategies.

CCRCs have also learned some important financial lessons. For example, upfront entry fees work well in many markets, and many owners and sponsors have learned how to lower financial risk for largely unpredictable future health care costs. To accommodate seniors who want to preserve capital and leave a legacy, many CCRCs now offer highly refundable entrance fees. Others offer a pricing option of paying a lower upfront fee (for the same unit). The tradeoff is that refundability obligation declines by 1.5 to 2.0 percent per month. This pricing strategy accommodates those seniors who either:

1. Want the same unit but have a smaller asset base
2. Those who are not concerned about leaving a substantial estate to their heirs

For more details, see Chapter 6.

Call to Action

It's time to move to the next generation of senior housing. Future chapters will clearly articulate how the senior consumer is changing. We must also change. Yesterday's product, market positioning and operations philosophy may not work successfully in the future.

Consider the following:

1. How will the 10 trends in Figure 2-1 impact your community?
2. Review Figure 2-2, your punch list for success. Are you really prepared to experience success in the future?

With each chapter, ask yourself this question, *"should I act now or wait (procrastinate)?"* Read on – I hope to help you provide a blueprint for the future.

FIGURE 2-2
REVIEW THE PAST WITH 20/20 HINDSIGHT . . . BUT LOOK TO THE FUTURE WITH AN ENTREPRENEURIAL VISION

1. **This is a time for doing a better job of operating existing senior living communities.**
2. **There is a need and a tremendous opportunity to focus on at least five fundamentals:**
    - Sharpened and zero-based operations
    - Offering a high value, market-response product and service delivery system
    - Pricing that covers costs and demonstrates affordability, value and competitiveness
    - Recognizing the subtly changing psychographics of tomorrow's senior consumer
    - Focusing on *individualized* quality of life
3. **Existing owner/operators and sponsors have a tremendous opportunity (and a responsibility) to optimize operations for the various stakeholders:**
    - Owners/operators/sponsors
    - The residents and their families
    - Lenders and investors
4. **Capitalize on existing barriers to entry. Newcomers into the market will face the development and construction costs of today and tomorrow:**
    - Yet pricing may have to be competitive with many of the existing well-conceived communities

      Unless . . .
    - The provider can offer a higher value community
5. **Product, price, value and choice will be top market-responsiveness initiatives in the future.**

   Benefit from 20/20 hindsight . . . but plan for the future with an entrepreneurial vision.

Moore Diversified Services, Inc.

CHAPTER 3

THE COMPLEX SENIOR LIVING CONTINUUM

The Challenges and Opportunities of Overlapping Options

The Total Continuum of Senior Living and Health Care

There are two major forces at work shaping senior living options and impacting the "continuum of care." First, the *business sector* is focused on finding more efficient ways to expand and deliver services. Meanwhile, the *consumer market* is demanding quality, value, ambience, choice and affordability. These forces are generally interrelated, but sometimes in conflict.

Senior consumers are being offered a more complex senior care continuum as more comprehensive living arrangements, levels of care and ancillary services (home health, hospice, etc.) are emerging on senior living campuses. Ultimately, this means more competition for independent living and an increasingly complex business model. These more comprehensive living arrangements and care options include:

1. **Assisted living.** Communities are getting better and better at offering the residential/social model of assisted living. Dementia and Alzheimer's care units are more sophisticated than ever, resulting in stiff competition for conventional independent living.

2. **Community-based services.** Rehabilitation and home health care are among the community-based competitors becoming more sophisticated.

3. **Active adult housing.** Active adult housing and service-free senior apartments are frequently competing for the same market share, previously the exclusive territory of independent living.

Two Ways to View the Continuum

Most people are aware of the long-term care continuum. But many are not aware that there are two ways to view this continuum. It all depends on your perspective:

1. **The Horizontal Continuum.** The consumer's perspective is illustrated in Figure 3-1. View the horizontal continuum from left to right as living and health care options that respond to increasing age and assistance in living needs.

2. **The Vertical Continuum.** The vertical continuum is the way business and managed care professionals view strategic product positioning (Figure 3-2). Instead of the hospital being an end point, it is a place to begin. I'll discuss this concept more in the pages that follow.

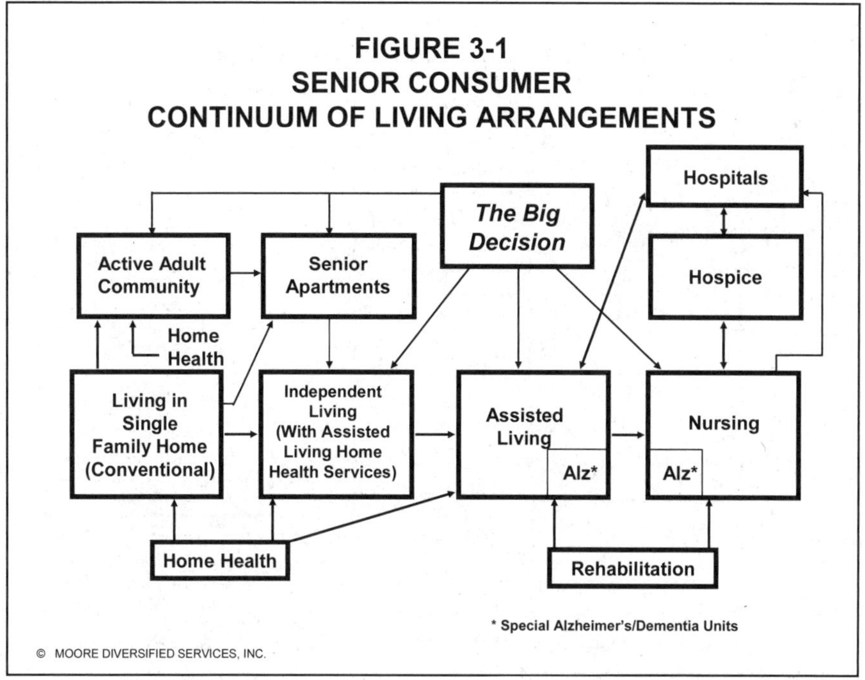

Current Trends Shift the Continuum

In the past, senior housing and health care professionals thought of the continuum that influenced their strategies as something that moved horizontally. The emphasis was almost exclusively on the senior consumer (Figure 3-1). At the left side was the senior's current home, while the other end was typically anchored by a hospital, the ultimate in health care service delivery, which has changed greatly. Managed care, industry consolidation and aggressive cost containment strategies ushered in a new *vertical* continuum (Figure 3-2).

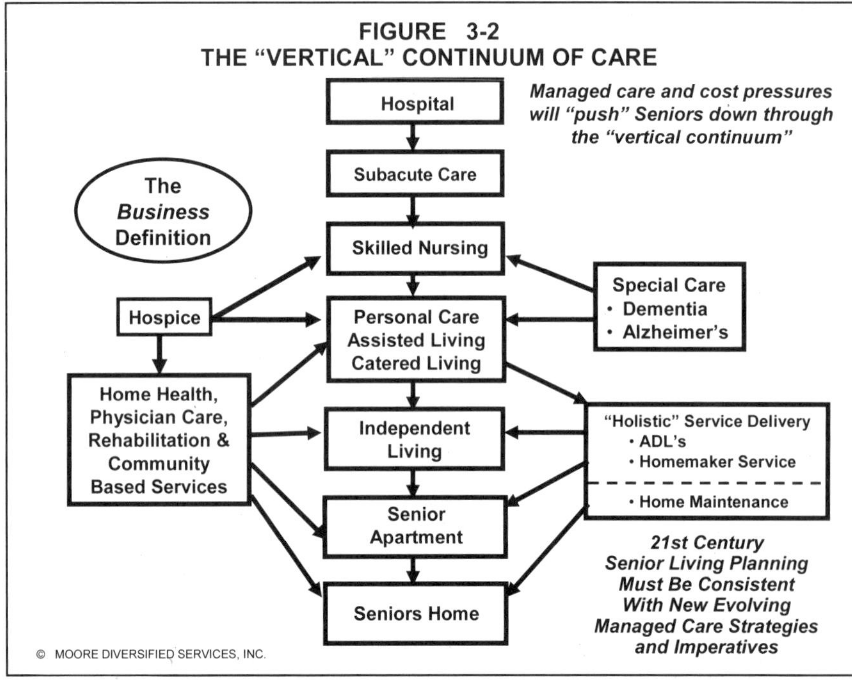

In the vertical structure, the hospital or other major health care provider is frequently the gateway to other health care services. After an acute care hospital stay, options include:

- Subacute care/rehabilitation
- Skilled nursing
- Special care/dementia units
- Assisted living
- Independent living
- Senior Apartments
- Active adult housing
- The senior's private home
- Home health
- Community-based services

Ultimately, this means that sponsors and owner/operators now have two moving targets on their radar screens to track – the *horizontal* continuum in the consumer market (the way consumers think) and the *vertical* continuum in the business/managed care sector (the way businesses operate).

There Are Four Assisted Living Market Models

A complex continuum could contain any of four fundamental assisted living market models:

1. Integrated with independent living
2. Freestanding assisted living community:
   - Possibly with Alzheimer's/dementia section
3. Assisted living integrated with skilled nursing
4. Assisted living as an integral part of a hospital campus

As you would expect, each model offers unique marketplace opportunities and challenges. Figure 3-3 illustrates these four models. For extensive details on the assisted living market sector, refer to my previous book, ***Assisted Living Strategies for Changing Markets, 2nd Edition*** (www.m-d-s.com).

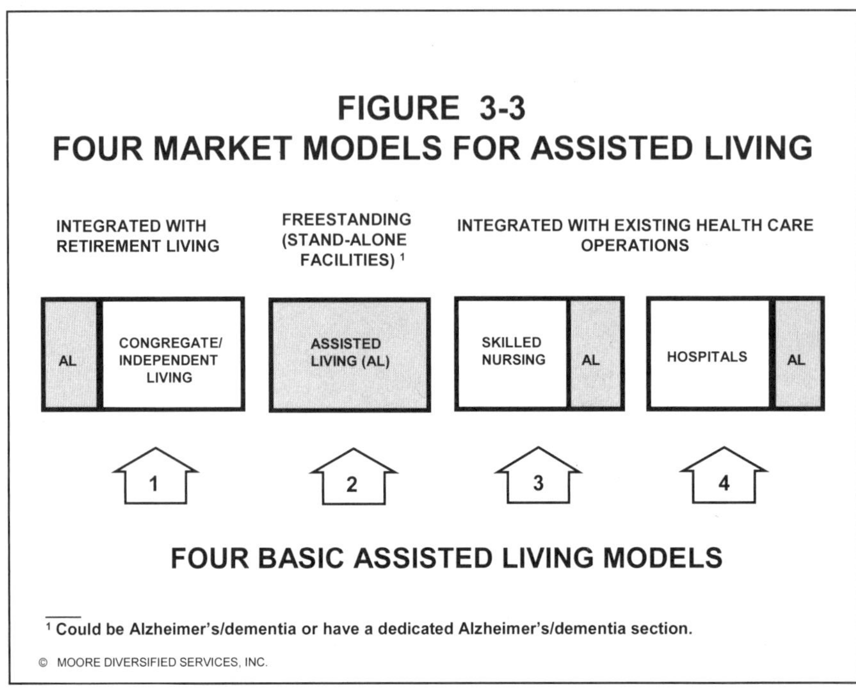

Actually a *fifth* market model may be emerging. I refer to it as the "holistic" approach to serving seniors. Some major sponsors and owner/operators now care for seniors in their private homes. In addition to delivering care, the relationship also serves as a marketing opportunity. When the senior is ready to move into senior housing, chances are the senior will stick with the company they know and trust. Operators also hope to leverage their existing resources by establishing an early home-based service delivery system.

History shows that, in U.S. competitive markets, senior living communities that offer either a full continuum of care (CCRCs), or at least a combination of independent and assisted living, have consistently performed better. History also shows that in the early 1990s, many owner/operators, particularly those in the for-profit sector, initially avoided getting involved in the day-to-day operations of assisted living. For the most part, they paid a heavy price for this procrastination. Adding assisted living services was one of the top three ways used to resuscitate a slow-moving or severely distressed senior living community which previously offered only independent living.

The Four Major Components of Senior Living

Senior living represents a very complex business model. There are at least four major components:

1. Real estate (bricks and mortar)
2. Hospitality services (shelter)
3. Restaurant (meal service)
4. Health care (assistance with ADLs[1])

The Consolidated Business Model

To be truly successful, you must address each of the four components as an ***individual*** business model. Let's call them "individual cost/profit centers." The four must be executed, however, in an integrated, ***seamless*** manner. This means that we should first optimize <u>each</u> cost/profit center and then operate them within the consolidated business model.

---

[1]Activities of daily living

"Carve-Outs" and Market Niches for Revenue Enhancement

With these four cost/profit centers in place and running efficiently, consider taking your organization to the next level by developing a market niche. A niche extends your senior living continuum. Specialized services can boost revenue while expanding the diversification of your overall continuum. These additional market niches include, but are not necessarily limited to, the following:

- Service-free senior apartments or for-sale condominiums
- Assisted living/residential care
- Special care (Alzheimer's/dementia):
  - In assisted living; residential/social model
  - In nursing; a medical model
- Assistance in living into independent living
- Wellness services
- Respite care
- Adult day care
- Rehabilitation
- Home health
- Community-based services
- Hospice

Many organizations struggle with deciding whether to outsource the above services or deliver them as an internal capability. It's a complicated decision involving many factors. There are two things of particular importance: expected resident acuity level and new business potential. A number of these market niches are covered in some detail in ***Assisted Living Strategies for Changing Markets, 2nd Edition*** (www.m-d-s.com).

Special Care Alzheimer's/Dementia "Carve-Outs"

Success in senior living is just like any business in that it demands one core skill: listen to your customers. If you are listening, you know that about 50 percent of those 85 or older have, at least, the early symptoms of Alzheimer's or some other form of dementia. Most sponsors and owner/operators must address dementia or they will experience unacceptable turnover.

These rapidly emerging trends of special care in Alzheimer's/dementia are being addressed by special purpose-built living options within traditional CCRCs. This is a good strategy, but be careful not to create complications or serious, confusing market sector overlaps within your continuum.

Alzheimer's/Dementia "Carve-Outs" Are Being Defined as Two Distinct, But Overlapping Market Models:

1. **Residential/Social Model:** Seniors with dementia but in *relatively good* physical health.

2. **Medical Model:** Seniors with dementia and *complex/deteriorating* health conditions.

These health related market niches can involve different service delivery models.

Two Basic Service Delivery Models

There are two basic service delivery models:

1. Service Provider. Typically, the owner/operator's permanent staff provides meals, housekeeping, laundry, activities, direct care ADL assistance, health monitoring and medical emergency response activities.

2. Home Health Agency Satellite. In this model, the owner/operator generally provides "shelter" type services and a licensed third-party home health agency focuses on medically-related services such as ADL assistance, case management and general health management.

Home Health and Senior Living

Home health is more than a stop along the senior living continuum. Home health services are part of a growing trend in senior living services. Many sponsors use licensed home health agencies to deliver care into both assisted living and independent living communities. Home health services are used because it helps solve state regulation dilemmas and Medicare licensing. Other operators use third-party home health services so they do not have to get into the complex health care business.

Providers also vary on how to charge for home health services. Some sponsors carefully bundle *both* shelter and care fees, while others separate the services. Those who separate the two charge ***their*** basic fees for shelter and services and pass on the ***separate*** home health bill to the consumer.

As a sponsor or owner/operator, you *must* create a seamless relationship. I've studied hundreds of communities and believe that success in offering home health services boils down to four key consumer-focused elements:

1. The resident and their family should feel like shelter and home health services are all one operation.

2. All services should be consistent, coordinated and seamless.

3. The total cost should come in as close as possible to a comprehensive "in-house" staffing model. Total operating expenses (per resident-day) must be competitive. We'll talk a lot about the resident-day concept in Chapters 24 and 25.

4. The bill the consumer receives should show consolidated charges whenever possible. Pricing must be understandable and competitive.

Finally, the consumer must always come first. Develop your home health partnering strategy from a consumer-driven perspective as depicted in Figure 3-4.

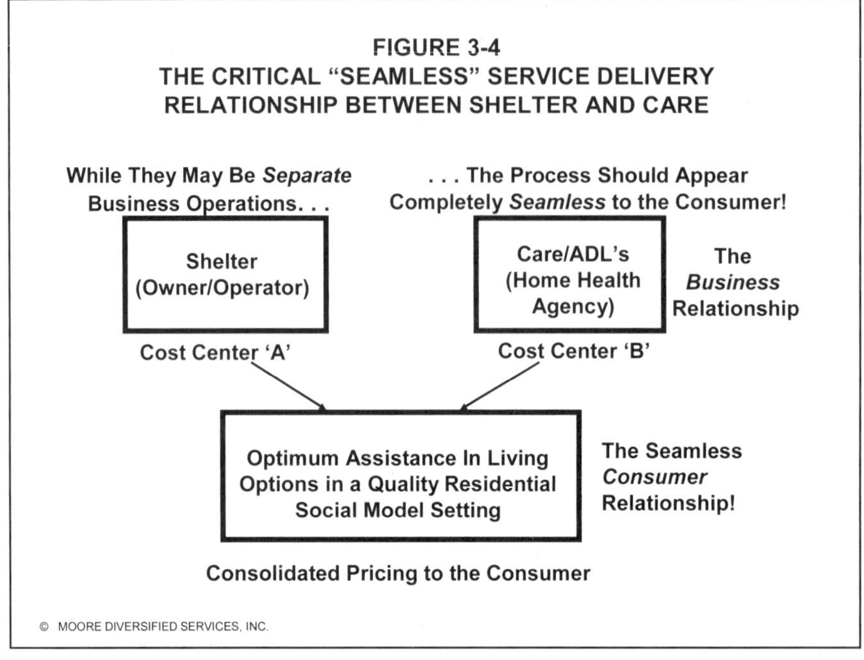

Market Sector Overlaps

If you found the continuums in Figures 3-1, 3-2 and 3-3 complex, here's something to consider: In real life, the continuum is even more complex. Lines get blurred and they overlap. For example, Figure 3-5 shows how assisted living clearly overlaps with the traditional business sectors of independent living and nursing. To understand this, look at Figure 3-5, and ask yourself three critical questions:

1. **When and how will I decide when a resident must transfer to another level of care within our continuum?**

2. **How will the resident and their family respond to this decision?**
3. **If I don't address this complex issue, will my independent living community rapidly become a "naturally occurring assisted living community?"**

Diagrams of the continuum seem pretty clear and understandable. But don't kid yourself. Most seniors don't really understand the continuum (at least it's not "top of mind") and most don't want to move through the continuum as their needs change. In the future, you will be hit with this dichotomy:

1. The Fair Housing Act might tell you that you're trying to move seniors *prematurely* through the continuum

   while . . .

2. State regulations and your staff may say you're not moving residents *soon enough!*

Chapters 8 and 9 address this complex aging issue in detail.

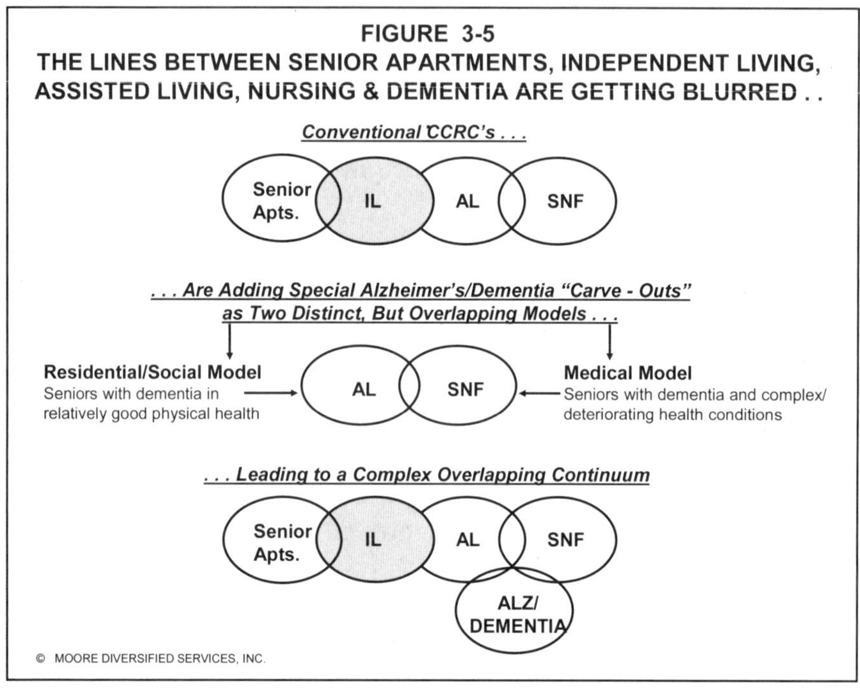

An equally important initiative is communicating more effectively with senior consumers and their adult children - including many who are geographically separated from their aging parents.

The future of senior living appears bright, but it won't be an easy ride. Increasing marketplace and regulatory turbulence will continue to challenge the industry. Astute operators will discover they can frequently expand their market penetration and enhance revenues and profitability by expanding their continuum.

Call to Action

Before moving on, consider the following:

- Review how future seniors will likely view the long-term care continuum.

- Do you plan to address the total life cycle and health care needs of the age 80+ senior consumer?

- Why or why not?

- If you offer home health services, would a family member agree that the relationship is really seamless?

The senior living continuum is not a simple block diagram or flow chart on one-dimensional paper. It must be multi-dimensional; representing the needs, complexities and confusion that seniors face late in life.

CHAPTER 4

THE CHANGING MINDSET OF THE SENIOR CONSUMER

Prospects and Residents are Demanding More as Their Value Perceptions Change

We all recognize the importance of *demographics* of seniors, but now we must also focus on their changing *psychographics.* In other words, the mindset of today's seniors.

A New Generation of Seniors is Emerging

Today's seniors will expect much more from our senior living communities. The typical prospect of the recent past is an 80- to 84-year-old senior who grew up during the Great Depression and World War II. The Depression produced a generation of fiscal conservatives. By the time of the Vietnam War and the rebellions of the 1960s, this group was in their 40s. They reached mid-life in the 1970s as members of the "***The Establishment***" and many were approaching at least early retirement planning during the boom/bust cycles of the 1980s and 1990s.

Companies and their high-powered advertising agencies have spent billions of dollars courting young and middle-aged consumers – the Baby Boomers. Yet very little has been done to truly understand and respond to the mindset of today's older senior consumer. In senior living, this has frequently resulted in misdirected or wasted marketing efforts – and many vacant units.

It's time to redouble your efforts at understanding today's age 75-plus consumers while becoming more savvy about how you market to them. Actually, quite a lot is known about the mindset of the senior consumer; the challenge is translating this knowledge into practical communication and marketing strategies. Take, for example, pricing. Most of us know we should sell *tangible value* before *price*. But, in our zeal to tell our story, we forget that the process involves three very important steps:

1. Truly understand the senior consumer mindset
2. Identify and correct common senior misconceptions (Chapters 5 and 6)
3. Deploy consumer-focused, market-driven positioning (Chapter 7)

Significant Birthmarks of Today's Seniors

First, realize that you are dealing with senior consumers who have experienced a number of life-changing events, let's call these ***significant birthmarks***. Figure 4-1 summarizes these birthmarks for some of today's 80-year-old seniors, the slightly younger Depression-era children and the oldest Baby Boomers. Let's focus on today's 80-year-old senior and his or her birthmarks:

FIGURE 4-1
BIRTHMARKS OF YOUR FUTURE RESIDENT

Year	Age	Major Life Event/Birthmark
1965	37	Possibly an active participant in University of Berkeley Vietnam Protests Or . . . Romped in the mud at Woodstock!
1975	47	Corporate Employee Convert
1985	57	Victim of Corporate Downsizing
1995	67	Fiercely Independent/Very Discriminating
2002	74	Savings rates at historic lows Stock market down over 23% (S&P 500 Index)
2009	81	*Your Resident in 2009 ???*

Will the resident of tomorrow accept your definition of today's status quo?

- ***The Depression Era (1929 to 1939).*** When I conduct senior focus groups, I always ask, ***"Does having lived through the Depression in any way affect your financial decision-making today?"*** The answer is always a resounding ***"yes."***

- ***World War II (1940-1945).*** GIs came home from the war, married, bought homes and had children in record numbers (the Boomers). These veterans were motivated to make up for lost time. After getting educated under the GI Bill, they built businesses, careers and personal savings. Building savings was usually a slow, but pragmatic, process.

- ***The "Gray Flannel Suit" Era (1946 – 1960).*** During this period, many men entered the corporate world prepared to spend their careers with one employer. They were generally "team players" – conforming, spending their time responding to the requirements of their employers as they worked through their careers.

- ***Vietnam Era (1960 – 1974).*** This troublesome period created large groups of disillusioned veterans and many "mavericks". A large portion of "the establishment" did not accept these nonconformists, which only triggered further rebellion against "the establishment".

- ***The Rebellions of the 1960s (1960 – 1970).*** This time period partially overlapped the Vietnam Era and created considerable opposition to global and local conditions and the general "status quo".

- ***Woodstock (1969).*** The Vietnam Era, the rebellions of the 1960s and Woodstock represented unforgettable birthmarks. In the 1960s, the age of today's 81-year-old senior was approximately age 33 to age 43. We must understand that their mindset was influenced by an entirely different set of conditions than the seniors who we currently know, those who have opted for senior living over the past 10 years.

- ***Economic Boom (1990 – 1999).*** During these very favorable financial times, today's 81-year-old senior was progressing from approximately age 63 to age 72. Things were going very well from a financial perspective. They felt very good about their financial future and security. They were comfortably planning for the advanced stages of retirement.

- ***High Tech Bubble Burst/Economic Recession (1999 – 2002).*** Just at the point when many seniors were making the big decision to move into senior living, most saw some of their financial savings devastated by low interest rates or plummeting stock market values (see Chapter 37 for more details). Many wondered if they could afford to permanently retire much less move into an "expensive" senior living community.

- ***Low Savings Rate/Lost Investments (2001 – 2009).*** In early 2009, interest rates on savings accounts hit 40-year lows. The stock market recovered somewhat in 2003. Most had modest gains in 2004 through 2007. However, in 2008, the market declined significantly and by mid-2008, a "bear market" (a 20 percent plus decline) was declared. Clearly most seniors still have a smaller equity portfolio in 2009 than they did in 2000.

In summary, an 81-year-old senior in 2009 was 7 in 1935 and 14 in 1942. The events they and their parents experienced in their early life molded the senior into a fiscal conservative, someone who is always thinking about and preparing for the next Great Depression. During mid-life, they became more outspoken and less likely to accept the status quo.

A Senior's Financial Life Cycle

The financial life cycle of today's senior involves three major phases:

- *In the early years*, they concentrated on raising and educating their children while starting to accumulate moderate but steadily increasing savings.

- *In midlife*, they optimized their lifestyle in a non-extravagant manner and started building a modest estate destined to be a future safety net and a legacy to their children.
- *In their later years*, they have focused on living the good life in a conservative way while working hard to sustain independence. Health concerns seem to surface almost daily for many seniors. But their concerns about health have more to do with avoiding a future financial catastrophe than their own mortality.

The Changing Paradigm

Today's 81-year-old widow could have protested during the Vietnam Era, participated in the rebellions of the 1960s and might possibly have romped in the mud at Woodstock! We can no longer simply say, ***"Welcome to our community and enjoy our offering of the status quo."***

Tomorrow's senior living marketing prospects are no longer "the usual prospects." They are raising the bar of expectations and will be much more articulate in expressing their wants and needs.

A word of caution: Don't get misled by the opinions expressed by your *existing* residents. These opinions may no longer necessarily reflect the changing mindset of your *future* residents.

It's also high time to focus on the little details that matter most to today's and tomorrow's seniors. For example, I can't tell you how many times I call into a senior living community and, when put on hold, hear the favorite rock music of the receptionist. What I should be hearing are tunes of the 1940s and the WWII era.

By the way, we're starting to see increased publicity regarding senior living for the Baby Boomers. Yes, the Boomers are aging, but no, they're not yet ready for senior living! In fact, the oldest Baby Boomer will be 63 in 2009 and it will be at least 2021 before that oldest Baby Boomer is age 75. However, the Boomers will continue to be a major influence on the decisions of loved ones considering CCRCs, independent living and, of course, assisted living.

Today's seniors also place a high priority on leaving their children a financial legacy. Although men were typically the breadwinners, women - in their very important supporting role of homemaker – developed a similarly conservative philosophy regarding personal finances.

Selling Choice and Perceived Value

Throughout life, seniors have made most purchase decisions by balancing affordability, choice and their perception of value. Due to a lifetime of financial conservatism, many seniors are now in a position to focus primarily on choice and value. In fact, many have been making value choices for the better part of their lives. They don't always opt for the lowest price commodity. Many buy Buicks and Cadillacs, for example – not Chevrolets. They dine at the nicer restaurants and buy brand name clothes from the better department stores – not necessarily Target or Sears. They also travel extensively.

The Price Sensitive Dilemma for Senior Living

Almost every major product and service aimed at seniors attempts to sell seniors on value, affordability and, where appropriate, quality of life. Yet, when many seniors face the most important decision of the rest of their life – where to live – it seems that we have not done a very good job showing them that senior housing is a good value.

Another challenge is to change the misconceptions that exist about senior housing. Chapters 5 and 6 deal with some significant senior misconceptions. Change will be subtle, but definite . . . kind of like the aging process we're all experiencing!

Call to Action

Before moving on, consider taking these steps:

- Sit with marketing and other key staff to discuss who you are really selling to. Does your marketing message match what today's seniors want and need to hear?

- List ways to modify your marketing message so that subtle changing "birthmarks" are taken into consideration.

The psychographics of the market are changing. Many of yesterday's marketing strategies and positioning will not work effectively in the world of tomorrow.

CHAPTER 5

MISCONCEPTIONS STIFLE SALES

Turning Deal-Breaking Sales Objections Into Win-Win Strategies

Let's face it, we don't always respond effectively to consumer misconceptions. We frequently fail to properly communicate with frustrated and ill-informed adult children. Misconceptions and lack of knowledge can slow down the decision-making process and leave room for sales objections. The challenge for sales and marketing professionals is to work through these objections.

Senior consumers evaluate senior living options with both concern and skepticism. As addressed in Chapter 4, growing up during the Great Depression has left today's seniors with permanent birthmarks that heavily influence their decisions.

Four Serious Misconceptions

If we want to sell to seniors, we must first understand that seniors come to us with misconceptions that impact their decision to move in. There are four serious misconceptions to be aware of:

1. **Cost of Living.** Most seniors underestimate their *current* cost of living. They think most senior living options are very expensive and not affordable. See Chapter 38 for some valuable details on how to address this complex issue.
2. **Inflation Concerns.** Seniors have an understandable concern about future inflation. They fear they will outlive their assets.

3. **Leaving a Financial Legacy.** Seniors are heavily focused on leaving a financial legacy to their children. They feel that living in senior housing could wipe out much of their net worth – assets accumulated over a lifetime of conservative financial planning.

4. **Health Care Cost Misconceptions.** Many seniors do not have a good understanding of their Medicare and Medicaid benefits as related to the cost of covering nursing care, making seniors unaware of how much they may realistically have to pay for future health care costs.

These misconceptions form a flawed and dangerous mindset. Some seniors think they are being prudent and conservative by delaying a decision to move into senior housing. In fact, their inaction could actually be more costly. Being unaware of the options available to control future health care costs can actually put seniors at risk to significantly deplete their assets. Senior living options typically are viewed as a financial burden or threat when they should actually be seen as a way to enhance a person's lifestyle, while at the same time introducing a prudent financial safety net.

With Many Seniors, "Misconception" is Their "Reality"

Here is a real world exchange between a mother and daughter:

"Kim, I appreciate your concern but, really, I'm just fine. Sure, I have an occasional 'spell,' but I can always rely on you and, if necessary, I'll call 911. That senior living brochure from

The Gardens at Westridge looks just like a glorified nursing home to me. Besides, I'm not ready yet, but when it's time, my Medicare program will cover all of the costs of a nursing home as long as I need it. If not, there's that other program called Medicaid which also provides coverage. And remember, we signed up for that Medigap program. Isn't Medigap like the long-term care insurance plans I'm starting to hear about on television?

"I don't know the total cost of a nursing home, but I'm sure it's all covered. The Gardens at Westridge will probably raise their prices as soon as I move in. Besides, there's no way that I could afford the $2,400 a month 'rent' that's in their brochure – my current cost of living is only about $700 a month. How in the world could I afford to pay that upfront fee? That would take most of my savings. I read so many bad things about places like The Gardens in the newspaper."

After listening patiently, Kim responds, ***"Mom, you're not really looking at this situation objectively. I, too, felt our situation was hopeless until I did some homework and discovered some surprisingly different results. Here's the bad news. Your Medicare covers only skilled nursing costs under very specific conditions and for an extremely limited time period. The Medicaid coverage would not apply unless you have used essentially all of your savings including the equity from the sale of your home. And I learned that your Medigap policy is <u>not</u> like long-term care insurance.***

"Now for some good news. You'll be moving into the independent living portion of what they call a 'Continuing Care

Retirement Community.' Many of us may eventually need nursing, but Mom, with your current income and assets, I've learned that we now have a better option.

"Remember, The Gardens at Westridge told us that they have increased their monthly fees by only about 4 percent per year since 2000. They reminded us that their cost inflation is not unlike the cost-of-living increases that we all experience with food, utilities, real estate taxes, insurance, etc. Mom, your cost of living is really not $700 a month. I looked at your monthly check stubs and was shocked to discover that when you factor in real estate taxes, home repairs, insurance premiums and other bills that you don't pay every month, it's really more like about $2,200 per month! I know you want to leave the house and your savings portfolio to us children – but, if we sold the home today and used some of the proceeds for the one-time entrance fee – while putting the rest of the proceeds into your savings account, you could afford to live at The Gardens at Westridge – and still leave most of your savings portfolio to us. And remember, at the end of your stay at The Gardens, they will refund 90 percent of the entrance fee. Mom, we only want what's best for you at this point in life.

"I also talked to the chairperson of the resident council at The Gardens. She told me that the press sometimes focuses on isolated cases and that the newspaper stories frequently do not match the true feelings of the majority of families and residents. The resident council member also said the press almost always misses a very important point: Seniors and their families want choice in the later stages of life!"

If there's anything unrealistic about the above scenario, it's the fact that a typical daughter may also have these same misconceptions and may not be armed with the kind of detailed, accurate information reflected in this example.

Deal-Killing Misconceptions

As senior living professionals, we have to anticipate and respond to customer misconceptions in the early stages of the sales and marketing process. With a more detailed game plan, we can substantially improve the performance and acceptance of senior living.

These misconceptions can stifle sales. We tend to celebrate the 3 percent of the market that moves into our community, but we fail to determine why the other 97 percent of prospects got away. Lost prospect surveys reveal some surprising but consistent results. Typical responses include:

1. ***"Your community was just beautiful, but it was too expensive, and I'm sure I could not afford it."***

2. ***"I liked everything I saw, but I worry that you will increase your pricing and I will outlive my assets."***

3. ***"Your monthly service fee seems unrealistically high. That's an awfully high rent payment."***

Keep in mind that these responses came from prospects who were previously determined to be ***asset and income qualified***.

These misconceptions present enormous obstacles for sales and marketing professionals. A successful response will require sophisticated and redoubled marketing efforts in the future. Sponsors, owner/operators, and most sales and marketing professionals pride themselves on organization and selling techniques, but very few truly understand how to get inside the minds of seniors. To succeed, you must help seniors make very important financial planning decisions.

Seven Steps to Professional Sales and Marketing Success

Here is an outline of seven strategies that will help you execute a sophisticated sales and marketing program:

1. Think about how you would advise your parents. Honestly answer the questions, ***"Could I sell my community to my parents?"*** and ***"Could I effectively sell against my own community?"*** The answers to these questions may be painful, but addressing them allows you to walk in the shoes of your senior prospects (or those of their adult children).

2. Establish value by stating, *"There's no free lunch."* Seniors will understand that statement, and they'll appreciate your honesty. Use the "no free lunch" philosophy to support your position of affordable cost and modest annual increases. Stress the high value that seniors will experience by living at your community.

3. Correct classical misconceptions early in the sales process. I've found that making the following point works wonders: ***"Seniors like yourself have told me that once they tally all of***

their current living expenses, they find that their current cost of living is much higher than their initial, top-of-mind estimate." This is a delicate way of saying that the prospect's cost of living estimate is probably erroneous and needs to be put in perspective before senior living pricing can be discussed. This technique shows value and helps avoid sticker shock.

4. Build value before discussing price. Price is the ***first*** thing seniors touring your community want to know - but it is the ***last*** thing you want to tell them. That's easier said than done, but one technique that frequently works is to say, ***"I know our prices are most important to you, Mrs. Barker. If I may first show you what we offer here at The Gardens at Westridge, we'll then discuss price in great detail. I'm confident you'll find the price to live here surprisingly affordable when compared with your current financial situation."***

5. Address senior's concern of outliving their assets. Explain cost of living and affordability to them like this, ***"If someone tells you that prices at a senior living community will never increase, they're being less than straightforward, or they really don't understand the business of serving seniors. I can tell you that here at The Gardens we can control inflation better than an individual living in one's own home. Our prices have increased only 3 to 4 percent a year since 1990."***

6. Put the senior's future financial threats in perspective. Say something like this, ***"In the past, nursing homes were among the only options for seniors. With nursing home costs typically ranging between $45,000 and $60,000 or higher per year, a senior's financial legacy to their children could easily disappear.***

While there are no absolute guarantees, senior campuses like ours can now provide a full spectrum of future care at lower costs. This allows us to provide a substantial safety net for our seniors, helping them avoid the most serious financial threat they would likely ever face."

7. Finally, deliver on a very important promise. Here's how to say it: ***"Mrs. Barker, if I could assure you that you can afford to live here at The Gardens for equal or less than your current cost of living, plus leave a major portion of your home equity and current savings portfolio as a financial legacy to your children, would you make the decision today to join our community? I want to further assure you that future increases in your monthly service fee will very likely be less than what you would experience in your own home."***

Using these and other strategies, you can clarify misconceptions and turn deal-breaking sales objections into win-win strategies for both you and the seniors you serve. Chapter 6 contains more details on these senior living pricing misconceptions and sales objections in a problem-solution format.

Call to Action

Before moving on, consider the following:

- Is your marketing staff really "getting inside the minds" of seniors on important issues?
- Is your sales and marketing staff helping seniors make financial planning decisions as part of the sales process?

- Which of the seven selling strategies addressed in this chapter still needs to be worked into your sales process?

Misconceptions are deal killers! We have an ethical and moral obligation to seniors and their families to honestly help them clarify financial misconceptions as they plan for the future.

CHAPTER 6

CONQUERING SENIORS' MISCONCEPTIONS ABOUT COST

Seniors Must Understand They Can Still Leave a Financial Legacy to Their Children

"Forget the warm and fuzzy talk, what does this place really cost?" That's what Mrs. Barker is thinking during your marketing tour. As I said in Chapter 5, that's because ***the first thing seniors want to know is the last thing we want to tell them.***

At age 75 or older, seniors must make some of the most difficult and important decisions of the rest of their lives. Understandably, many are looking for a way to delay this complex decision. Misconceptions and decision procrastination are the two most significant challenges for sales and marketing professionals to overcome.

Four mental roadblocks surface repeatedly as deal killers. Let's look at these four misconceptions, first addressed in Chapter 5. This time, however, I'll address them from a problem-solution perspective:

Problem #1: Cost of Living. In formal focus groups and informal discussions with thousands of seniors, I have consistently found that they lack a clear understanding of their current cost of living. Seniors typically forget the cost of real estate taxes, home repairs, insurance premiums, and other bills they don't pay every month when estimating their expenses. Some even underestimate bills that they do pay each month. It's not unusual for seniors with minimum annual incomes of $30,000 to $35,000 or more to initially estimate their current cost of living at between $1,000 and $1,200 a month. After some objective, non-leading and in-depth probing, many of these same seniors revise their estimates to between $1,800 to $2,200 per month. Chapter 38 deals with this challenging situation in great detail.

With these types of misconceptions, picture the sticker shock many seniors experience as your sales professional proudly announces what it costs to live at your community. Many seniors may think your community is very nice but clearly overpriced. Some feel they certainly could not afford to live there even if they wanted to.

Solution: ***Address these misconceptions during the early stages of the sales encounter.*** Most marketing brochures have a cost-of-living comparison sheet. These are good, but they are not enough. You first have to plant some seeds: **"Mrs. Barker, seniors like yourself who live in private homes tell us that their current cost of living is between $1,800 and $2,200 a month. Of course, some budgets are higher and some are lower. But you must factor in periodic expenses such as real estate taxes, insurance premiums, ongoing home maintenance and other important cost-of-living items."** This non-threatening dialogue can be very effective in tactfully correcting misconceptions and laying the foundation for selling value.

In Chapter 38, I provide a comparative cost-of-living analysis between senior living and living at home. I also show you how to present a senior's cost of living estimate in an easy to comprehend manner. You may find the results surprising and favorable.

Problem #2: Inflation Concerns. Many seniors worry that the service fee increases will be arbitrary and far exceed any inflation they would experience if they just stayed in their current homes.

Solution: ***Make sure the customer knows that your price increases are not arbitrary.*** Address them as "normal inflation." Explain that a senior living community manager faces the same types of cost increases for food, utilities, taxes, and so on, just as any homeowner. Also point out that a well-run community can curb inflation better than any ordinary consumers through increased purchasing power and operating economies. Bear in mind that what might appear to be nominal increases to you may present serious concerns for your residents. With initial service fees of $2,200 a month or $26,400/year, a 4 percent annual increase would mean Mrs. Barker's annual outlay would increase by almost $6,000 from $26,400 to over $32,000 over a five-year period.

Problem #3: Leaving a Financial Legacy. Leaving a legacy. Return of capital. Preservation of assets. These are the magic sound bites in market positioning for seniors. Most seniors are preoccupied with leaving a financial legacy to their children and grandchildren. In the process, they frequently underestimate the value of their existing pent-up home equity, although chances are it's considerable.

Solution: ***Make this consumer desire work for you.*** If you offer a market rate rental, your price positioning should be: ***"Mrs. Barker, we think you should maintain complete control of your valuable assets and manage them as you choose."*** Make sure Mrs. Barker understands that since your monthly rents are based on market-competitive rates, she will not likely deplete her savings portfolio due to arbitrary price increases. In fact, if she is a current homeowner, she will be putting her newly liquidated net home equity to work for her now and will still be able to leave most of it to her estate. Chapter 35 addresses the issue of whether a senior's home is an asset or an opportunity cost (actually it's both).

If your community charges an entry fee, consider offering one pricing option that is largely refundable (80 to 90 percent). Or try a lower entry fee with declining refundability for seniors with more modest assets, or for those without significant estate concerns.

Problem #4: Price-Value Perceptions. Seniors are typically far from understanding the value of the services your community offers. As one senior told me, ***"Heavens, I've never paid that much rent before."***

Solution: ***We are in a service-enriched, value-enhanced benefit-driven business.*** We have to communicate and sell uncomplicated, honest value. But that's easier said than done. We must sell a value package of *bundled benefits*, not *individual features*, or just price points.

The ultimate test of how well you have developed and positioned your pricing strategy was initially addressed in Chapter

5. It involves whether or not you can deliver on this promise: ***"Mrs. Barker, what if you could live here at the Gardens of Westridge for the same or less than your cost of living today - and still leave most of your current estate to your children? We can provide you with the kind of living arrangements and services that we've discussed for no more than your current cost of living."***

And if your pricing includes entry fees you might add, ***"The largely refundable initial entry fee that you pay now will likely be no more than the net proceeds realized from the sale of your home. So the entry fee can be paid by your net home sale proceeds. This means you can still leave most of your home sales proceeds and current savings portfolio to your estate."***

Before making your pitch, make sure you can back up your claims and promises. Residents should generally pay no more than 65 percent of their ***after-tax cash flow income*** for *independent* living monthly service fees, or about 80 percent for *assisted* living. There is evolving anecdotal evidence that a number of seniors are actually experiencing higher senior living spending ratios. Some may even be spending down their assets, and/or receiving financial assistance from their adult children. But, assuming normal and conservative industry standards, it takes a total annual income of approximately $50,000 (pre-tax) to cover a typical independent living monthly service fee of $2,400. Does that surprise you?

Let's look at the numbers:

- $2,400 per month x 12 = $28,800/year
- Only spend 65 percent on independent living monthly service fee: $\frac{\$28,800}{.65}$ = $44,310/year
- Must pay obligations in *after-tax* dollars[1]: $\frac{\$44,310}{.90}$ = $49,230/year

Spend-down is a possible option, but it must be approached with extreme caution.

As marketing senior living communities becomes more sophisticated and competitive, it is imperative that we understand both the ***perception*** and the ***reality*** of senior consumer affordability. Some owner/operators have been encouraged by recent anecdotal evidence indicating that many seniors are spending all of their available income on monthly service fees, and that some are even spending not just the interest but at least part of the principal in their savings portfolios. Don't count on those very aggressive spending patterns to justify a project that would otherwise have a marginal market response and less than optimal financial feasibility.

Chapter 38 offers some innovative new high technology ideas to solve some of the old classical financial planning challenges that have been discussed in this chapter.

---

[1] This example assumes a senior's average tax rate is 10%.

Call to Action

The ***"don't ask – don't tell era"*** regarding senior consumer finances is over! It's time to enter into frank, open and diplomatic financial discussions with your prospects. Most seniors really want to talk about financial details.

Before moving on, consider conducting training sessions on overcoming common misconceptions about the cost of senior living.

CHAPTER 7

ADVANCED MARKET POSITIONING PLATFORMS

Getting Inside the Minds of Seniors and Their Families

In spite of approximately 20 years of intensive advertising and public relations efforts, seniors and their families *still* know very little about senior living. It's true seniors think about their health every day, but it's not until there is a crisis that they – or their children – usually search for viable options. In senior living, that's termed a "wake-up call." Let's hope that many consider your community the most appropriate option to resolve their family dilemma. The reasons can be very simple – especially when effective market positioning strategies are deployed.

Market Positioning for Senior Living

CCRCs respond very effectively to the need-driven, health-related concerns of the senior. CCRCs are also a cost-effective and emotionally acceptable alternative for many adult children – caregivers faced with a growing family dilemma or crisis involving complex emotional and financial decisions. For both seniors and their adult children, I have a very simple but powerful senior living market positioning statement.

"Senior living communities provide a surprisingly affordable living alternative offering ambience, dignity and maximum independence for many seniors in their later stages of life."

Market positioning is an industry buzzword that has been around for 25 years. Most marketing professionals think they know what it means, however, marketers frequently ignore or misapply the critical strategies and tactics required to effectively position their community in the senior marketplace.

Positioning is not simply what one does to alter a product or service – it involves a pragmatic strategy for getting inside the minds of seniors in order to elicit a strong, favorable, and decisive response to what the senior living community offers. Most communities offer a reasonable match or attraction with respect to the needs of the senior marketplace, but this is where many marketing strategies stop. Operators across the United States are missing the mark. Frequently, this match is communicated almost exclusively in terms of *features* and *amenities*. It turns out that directly recognizable *benefits* and *affordability* are almost the only things that really count with most seniors.

Features vs. Benefits

One of the biggest traps marketers fell into in the 1980s and early 1990s was becoming preoccupied with their community's beautiful features and amenities. While these attributes may define the product in some arenas, they do not provide the necessary emotional link with the consumer. The success stories in the industry now are those astute owner/operators who are clearly selling benefits sharply focused on the true needs, emotions and established buying behavior of the senior. Some may dismiss these discussions of features versus benefits as merely a preoccupation with semantics, but rest assured that very expensive marketing campaigns can succeed or fail based on these subtle distinctions.

Features and amenities are largely a reflection of the sponsor's thinking and are typically situation-driven. The secret to success is communicating real *benefits* that reflect the pragmatic thinking and emotions of seniors – and that means being market-driven.

Structuring and implementing high-impact market positioning strategies accomplishes the following:

- Sharpens the prospect's perceptions by focusing on needs, emotions, and benefits.
- Motivates the prospect to seek and evaluate significant information.
- Eliminates fatal misconceptions.
- Addresses and counters common sales objections and accelerates the decision-making process.
- Clearly communicates a community's strengths (benefits) while effectively addressing weaknesses.
- Defines a specific *call to action* – what, specifically, do you want the prospect to do?

Benefit-driven senior living communities respond to the emotions and needs of seniors. Their messages get to the heart of the real issues. *Situation-driven* communities either miss the mark completely or, at the very least, avoid or delay decision making.

"Moore's Law" of market positioning goes something like this: ***If the staff has difficulty clearly explaining the benefit-driven attributes of the community among one another, there is no way the external marketplace will effectively get the message.*** Market positioning must be communicated using a memorable and distinctive message to seniors who are already being saturated by various media.

Turning Challenges Into Opportunities

Sales and marketing of seniors housing relies heavily on a positive outlook, but it is also very necessary to dwell on some sobering realities and challenges. Some of these challenges include:

- Most seniors really do not want to move out of their home full of love and memories.
- Seniors are typically not into buying a wide variety of material things.
- Many live with the permanent scar of the Great Depression and they are afraid of outliving or spending down their lifelong savings.
- Seniors will use discretionary income and assets to purchase positive experiences, security, and solutions to life's challenges – *as they perceive them.*
- A senior's primary motivation for opting for retirement communities is still very need-driven.

Failure to recognize these marketplace realities has led many expensive marketing programs astray – sometimes resulting in a stalled project. Many seniors were not emotionally or technically prepared to respond to some of the marketing approaches frequently used in the 1990s. Compounding the *"I'm not ready yet"* response and the *"When it's time"* rationale are some surprisingly consistent (and sometimes fatal) misconceptions. These misconceptions, addressed in Chapter 5, cloud seniors' attitudes regarding senior living communities.

Seniors consistently underestimate their current cost of living. Nonrecurring expenses such as real estate taxes and home maintenance are frequently forgotten. Many therefore, lack a valid basis for cost comparison when exposed to retirement community costs. This has led to the misconception that many senior communities are very expensive and perhaps not affordable. This misconception is compounded when some seniors see an (erroneous) inverse relationship between increased quality and ambience versus cost/perceived value.

Seniors think about their health every day. While health may be the number one concern for seniors, most demonstrate little understanding and have significant misconceptions regarding the limitations of their current health care coverage. Most do not understand their Medicare or supplemental policy benefits for nursing or custodial care needs. Despite their prudence and conservatism, seniors tend to ignore the biggest financial threat that more than 40 percent of them will face in the future.

These misconceptions can be clarified through effective market positioning and a new technique called prospect conditioning. This involves seniors talking candidly about their situation in small groups. When effectively implemented, seniors demonstrate a dramatic change in attitude and respond much more favorably to the offerings (benefits) of well-conceived senior living communities.

All of this seems to paint a fairly negative outlook for senior living. Nothing could be further from the truth. What this thinking really does is to lay the necessary groundwork for the repackaging and repositioning of retirement community offerings.

Effective implementation of market positioning will lead to a progressive, benefit-oriented selling strategy. These positioning strategies can dramatically improve the success of 21st century marketing programs.

Positioning From a Financial Perspective

There are some basic, innovative strategies that can be deployed to enhance the operational performance of senior living communities. To start with, we must narrow the gap between two sets of desirable outcomes for both sponsors and consumers.

Sponsors and owner/operators need new and sharpened market positioning that helps them sell the primary benefits the community offers: product, price, value and choice. But those favorable offerings don't become truly evident until the senior is focused on the *financial benefits* of making this most difficult decision. Sponsors are also seeking new approaches to capital formation while overcoming seniors' rational and emotional concerns about finances.

Seniors want to live out their final years with physical and financial security, having a comfortable living arrangement that offers ambience and dignity while enhancing maximum independence. Many also want a living arrangement that avoids the increasing hidden costs and growing hassles of home ownership. However, many seniors and their families fail to focus on a sound financial plan that preserves their assets, allowing them to leave a legacy. For many, this is one of the important "scorecards" in life. A senior's financial plan should allow them to leave a flexible, liquid estate while offering them a tangible direct or indirect investment return on any upfront costs, such as entry fees, etc. from their senior living "investment".

These sponsor and consumer-desired outcomes really come together when we position our senior living options as a prudent and necessary financial planning tool. Consider this market positioning platform:

21st CENTURY SENIOR LIVING MARKET POSITIONING

"Senior living can be a prudent and practical financial planning imperative – just like health insurance, life insurance, wills and estate planning."

There are at least 25 senior living personal financial and investment positioning strategies. Here are six along with references to other chapters that contain more detail:

1. **Hassle-free living** that avoids the increasing hidden costs and growing complexities of home ownership for seniors over age 75. The key challenges these seniors face are increasing real estate taxes, complicated home maintenance and upkeep, and escalating insurance and energy costs. A common concern is the loss of future home value appreciation when opting for senior living. This concern is usually more than offset by the more contained cost of senior living while realizing financial returns through investing liquidated home equity. Refer to Chapters 35, 36, and 37 to develop details for your market positioning strategy.

2. **Hedging many of the risks of runaway health care costs** by accessing reliable, high-quality services on an as-needed basis within a senior living CCRC. This is a high-value alternative to premature nursing home admission, ineffective and costly home health services, or the delay of necessary preventive or corrective health care initiatives (Chapters 3, 9, and 10).

3. **Home equity is a $1 trillion national asset** and, for seniors, that is really at the core of their financial planning resources. Progressive communities are showing seniors how to put their liquidated home equity to work now – while preserving most of this cash plus their current savings portfolio principal as a legacy to their estate. If you charge upfront fees, you should also show a direct or indirect return on the senior's investment (Chapters 35, 36, and 37).

4. **Prudent spend-down plans** may be necessary for some in order to private pay for desired services that maximize independence and quality of life. Over 70 percent of the patient days in institutionalized nursing homes are paid for by Medicaid

because many of the patients have spent down their assets at a much faster pace than is really necessary with today's senior living options. You should show seniors how to avoid unnecessary spend-down, while offering them reasonable approaches to prudently planned spend-down that will not leave them destitute within the period of their remaining expected life (Chapter 38).

5. **Tax shelters** are not just for high rollers or sophisticated Wall Street investors. Advise seniors that under specific conditions, they can deduct a moderate portion of a CCRC's monthly service fees and initial entry fee as a legitimate medical tax deduction (Chapter 42).

6. **Creative pricing by sponsors** shows seniors how to put their home equity to work now – while preserving most of it along with their current savings portfolio as a legacy to their estates. Let's face it, a $200,000 refundable entry fee that declines in refundability by 1.5 percent per month results in a real cash cost or *spend-down* of $3,000 per month or $36,000 per year. And that's in addition to the monthly service fee they're paying (Chapter 42). Many sponsors are changing pricing plans that worked in the past, but are currently facing increasing marketplace resistance.

A word of caution: *Some of today's "traditional pricing" may become obsolete as the industry responds to changing psychographics and focuses on more innovative resident-centered financial strategies. Chapters 40 through 42 address pricing strategies in detail.*

It's time to take a new look at an old problem. Most of us try to hedge future lifetime risks. We have wills, trusts, and life insurance and sometimes even long term care insurance. We try to make sure that we have enough retirement income to live a normal lifestyle. But after age 75, many seniors' lifestyles are far from normal – and frequently little thought has been given to the real threats of preserving an estate accumulated over a lifetime of conservatism. Many older seniors have "planning denial," but astute senior living sponsors can help immeasurably while sharpening community performance.

No one's final years should be seriously compromised in order to maximize the financial aspects of their estate. We have an opportunity (and an obligation) through sound market positioning to show seniors how that final phase of their life can be influenced by an optimum, financially responsible plan.

In spite of the significant potential for very favorable market acceptance, the concept of senior living is still largely misunderstood by the consumer marketplace – and surprisingly by many sponsors and owner/operators. While effective market positioning has proved to be very successful for some sponsors, others seem to either ignore or not be aware of the value of positioning strategies.

Your ideally conceived senior living community is not just bricks and mortar. It is also far more than just shelter, quality food service, housekeeping and health care. Guilt-ridden adult children and professional referral sources (doctors, discharge planers, etc.) need to hear another important market positioning statement:

"CCRCs must have a strong, but largely invisible, medical basis as the solid foundation for their internal resident care and operating philosophy."

Finally, can you effectively deliver on this market positioning statement – which is really a primary objective of older seniors?

"To provide seniors with dignified, appropriate, necessary and cost-effective living options and choices to accommodate their changing needs as they proceed through the later stages of life."

This book has taken a problem-solution approach to a myriad of senior living challenges. Within each solution scenario is a new market positioning opportunity.

Call to Action

Stop running long enough to take the following steps: 1) evaluate the effectiveness of your current market positioning platforms (assuming you have some!) and, 2) identify at least one new market positioning statement that you could use in your community.

Clearly defining market positioning is not easy. It forces you to clarify your *features* versus *tangible benefits* and assess market responsiveness. Finally, you must clearly communicate where you stand versus your competition.

CHAPTER 8

PROVIDING INCREASED ASSISTANCE TO INDEPENDENT LIVING RESIDENTS

Responding To A Resident's Increasing Needs Presents a Huge Sponsor and Owner/Operator Dilemma

Many sponsors and owner/operators are involved in both assisted living and independent living. These living arrangements are typically separated.

But now a human drama is unfolding in independent living communities across the United States. It's one that can have an enormous impact on the future of your CCRC or independent living community. That's because your existing independent living residents have aging-in-place needs – and, at the same time, your community must remain fully market-responsive to new residents. This is often viewed as a no-win situation.

"Aging-in-place" is a commonly-used phrase in the senior living industry today. Most sponsors feel they basically understand what it means. But as a community ages, sponsors and owner/operators are gradually realizing that the aging-in-place concept represents huge operational and marketing challenges.

In my work with senior living clients, I've lived briefly in over 130 communities. I do this to witness the actual senior living environment up close and personal. I dine with the residents whenever possible. One night at dinner, Mary, an 85-year-old widow said, ***"Jim, I really don't want to go to the <u>Big House!</u>"*** She went on to describe the prison that was referred to in that famous old James Cagney movie. Fred, also 85, chimed in, ***"Jim, I'm not concerned about death or dying, what troubles me is the path I'll have to take to get there."*** Another resident said, ***"I really love Helen, but it troubles me to see her every day in her current state . . . I know but for the grace of God go I."***

These statements reflect both concern and reality for many seniors.

The Dilemma Defined

Aging-in-place describes the gradual deterioration of the health of residents in senior living communities. It is one of the most predictable trends in senior housing today. Aging-in-place is also one of the most difficult trends to manage effectively *and* compassionately. Average annual resident turnover rates range from:

- 24 to 40 percent for independent living.
- 41 to 67 percent for assisted living communities.
- 18 to 22 percent for CCRCs – lower off-the-campus turnover because residents are typically transferring within the comprehensive continuum.

Sponsors and owner/operators have a natural tendency to increase the level of services to reduce turnover. But as aging-in-place becomes an increasingly dominant trend within independent living, practical, effective and consistent responses to this dilemma often elude even the most experienced and innovative sponsors and owner/operators. The issue is easily defined, but difficult to address. Here is the issue: ***To what degree are you willing to deliver health-related assistance to your residents who live in independent living?***

Don't answer this question quickly. First, consider two other key questions:

1. ***How and when specifically should you facilitate a resident's move to a higher level of care?***

and . . .

2. ***Should you embrace or avoid a naturally occurring assisted living community?***

Sponsors and owner/operators are also realizing this is not an autonomous internal decision.

The Assistance in Living Concept

Dealing with aging-in-place in independent living is, at best, extremely complex. There is a strong temptation to procrastinate or make shortsighted, short-term operational decisions. Many astute operators create distinct living and care continuums that include active adult housing, independent living, assisted living, special Alzheimer/dementia units, and nursing. But others offer assistance in living (AIL) services, which offer as-needed assistance with the residents' activities of daily living (ADLs) to independent living residents. The theory is that care is portable and we can do great things with technology. But are these AIL decisions *strategically correct?*

Short-Run Tactics – The Quick Fix

The quick fix sounds good because, in the short run, providing assistance in living services is good for the residents being served. It also appears to solve immediate aging-in-place problems and slows down turnover. If properly priced, the AIL concept can also provide the sponsor with ancillary income and a hedge against operating expense cost creep. But this short-run solution can frequently trigger serious long-term problems.

Some sponsors are using licensed, third-party home health agencies to deliver the "*medical component*" of service delivery, while they continue to focus on the "*shelter component*." Properly executed, this can appear to be a viable, reasonably seamless concept. However, the strategy is frequently not truly market-driven or resident-centered. Home health or assisted living charges are frequently billed separately from the monthly service fee and often appear fragmented, excessive, inequitable, and confusing to the resident.

Long-Run Impacts – The Self Selection Process

If you deliver AIL services to your *independent* living residents long enough, a large percentage of seniors will become *assisted living* residents. Many will experience various stages of cognitive impairment. To compound this challenge, the profile of new residents moving in will likely change. New prospects visiting communities that offer extensive AIL services to independent living residents increasingly judge all residents there as "older, frailer people." Many prospects and their families tend to make move-in decisions based on how they perceive the existing resident population. In this scenario, older, frailer seniors may be the ones to feel that the particular community is right for them. Thus, new move-ins tend to be the result of a *self-selective process.* By appealing to an older, frailer population, you compound and accelerate the cumulative aging-in-place process of the community's resident population.

You Must Respond to Two Types of Conditions

Assistance in Living (AIL) for seniors can involve one or both of the following conditions:

- ***Chronic Condition*** is the natural changing health status of seniors as they age. The need for assistance with the Activities of Daily Living (ADLs) gradually increases with time – including addressing the special needs of those seniors experiencing various levels of Alzheimer's or other related dementia. The *process* is generally predictable. What's more difficult is being certain of the most appropriate ways for care providers to *respond.*

- ***Episodic Condition*** is a sudden change in health status due to an "episode" such as a hip fracture or stroke. This usually triggers an abrupt increase in ADL needs, and sometimes a permanent change in the need for sheltered living arrangements. Here, treatment and procedures are well defined, with recovery outcomes that are reasonably predictable.

Regardless of their initial conditions, most seniors age in place and eventually develop chronic health conditions.

Four Stakeholder Groups Are Involved in the Process

Let's take a look at the implications of aging-in-place from the real world perspective of four very involved groups:

1. ***Existing residents.*** Existing residents experience the growing complications of aging and are obviously trying to cope with their physical afflictions. They frequently experience fear, confusion, frustration and insecurity. Many either refuse to understand – or fail to recognize – the real implications of their changing health conditions. In other words, they're acting human.

2. ***Family members.*** Family members generally fall into one of two broad categories. They either deny that changes are occurring in their loved one's condition or they hope their loved one (and your staff) will miraculously cope with the situation. Some family members, but not enough, also recognize it's time to make some very difficult decisions.

3. ***Peers and neighbors.*** Peers and neighbors of ailing senior living residents who have not yet experienced serious aging complications don't want to be constantly reminded of the inevitable.

4. ***Professional staff.*** These professionals frequently find themselves facing three aging-in-place challenges:

- Providing love, patience, and compassion while addressing the changing needs of the residents.
- Working effectively with family members who simply refuse to deal objectively with bad news.

- The balancing act: upper management works to strike a delicate balance between delivering increasing levels of care into independent living, while facing complex and costly operations and marketing issues.

Complicating this balancing act is the sometimes conflicting compliance requirements between the national Fair Housing Act and unique state regulations. Some state regulations might require the movement of a particular resident to a higher level of care. On the other hand, Fair Housing may impose fines for moving the resident prematurely!

There are alternative approaches to delivering assistance in living to seniors. Meeting this enormous challenge is more than many owner/operators bargained for when they initially planned their high ambience, independent living community.

The chronic aging process of seniors has caused many older, conventional apartment buildings and condominiums to gradually transition into what is called a "NORC" – a Naturally Occurring Retirement Community. Meanwhile, *independent* living retirement communities are evolving into marginally efficient, less attractive, *Naturally Occurring Assisted Living Communities.*

Six Tough Questions to Address

The first step in attacking this aging-in-place dilemma is to address the six tough questions outlined in Figure 8-1. If you objectively respond to these six questions, you will probably recognize some potential problems.

FIGURE 8-1
YOU MUST ASK AND ANSWER
SIX TOUGH ASSISTANCE IN LIVING QUESTIONS

To avoid getting into trouble down the line as a result of delivering AIL services to existing independent living residents, ask yourself six tough questions now. Answer the following questions from the perspective of the years 2009 through 2014:

1. What is your optimum resident profile, for both your existing independent residents and new move-ins?
2. What will your future business model and market positioning look like? Will residents be independent with moderate needs? Or high acuity assisted living residents? Or a combination of both?
3. Will you have the capability to accurately measure levels of care, those actually delivered to each resident, in order to recover your increasing AIL costs?
4. Will your community be fully market-responsive if residents are charged for incremental increases in assistance with ADLs as they age in place?
5. As resident care needs intensify, can you deliver ADL assistance cost-effectively to randomly distributed independent living units throughout your community?
6. Are all of your care level policies in independent living consistent so that you do not "cannibalize" the other senior living options on your campus?

Moore Diversified Services, Inc.

There Are Some Viable AIL Strategies

Your long-term prospects may seem dim after answering the questions in Figure 8-1. However, there is some light at the end of that long, dark tunnel. In the next chapter, seven practical strategies will help you learn how to manage the aging-in-place dilemma. This includes more information on the option of creating an integrated, yet separate area to provide increased assistance in living within your independent living community.

Call to Action

Consider the challenges and opportunities of offering increasing levels of assistance in living for your residents in independent living. What are your biggest concerns? How will you address these concerns? Do you need to implement some new policies? When? Are you <u>really</u> comfortable with your answers to the questions posed in Figure 8-1?

CHAPTER 9

SUCCESSFULLY ADDRESSING AGING IN PLACE

Striking a Delicate Balance Between The Desires of Seniors and Long-Run Operator Viability

If your long-term prospects seem gloomy after trying to answer the questions in the previous chapter, consider adding a *separate, yet integrated* assistance in living *neighborhood* within your independent living community. With less personal living area and more services compared to the typical independent living community, an assisted living section is frequently the most cost-effective way to deliver optimum service to your aging residents for a reasonably affordable price. This can be accomplished through a purpose-built new design or by converting existing space.

Consider the *Separate*, Yet *Integrated* Neighborhood Concept

Does ***separate, yet integrated***, seem like an oxymoron? Can the concept really be seamless? Consider this brief overview:

1. Create two separate residential *neighborhoods* (independent living and assisted living) connected and integrated under the same roof.

2. Use common core areas, such as the commercial kitchen, laundry, maintenance, etc. to efficiently deliver services to both areas.
3. Provide *separate* satellite dining rooms for each living type, supported by the common commercial kitchen. (Most hotels with multiple restaurants use this system.)
4. Offer properly sized and separate public spaces (such as lounges) for each living type.

This purpose-built approach is what designers use today for a new community that plans to offer both independent and assisted living. But what about converting an older property? An independent living-to-assisted living conversion might look like this: One or two independent floors (or wings) become designated as assisted living. Small satellite dining rooms are created within the space converted to assisted living. Food from the main kitchen is delivered to a satellite warming kitchen where food is plated for assisted living residents.

This conversion will likely require gutting several revenue-producing independent living units to create appropriate staff space and satellite dining accommodations. You might also consider creating an Alzheimer's/dementia carve-out wing – providing a secure courtyard if the conversion is on the ground floor. Make sure you comply with existing building codes and licensing requirements.

Before deciding which strategy is right for you, ask yourself three key planning questions:

1. **What is the least costly way to help residents with growing ADL needs?** For the most realistic response, make a detailed cost comparison. Compare the cost of providing a dedicated

assisted living area versus providing ADL assistance to randomly distributed independent living units. Consider the impact on cost and your resident profile – both now as well as five, seven, and ten years from now. Remember, the most attractive *short-run* option may not always be the best *long-run* strategy. Look at several scenarios, such as providing ADLs for 10 percent of independent living residents now, versus the likelihood of the need growing to over 50 percent in several years.

2. **How will three very important senior consumer groups and their adult children feel about the strategy you're planning to adopt?** These three senior consumer groups include:

   - Existing independent living residents who need assistance with ADLs
   - Residents who are still relatively healthy
   - Potential new residents

   The obvious challenge is finding a service delivery system that will satisfy the first group without driving away the other two.

3. **Will your independent living residents be willing to move to the purpose-built assisted living arrangement at the appropriate time?** Despite the best of intentions, a multi-level, full-service senior living community can experience mediocre performance because of resident non-compliance. To help ensure that residents are willing to move when the time comes, you must develop very specific independent living resident admission and discharge policies. These policies must be enforced tactfully, yet consistently. The policies should describe specifically what services and care can be provided in each living arrangement. These policies must strike a delicate

balance between internal objectives, state regulations and Fair Housing criteria.

Pricing Strategy for Providing Assistance In Living (AIL)

If you plan to charge an extra fee for AIL – added to your basic independent living monthly service fee – it should be driven by the ***loaded cost of your direct care staff***. Figure 9-1 provides a pragmatic approach to determining the right pricing model.

Moving your independent living residents through the continuum will continue to present significant challenges. Figure 9-2 provides seven key strategies to consider when dealing with the aging-in-place challenge. Remember to always let two initiatives guide your decisions: The Fair Housing Act and the Americans With Disabilities Act (ADA).

Senior housing sponsors are obligated to provide appropriate, cost-effective assistance with ADLs for their residents. Besides the satisfaction of knowing you're doing the right thing, there could be other significant payoffs for those who effectively manage this challenge. For instance, communities that offer either full or modified life care contracts could lower their health care benefit costs. This is because you can, when clinically appropriate, substitute formal assisted living or temporary assistance-in-living services in place of higher-cost nursing home admissions. Use the implied strategies and tactics of Figures 9-1 and 9-2 to develop your resident aging-in-place position. Do it now . . . not later!

FIGURE 9-1
ARE YOU RECOVERING THE FULL COST OF DELIVERING ASSISTANCE IN LIVING?

INPUT ASSUMPTIONS:	
Base CNA/Resident-Aide Hrly $:	$10.00
Fringe Benefits @	25.0%
Indirect Time @	20.0%
Overhead Allocation:	15.0%
Desired Profit/EBITDA Margin:	35.0%

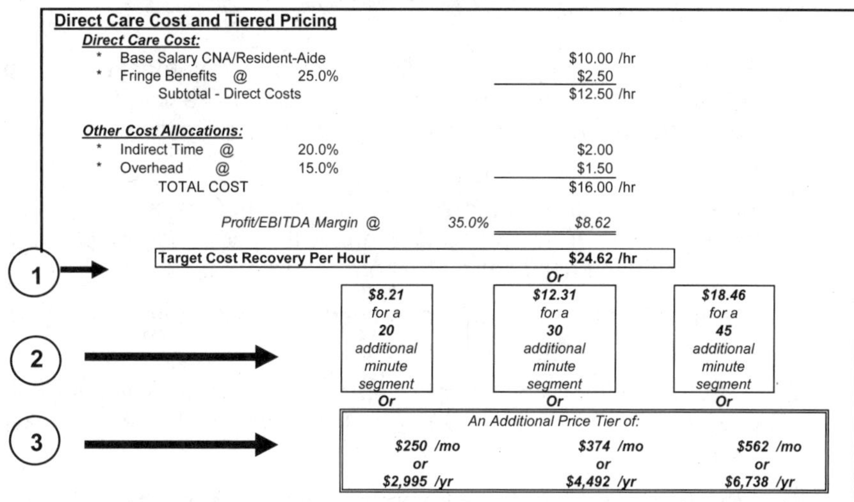

Direct Care Cost and Tiered Pricing

Direct Care Cost:

* Base Salary CNA/Resident-Aide			$10.00 /hr
* Fringe Benefits @	25.0%		$2.50
Subtotal - Direct Costs			$12.50 /hr

Other Cost Allocations:

* Indirect Time @	20.0%		$2.00
* Overhead @	15.0%		$1.50
TOTAL COST			$16.00 /hr
Profit/EBITDA Margin @		*35.0%*	*$8.62*

(1) **Target Cost Recovery Per Hour** **$24.62 /hr**

Or

(2) ***$8.21*** *for a* ***20*** *additional minute segment* | ***$12.31*** *for a* ***30*** *additional minute segment* | ***$18.46*** *for a* ***45*** *additional minute segment*

Or

(3) *An Additional Price Tier of:*

$250 /mo	***$374 /mo***	***$562 /mo***
or	***or***	***or***
$2,995 /yr	***$4,492 /yr***	***$6,738 /yr***

Are you recovering the cost of your AIL services being delivered into independent living? It's a three step process as indicated above:

(1) Determine the *loaded* hourly rate of your direct care staff.

(2) Base your charges on the actual direct care time used by each resident.

(3) Develop monthly pricing tiers accordingly.

You should also reconcile the actual *number* of FTEs it takes to deliver the care in order to ensure complete cost recovery. Refer to *Assisted Living Strategies for Changing Markets* for more details (www.m-d-s.com). **Moore Diversified Services, Inc.**

FIGURE 9-2
THE TOP SEVEN STRATEGIES FOR DEALING WITH AGING IN PLACE

These seven strategies are *imperative* when dealing with the aging-in-place issue:

1. Deal with the problem *now,* because it will surely intensify, rather than diminish, with time.
2. Resist simplistic "politically correct" approaches that accommodate individual independent living residents in the ***short-run***, but create extensive community problems in the ***long-run***.
3. Clearly define the circumstances under which a resident must move to another living arrangement in the residency agreement. Use negotiated risk contracts where appropriate.
4. Clearly communicate policies, procedures, and admission criteria to new residents and their families.
5. Get your resident council involved as peers in the policy-making process. This helps your residents feel they are part of a positive solution.
6. Closely monitor each resident's health status on a continuing basis.
7. If you operate an older community, consider developing a second-generation, new independent living section or building that will replace the existing one as aging residents gradually (and inevitably) convert the initial community into a ***"naturally occurring assisted living community."***

Whichever route you follow, you must adopt certain strategies <u>now</u> in order to effectively plan for the future.

Moore Diversified Services, Inc.

Call to Action

Before moving on, consider the following:

- Answer the three key planning questions I outlined in this chapter. Carefully consider the pros and cons of each issue.

- Review the seven strategies in Figure 9-2. Which aging-in-place strategies does your community need to work on?

Finally, run your own numbers using the template provided in Figure 9-1.

SECTION TWO

Design and Development

Issues And Strategies

CHAPTER 10

DEVELOPING A NEW SENIOR LIVING COMMUNITY

Don't Break Ground Without Correctly Answering Ten Key Questions

When developing new independent living or CCRC projects, many owners and sponsors are tempted to make situation-driven decisions offering what *they* would like to provide – in the hopes that the marketplace will respond favorably. With luck, this method sometimes leads to success.

However, far more often, inadequate planning results in either a seriously distressed project or one with flaws that could have been avoided. The late 1980s provided the best examples of this. Many for-profit independent living communities offered the wrong products and services, or improperly aimed the *right* ones at the *wrong* market.

The Ten Planning Questions

A better approach is to study the market and learn what is really needed both now and in the future. Only then can you be certain you are providing the most market-responsive products and services. Once you've studied the market, you should be able to answer the following ten important questions from a *market-driven* perspective rather than from an emotional *situation-driven* position.

The Top Ten Development Questions To Answer in 2009 and Beyond

Let's cut to the chase and outline those ten very important questions, which will be covered in more depth later in this chapter. Consider this a development strategy punch list:

1. **What will be the extent of your total continuum of care?**
   - Independent living only
   - Independent living integrated with:
     - Assisted living
     - Special Alzheimer's/dementia unit
     - Nursing
     - Home health
   - Active adult housing
   - Offer the full continuum (see Figures 3-1 and 3-2 in Chapter 3)
2. **What is your expected resident profile?**
   - Majority are likely to be single females
   - 25% to 35% couples initially for a new community (then this ratio will decline rapidly over the first 5 years of operations)
   - Average annual turnover:
     - Assisted living, 41% to 67%
     - Independent living, 24% to 40% per year
     - CCRC, 18% to 22%
   - Entry age: Approximately 82/83+ for independent living
   - Low/moderate acuity (in independent living)

3. **Will you deliver assistance in living to independent living residents? How will you execute it? (Refer to Chapters 8 and 9.)**
   - Use your assisted living staff?
   - Use a third-party home health agency?
   - Decide how extensive home care services will be?

4. **Will you offer structured assisted living?**
   - Residential-social model
   - Medical model
   - Special care – dementia
   - Catered living

   } Will these be separate, stand-alone "neighborhoods"?

   - Using CCRC health center staff?

     or . . .

   - A separate home health agency. Will the agency be:
     - Owned?
     - Contracted?
     - Licensed?

5. **What will be the specific criteria for residents to move within your continuum?**
   - Strong, definitive independent living admission and discharge policies?
   - Criteria for assisted living admissions?
   - Criteria for skilled nursing admissions?
   - Specific policy for providing assistance in living within independent living?

6. **What will be your overall design philosophy and strategy?**
   - Number of units

- Unit Size
- Mix of units:
  - Studios (Be careful of obsolescence)
  - One bedroom
  - Two bedroom
  - Three bedroom
- Quality guest rooms/suites
- Hallways:
  - Straight/conventional
  - Recessed unit entry doors
  - Neighborhood/cul de sac
  - Pods/clusters
- Separate vs. connected buildings
- *Integrated,* yet *separated* "neighborhoods" (by level of care)
- Number of stories/floors:
  - *Vertical* growth minimizes *horizontal* walk distances to elevators/common areas
- High "flash value" strategies (see Chapter 11):
  - Exterior
    - Elevations
    - Roof lines
    - Main entrance to community
  - Public spaces
  - Entrance to living units
  - Interior design of living units

7. **How much staffing will your project require?**
   - Staffing guidelines and benchmarks:
     - Overall number of FTEs per resident in independent living – 0.25 to 0.31

8. **What will it cost to develop and operate your community? Some 2009 benchmark guidelines are provided in future chapters:**
   - Typical all-in development costs (Chapter 23):
     - Land
     - Construction
     - Soft costs
     - Financing
     - Etc.
   - Typical operating costs; total dollars per resident-day (Chapter 24)
   - Operating expense ratio } Chapters 24, 25 and 26
   - Operating profit margin }

9. **How will you price your project? (See Chapters 40 through 43)**
   - Flat (base) monthly service fee:
     - Independent living
     - Assisted living[1]
     - Alzheimer's/dementia[1]

---

[1]For tiered pricing details and guidelines for high acuity residents, refer to ***Assisted Living Strategies for Changing Markets*** by Jim Moore (www.m-d-s.com).

- Entry fee plus monthly service fee with entry fee being:
  - 100% refundable
  - Partially refundable
  - Refund amortizes to zero
    - @ 1.5% per month
    - @ 2.0% per month
- Fee simple ownership
- Condominium
- Co-operative

10. What are your initial fill-up/absorption expectations (for a 150-unit independent living community)?

- Initial in-rush upon opening (from pre-sales):
  - Could experience 20% to 25% occupancy
- Typical fill-up ramp after opening – Net of turnover:
  - Approximately 5 to 7 units per month could be realized with a professional sales and marketing program
- Expected time to stabilized occupancy
- With an initial annual turnover, you're always effectively in fill-up mode!

Sounds complicated? It's really not that bad when you tackle each question as a separate issue:

1. ***What will be the extent of your total continuum of care?*** Should you offer only independent living or the comprehensive services of a CCRC? Let's talk about both ends of the spectrum. Offering only independent living can be a recipe for failure as most seniors want to know that there is another living option on campus

for them to go, should they need it. No, they really don't want to consider moving into assisted living – but most want to know that it's there.

Offering skilled nursing can be music to the ears of those looking for the ultimate product solution. However, you must give very careful consideration to the current day complications and reimbursement trends of Medicaid and Medicare. Payor mix (private pay, Medicare, and Medicaid) is critical to the success of today's nursing operation. A large sector of the market responds very favorably to communities that offer a total continuum of living arrangements. Review Figure 3-2, the vertical (business) continuum, and Figure 3-1, the horizontal (consumer) continuum, shown in Chapter 3.

Also, when choosing your continuum of care, consider the two basic models:

- **Independent living** with a modest assisted living neighborhood – *integrated* yet *separated* within the community.
- **A CCRC** with independent living, assisted living and nursing.

The key question to answer is, ***"Will I be a legitimate player in my competitive marketplace, and if not, how will the other players impact my game plan?"***

2. ***What is your expected resident profile?*** A classic example of situation-driven thinking involves planning for a majority of couples being active, vibrant and just wanting the leisure lifestyle. Many well-intended, but naïve, developers say, ***"You just don't understand, we are going to be different."*** This philosophy is typically an early indicator of a slow moving, troubled project.

Most seniors who are responding to the independent living market or CCRCs have already had one of life's wake-up calls. That means some health related event has already occurred even though the person appears to be an active, independent living prospect. Sure, there are some pre-planners who want to move into full continuum retirement communities while they are still very active and able to do all the planning themselves – but these people are relatively rare, percentage wise. The average entry age into senior living today is older than 80. Couples are relatively rare. You would be fortunate to get more than 30 to 35 percent of couples during your initial occupancy.

3. ***Will you deliver assistance in living to independent living residents?*** While this sounds like an obvious and simple approach to expanding the flexibility of your services to residents, the consequences can be quite complex. Chapters 8 and 9 deal extensively with the challenges and opportunities of providing assistance in living into independent living units. Carefully review those chapters before finalizing your plans.

4. ***Will you offer structured assisted living?*** The outline presented earlier in this chapter listed a variety of assisted living models. Assisted living as a stand-alone product has had a significant influence in the senior living market in the last ten years. It certainly should be part of your overall product/ service offering for your new or expanded campus. In addition to the suggested components presented in the previous outline, you might refer to my previous book, ***Assisted Living Strategies for Changing Markets.*** [1]

[1] Refer to www.m-d-s.com

5. ***What will be the specific criteria for residents to move within your continuum?*** Moving residents within your community can present a serious dilemma if you offer two alternative situations with a very blurred line between them. In one situation, the community might ask residents to move prematurely because their frailty "doesn't look good" in the independent living section of your community. In contrast, another community might keep residents in independent living too long, putting the resident (and the community) at risk for an unfortunate accident or event. Chapters 3, 8 and 9 deal with this difficult situation.

6. ***What will be your overall design philosophy and strategy?*** This complex issue has three major components – consider living units, common space, and project size:

- **Living units** have evolved from affordable studios in older independent living communities or CCRCs to significantly larger apartments. Essentially, studios have become obsolete; many have been converted into one-bedroom units by combining adjacent studios. Today, there is an evolving trend involving a heavier concentration of two bedroom units. Like the studio to one bedroom conversion, we are now seeing considerable one bedroom to two bedroom conversions. Chapter 11 addresses other significant living unit trends.

- **Elaborate common spaces** are nice, but are becoming increasingly expensive. Newer communities appear to have higher perceived value than those that are at least 10 years old. Good design of common spaces involves a delicate balance between delivering high ambience, efficient space planning, and cost.

- **Optimum project size** requires a delicate trade-off between maximizing the number of units in order to spread capital and operating costs across more units while avoiding marketplace risk by overbuilding. For independent living and CCRCs, industry experience indicates that a total of 150 to 180 revenue-producing units should result in good financial/operational efficiency. There could also be a second phase of the development plan if the initial offering is successful.

Obviously, entire books have been written regarding senior living design, however, the outline contained in this chapter and the details contained in Chapter 11 provide guidance as you proceed down the design path.

7. ***How much staffing will your project require?*** Since labor costs represent more than 60 percent of the total operating costs for independent living and CCRCs, give very careful consideration to value engineering your staff. You must optimize your full time equivalent (FTE) employee counts and balance this with operational efficiency – without compromising standards of care or quality of life. Chapters 24 (operating expenses), 28 and 29 (operations analysis and benchmarking) address this important issue.

8. ***What will it cost to develop and operate your community?*** This involves myriad issues that start with your total all-in capital costs and how these costs will be covered with a combination of debt, equity, and possibly entry fee proceeds. The next important area of costs includes the critical fill-up period where you will naturally experience significant levels of negative cash flow. The question is, ***"How much negative cash flow is appropriate and how much can be avoided with appropriate planning?"*** Finally, the stabilized operation of your community must deliver certain key operating metrics per resident-day as well as acceptable operating expense ratios and profit margins. The following chapters address each of these important issues:

- Capital costs (Chapter 23)
- Operating expenses (Chapter 24)
- Operating profit margin (Chapter 25)
- Income statements (Chapters 26 and 27)

Finally, all of this is driven by how you ultimately price your project.

9. ***How will you price your project?*** Detailed pricing strategies are contained in Chapters 40 through 43. These chapters provide important guidelines for properly pricing various senior living options.

10. ***What are your initial fill-up/absorption expectations?*** For a 150-unit independent living community you should expect a fill-up after opening of approximately four to six units or six to eight units per month – net of turnover. In fact, you will have modest turnover even during initial fill-up! If you've done your pre-marketing properly, you can also expect an initial in-rush of residents moving in when the doors open due to pre-sales. This typically represents 20 to 25 percent of total units available.

Keep in mind with annual turnover for independent living in isolation is approximately 24 percent to 40 percent. For a new CCRC community turnover (death or leaving the campus) is approximately 18 to 22 percent, you are essentially always in fill-up mode!

The Senior Living Industry is Maturing

As the senior living industry continues to mature, two new trends are emerging:

1. The market is gradually becoming more educated and sophisticated with respect to the available continuum of alternative living arrangements and health care options.

2. The senior consumer and their families will give you very little consideration or compassion for your mistakes and unacceptable trade-offs.

State-of-the-art senior living can be a surprisingly affordable living arrangement for seniors in the later stages of life. But your project won't be successful if you fail to properly answer the ten questions in this chapter fully and honestly during your planning phase.

Call to Action

Completely answer the critical ten development questions. Finally, I've saved the most important question of all for last:

*"**Under what conditions would your own mother willingly, and with your support and blessing, move into your community?**"*

You only get one chance to get it right. Read on for some additional market-responsive approaches to CCRC design.

CHAPTER 11

MARKET-RESPONSIVE APPROACHES TO CCRC DESIGN

You Get Only One Chance to Get it Right!

You've just been assigned the role of fine-tuning the interior and design of a CCRC. Your job is to add *benefits* that will wow the residents – without blowing the budget. What high impact *benefits* do you add?

In Chapter 10, I identified ten key questions to answer as you develop your new independent living and CCRC design strategies. Some of those questions had design implications, such as: What is your overall design philosophy? What is the optimum project size?

In this chapter, I'll introduce you to the design features and benefits that make the biggest impact. Seniors will subliminally translate these "features" into "value". Keep in mind that ultimately we're selling value – not individual features.

The Non-Institutional Design Strategy

Your new community will be the final home for hundreds of seniors accustomed to a lifetime of comfort in homes filled with memories. Your design should offer comfort, ambience, and the perception of good value. This means providing features, benefits, and amenities, such as:

- Carpeting, high quality wood, or tile in all areas
- Significant millwork – go the extra mile on door frames, crown moldings, baseboards, etc.
- Solid core, paneled doors
- Drapes and window treatments
- Aesthetically pleasing wall coverings in living units and public spaces
- Hallways with reasonable width and innovative design techniques (breaks in the vertical and horizontal surfaces, wall covering, lighting, etc.) to minimize the "tunnel effect"
- Traditional artwork
- Non-institutional furniture (furniture that belongs in a *home*, not a *motel*)
- Ceiling heights consistent with total size (area) and volume of a particular space
- Soft, incandescent lighting fixtures (vs. harsher fluorescent) that meet the growing visual needs of seniors:
    - In 2009 and beyond, there will have to be a delicate trade-off made between incandescent lighting and the newer, energy efficient, long life fluorescent bulbs and LEDs.

While the overall community and the individual living units are certainly positioned as the seniors' new home and legal residence, the "look" of the public spaces should give the impression of a well-conceived country club. Your community should send subtle signals of comfortable, moderate luxury.

Your design concept should also reflect a highly residential structure developed within local building code requirements and state licensing regulations.

First Impressions Are Critical

First impressions are everything. The first visual impression that your community gives to seniors and their loved ones could well be the primary deal maker or breaker. Your total offering must pass five competitive and consumer preference tests:

1. Strong *first impression*
2. Superior *product*
3. Affordable, reasonable *price*
4. Perception of high *value*
5. Optimum resident *quality of life*

In more than 900 focus groups, and in my personal "mystery shopping" in more than 750 markets in 49 states, certain favorable attributes are common themes of successful communities:

- **A strong sense of entrance.** From the time they first turn onto your campus roadway, seniors and their families start forming both conscious and subliminal impressions. Ideally, the first entrance into the campus should be a mini-boulevard with a small divided lane or island and perhaps a "monument," such as an attractive sign indicating the name of your community.

After the prospect enters your campus, the next sense of "entrance" will be your main front entrance and any roofed extensions or porte cochere covering the driveway near the main doors. Properly designed, these extensions provide shelter from rain and the hot summer sun. Does appropriate, quality signage get the consumer to your main front entrance hassle free? Then, does it tell the visitor or prospect where to go *within* your campus (main building, marketing, etc.)?

- **Building elevations and roof lines.** A well-designed community should have "breaks" in its exterior elevation and interesting roof lines. This means that the vertical walls of your community should be accented with balconies on the upper floors, possibly vertical columns, and other breaks in the elevations, rather than a flat vertical surface that lacks interest or appeal. Roof lines should have peaks or gables.

- **Exterior window treatments.** One of the best ways to avoid the impression of institutionalism is to have interesting window treatments. This can be done with blinds, shutters or other design treatments influenced by your part of the country. Use attractive architectural themes that are prevalent in your area.

- **First impressions of the interior.** When a prospect walks into your vestibule or lobby, he or she wants to get a warm feeling of quality and ambience. Be careful not to overdo the impressions of "luxury." Depression-era seniors are concerned by opulence. They may perceive too many "extras" as extravagance and the basis of inflated prices. Always remember: Most prospective residents and their families will be on the lookout for signs that you might charge them too much. Your public spaces should convey warmth, ambience, and value – but not extravagance.

- **Approaching the individual living units.** Senior living communities will typically offer units that are "double-loaded" off of interior hallways. That means that the entrances to the senior living units are on both the left and right side of the interior hallway. It is important that these hallways be at least eight feet in width and have breaks rather than long, extended, tunnel-like flat walls that sometimes emphasize that long walk to the dining room! The doorway to the individual living unit is the entrance to the senior's <u>new home</u>. Where possible, it should look like a front door. Install solid-core paneled doors, and a reasonable amount of millwork (wood trim) around each door. In addition, the doorway can be "notched" or recessed rather than part of a long, extended wall. Direct and indirect lighting, colors and wall coverings can add the final quality accents to this important area of your design.

- **Individual living units.** Studios or alcove units offered in older independent living communities present serious marketing challenges because they are too small and hard to sell. Avoid studios/alcoves except when offered in <u>very limited</u> numbers as part of a very specific affordability strategy in your market.

Unit types and mixes are so critical that I've created two sample specifications for you to use as best practices. Figure 11-1 shows typical design configuration scenarios for two possible value strategies:

- Moderately priced "*Pontiacs*"
- High value "*Buicks*"

Just like different automobile models, each of these designs must be appropriately priced. This is discussed in more detail in Chapters 40 through 42.

FIGURE 11-1
TWO TYPICAL INDEPENDENT LIVING DESIGN SCENARIOS
(For a 150-Unit Project)

Remember, these are typical scenarios. Many variations are possible based on project-specific situations.

Unit Type	Moderately Priced *"Pontiac"* No. of Units	Unit Mix	Living Area (s.f.)
• Studio/Alcove[1]	5 units	3%	550 s.f.
• One Bedroom	60	40	650
• One Bedroom w/ Den/Office	35	23	800
• Two Bedroom	50	34	1,000
Total	**150 units**	**100 %**	**800 s.f.[2]**

Unit Type	High Value *"Buick"* No. of Units	Unit Mix	Living Area (s.f.)
• Studio/Alcove	-	-	-
• One Bedroom	50 units	33%	750 sf
• One Bedroom w/ Den/Office	35	24	995
• Two Bedroom	50	33	1,200
• Two Bedroom Deluxe/Penthouse	15	10	1,500
Total	**150 units**	**100%**	**1,032 s.f.[2]**

[1]Provide studios only if you have a very unique and affordable pricing option.
[2]Weighted average.

Moore Diversified Services, Inc.

High Impact Design Features

There are a number of subtle, but very important, design features that should be carefully considered in your overall state-of-the-art independent living design. These features must be a delicate trade-off between *functional use* for seniors and *perceived value.* Seven important design features include:

1. Full-function kitchens – Even if you're serving three meals a day to relatively old, frail seniors, state-of-the-art independent living communities commonly offer full-function kitchens. That means a galley kitchen (U-shaped) with dishwasher, disposal, medium-sized refrigerator, countertop range, oven and other features. This "investment" in particular plays on the perceptions of the senior and their family, rather than being a true future functional utility. In reality, they may use it infrequently, but most want the full-function kitchen as a design amenity.

A convincing statement as to the quality of your community can frequently be the decision to use high quality (and relatively expensive) solid core cabinet doors and granite countertops in both the kitchen and bathroom. This design philosophy is an extension of the very high quality, solid core paneled front door to the living unit.

2. Tubs vs. showers – While many of today's seniors are part of the "tub generation," most struggle to negotiate the tub rim. The most common design decision is to have tub-shower combinations (with non-institutional hand rails and seats). If you use tubs, make sure you install the new design with a low vertical height rim. In two-bedroom units or other configurations where there are two full bathrooms, the second bathroom typically contains a roll-in shower which seniors can enter using either a walker or a wheelchair.

3. **Walk-in/walk-through closets** – This is a high value item for seniors. By that I mean, a walk-in or walk-through closet of modest size makes a quality statement about the unit and tends to take away some of the concern that the senior is moving into a relatively small apartment compared to their home.

4. **Counter space in bathrooms** – Just as you observe when you stay in a hotel, some bathroom counter space designs are adequate; others are not. It is prudent to allow sufficient counter space, which could even include extending the countertop over the water tank of the commode. Seniors living in these relatively small units need all the space advantages that you can provide.

5. **Washer-dryer option** – This is often a difficult decision to make. Most seniors would indicate they definitely want washer-dryer options when, in fact, many owners get along just fine by offering common laundry facilities on each floor for residents to use (usually at no cost). However, innovative sponsors can offer their residents an option. It goes something like this: ***"We can provide you with either a stacked washer-dryer in your unit or you can use that same space for high efficiency storage."*** Some sponsors use the stacked washer-dryer (retail value of approximately $800) as a "charter member" move-in decision incentive. This offer always has a deadline.

6. **Auxiliary storage** – As you can imagine, there never *appears* to be enough storage for seniors moving from their homes. Some communities will provide private, locked storage in subterranean "cellars." Those who offer covered or enclosed parking sometimes provide a storage unit at the front end of the enclosed parking space. Others provide storage "cabinets" that can be accessed from the balcony of the resident's unit. This usually compromises some of the high value balcony space and may not always be a good alternative.

7. Covered/enclosed parking – This is primarily an issue of climate and preference. In northern locations, it is not unusual for seniors to pay $50 to $75 per month for covered parking (not weather enclosed). For underground, climate-controlled parking, seniors frequently pay an extra initial one time fee of $5,000 to $7,500, plus a modest increase in monthly service fee for that option if they pay an upfront fee for their living unit. For a straight monthly service fee community (without an entry fee), residents pay approximately $125 per month for climate-controlled parking. Developing true underground parking will cost somewhere between $20,000 and $23,000 per space – you need to recover that investment from the residents who use the garage rather than assessing all of your residents for something many do not use or desire.

These are difficult trade-off decisions. In Chapter 19, I show you how to make some of these difficult capital investment decisions by determining how much you must add to a resident's typical monthly service fee to pay the additional debt service for various incremental capital investments. Conducting an incremental monthly service fee "sensitivity analysis" frequently will help you make this difficult decision.

Multiple living unit configurations grouped in *neighborhoods, clusters,* and *cul de sacs* are becoming common in assisted living and nursing designs. They can also be considered for independent living. They look very nice on a tour, and may be recommended by your CCRC design team. Before making this important design decision, you should have a full understanding of the costs – the initial capital needed, as well as ongoing operating cost impacts.

Call to Action

Consider a development project you may have worked on (or are currently working on). What changes would you make to that design based on what you now know? Also, consider the strengths and shortcomings of your direct competition. Look back with 20/20 hindsight and look forward with a creative vision of the future. Finally, you must always keep your new community's total all-in cost on your radar screen.

CHAPTER 12

THE OPTIMUM SIZE OF A CCRC

The Critical Tradeoff Between Operational Efficiency and Marketplace Risk

Once you've decided to build a CCRC, one of the most critical decisions will be how many units to develop. Overbuild, and many of your units will remain empty. Under-build and you doom yourself to permanent marginal financial performance or worse.

The optimum size decision represents an objective tradeoff between optimizing operational efficiency (more units) and marginal market feasibility (building too many units).

A financial sensitivity analysis will usually indicate that a well-conceived, freestanding independent living community should contain at least 135 to 150 units. In fact, many of the current industry models involving a more complete CCRC typically encompass more than 150 units. A small independent living project will have a higher financial break-even occupancy point than a larger one. Break-even occupancy is typically defined as just enough cash to cover both operating expenses and debt service payments.

However, you can't just arbitrarily increase the unit count to make your operations more efficient. You have to consider the resulting market penetration rate. From a market feasibility perspective, you generally should not assume an individual independent living project market penetration rate of more than 5 to 7 percent. Let's take a closer look. That means your project should not need to capture more than 7 percent of the total age- and income-qualified households within a properly defined Primary Market Area. And that's *after* allowing for important factors such as existing and announced competition and annual resident turnover of at least 18 to 22 percent for a CCRC. There must be a balance between optimizing financial viability and avoiding excessive marketplace risk. There's much more to consider in determining market feasibility. You should consult qualified industry professionals on this important matter.

Note: While a minimum of 100 units is marginally acceptable, your financials won't enter the truly optimum "sweet zone" until you develop and operate at least 135 to 150 revenue producing units. Most modern CCRCs are much larger.

The basic business principle is to spread fixed and semi-variable costs over an appropriate number of ***revenue producing units***. For CCRCs, that typically involves the total independent living and assisted living unit count. Nursing with characteristically low operating profit margins are usually excluded from this special analysis.

Typical CCRC Product Definition

Two recently developed comprehensive, large scale CCRC projects (in 2005/2006) have the following characteristics:

	Project A	Project B
• Independent living units	205	256
• Assisted living units	43	60
• Alzheimer's/dementia units	16	24
• Skilled nursing beds	60	64
Total Units-Beds	**324**	**404**
• Land area	17 acres	16 acres
• Unit density	19 units/acre	25 units/acre

These were large scale lifecare CCRCs with entry fee type pricing. Properly designed campuses with moderately lower unit counts will also perform successfully.

How Many Stories?

Deciding how high to build – how many stories to incorporate – typically involves restraints and tradeoffs. These include:

- Local building codes (height restrictions)
- Optimizing internal "flow" of staff and residents
- Overall operational efficiency
- On a typical floor, the walking distance from the farthest independent living unit to the elevator leading to the dining room (the higher the *vertical* building, the shorter the *horizontal* walk distances)
- Relative cost (type of construction)
- Available land, which impacts unit density and the configuration of the building footprint
- Providing safe, practical emergency evacuation of residents

Usually, all of the previously discussed factors dictate the ultimate configuration of your new independent living building or CCRC campus. Note that overall development and construction costs can vary as a function of the number of floors. As the number of levels increase, some costs decrease (land, foundation, etc.), while other costs tend to increase (elevators, type of construction, etc.). For very preliminary planning purposes, you can typically count on the density (approximate number of units per acre) to range from 15 to 25 living units per acre for a two- to three-story building. This includes not only the building structure, but roadways, parking spaces and the overall site infrastructure.

One vs. Two Bedroom Trade-offs

Figure 12-1 outlines some typical decision trade-off factors.

FIGURE 12-1
RUNNING THE NUMBERS . . .
ONE-BEDROOM VS. TWO-BEDROOM UNIT[1]
(A Typical Scenario in 2009 Dollars)

	1-BR	Vs.	2-BR	Percent Increase
• **Living Area S.F.**	750 sf		1,200	60%
• **Typical All-In Cost Per Unit[2]**	$150,000		$170,000	13%
• **Monthly Service Fee**	$ 2,100		$ 2,650	26%
• **Operating Expenses Per Resident-Day**	$ 45.00		$ 60.00	33%
• **Typical Resident's Qualifying Income (Pre-Tax)**	$44,000/yr		$55,000/yr	26%

[1] Refer to Figure 11-1 in Chapter 11 for typical design scenarios.
[2] Refer to Figure 23-1 in Chapter 23 for detailed definition for all-in cost per unit.

In the late 1990s, *studio units* in independent living became essentially obsolete from a marketing perspective. Now, increasing marketplace pressure is being placed on *one bedroom units*. The unit mix of newer communities is placing heavier emphasis on two bedroom units.

Building Efficiency

Figure 11-1 in the previous chapter summarizes typical space profiles for a 150-unit independent living community. Your profile will evolve from your unique and detailed design and space planning effort. However, the ideal "envelope" might look something like that summarized in Figure 12-2.

FIGURE 12-2
A TYPICAL 150-UNIT INDEPENDENT LIVING COMMUNITY SPACE PROFILE

	Two Design Scenarios[1] "Pontiac"	"Buick"
• From Figure 11-1: The weighted average net living area	800 s.f.	1,032 s.f.
• Total livable area (150 units)	120,000	154,800
• Common/public space and circulation	30% or 51,430	35% or 83,350
• Total area under roof	171,430	238,150
• Weighted average gross area	1,143 s.f. per unit	1,590 s.f. per unit

Total livable area (the living units) within independent living typically represents approximately 65 to 70 percent of the total (gross) area under roof.

[1]Refer to Chapter 11 for a more detailed discussion of these design scenarios.

Moore Diversified Services, Inc.

Lessons Learned

In my experience in working with past design and development communities, I've learned some important lessons. These include paying special attention to two areas frequently overlooked:

1. Administrative space – Many sponsors and owner/operators make the mistake of not allocating enough administrative office space. This involves management, sales and marketing and other office support functions. Make sure your designers block out each and every functional space that you and your staff identify as necessary and be sure that the resulting size of each space will properly satisfy your future needs.

2. Phasing - During the initial phase, consider the size and scale of your commercial kitchen and dining area with respect to a possible *future expansion.* Some of our clients initially oversized the commercial kitchen design and considered expanding the dining room design using a factor of approximately 25 square feet per chair – thus preparing for the possibility of an orderly second phase.

These and other forward looking considerations are an important part of the initial design strategy.

Five Effective Design Planning Strategies

Before moving on, let's take a look at five design concept considerations that can lead to a successful project:

1. Analyze the size of the market – Accurately determine the size and depth of your market so that you know how many units you can realistically fill in the competitive marketplace.

2. "Value engineer" your project with a passion – Value engineering means reducing cost in ways that do not adversely affect quality, ambience, ongoing maintenance or operational efficiency. A sound senior living project usually can't tolerate "Cadillac" designs, cost overruns or inefficient operations (see Chapters 20, 23, 24 and 25).

3. Confirm adequate cash flow from profit margins – Be sure you can cover annual debt service payments by at least 1.3 times your net operating income (refer to Chapter 26).

4. Use economies of scale – Consider the practical financial economies of scale that might be realized if your new independent living project is an integral part of an existing CCRC or health care campus. This results in more total revenue-producing units to spread both fixed and some semi-variable costs.

5. Consider growth – Study the possibility of orderly, prudent future expansion. This means creating a master plan for your community now – for consideration of additional units in the future, assuming a favorable initial market response to your community.

Finally, the "Rule of 10 for Designers." I often tell architects that if certain elements of their designs can save $1,000 per month or $12,000 in annual operating costs, the intrinsic value of their client's community is likely increased by at least 10 or 11 times the operational savings or over $132,000. That's because in 2009, potential buyers and appraisers will determine value by "capitalizing" the project's net operating income at about 8.5 to 9.5 percent (or less) to determine value. See Appendix C for the capitalization concept.

Call to Action

When it comes to independent living or CCRC design, you have only one chance to get it right. Conceiving and delivering cost-effective design represents one of the biggest challenges – and opportunities – for the future.

Double-check that your design includes enough administrative space. Also, does your master plan allow for future phasing? Evaluate the five design planning strategies covered in this chapter with your development team.

Remember, the future senior consumer is basically looking for their perception of favorable product, price and value . . . and they want choices.

CHAPTER 13

ACTIVE ADULT COTTAGES AND VILLAS

A Synergistic Growth and Revenue Enhancement Strategy

How would you like to bring a sharpened, market-responsive focus to your campus, as well as:

- Increase your resident's average length of stay?
- Provide a "feeder market" for your independent and assisted living?
- Optimize your resident profile?
- Improve your operating profit margin?
- Make productive use of available land?
- Put another $300,000 to $500,000 of cash in your coffers?

Better still, how would you like to accomplish all of this with limited capital and acceptable market and financial risk?

If this strikes your fancy, and you have some available land on your existing CCRC campus, consider adding active adult housing. While open space on the campus is certainly desirable, many sponsors and owner/operators now prefer to devote part of that land to active adult housing. Many continuing care retirement communities are located on a 20-acre or larger site.

An active adult community frequently consists of single family *detached* homes with living areas of approximately 1,500 to 1,800 square feet with garages. The resulting unit density is typically four to six units/acre. A higher density alternative would be single family *attached* duplexes, triplexes and quadraplexes with living areas ranging from 1,300 to 1,600 square feet with a density of six to eight units/acre. Figure 13-1 summarizes basic active adult product options.

Active adult housing can provide a very attractive alternative to your smaller CCRC apartments, which typically range from 600 to 1,200 square feet.

Active Adult Financial Synergy

Adding 25 active adult cottages/villas with a reasonable land cost allocation of approximately $20,000 per unit has a big payoff. Developing the land allows you to realize another half million dollars of land value that you probably already own free and clear. In addition, you can take the $500,000 land cost allocation as a cash bonus from your project financing or unit sales. You could also contribute it to your project as part of your financing plan's equity contribution[1].

Successfully implemented, you will now be spreading much of your *existing* fixed costs (executive director, general administrative costs, etc.) across *additional* revenue-producing units. You will also realize ongoing increases in cash flow after paying all operating expenses and mortgage payments. This increase will likely range from $4,000 to $5,000 per unit per year or a total of approximately $120,000 per year for those 25 additional units.

[1] Some markets can easily justify a higher land cost per unit allocation.

FIGURE 13-1
MENU OF BASIC PRODUCT OPTIONS FOR
ACTIVE ADULT COTTAGE/VILLA COMMUNITIES
(Physical design integrated within the overall campus master plan)

1. **Single Family - *Detached*:**
   - Living area: Approximately 1,500-1,800 s.f.
   - Garages
   - Unit density: Approximately 4 to 6 units per acre
   - Possibly a zero lot line design

2. **Single Family - *Attached*:**
   - Duplex
   - Villa
   - Quadraplex

   } Living area: 1,300 to 1,600 s.f. - with garages
   - Unit density: Approximately 6 to 8 units per acre

3. **Some Design Features**
   - Fireplace
   - Security system
   - Attic storage
   - Window shades and treatments
   - Appliances – full function kitchen
   - 24-hour personal emergency response system
   - Private yard/garden space

4. **Criteria for Determining The Need For A Separate Club Building**
   - Analyze whether you can offer the same benefits and amenities contained in the public spaces of the central independent living building
   - An additional club building is normally not needed on a full continuum campus unless there is an unusually large number of cottages/villas (50 units or more)
   - Consider the incremental cost (avoidance) trade-off
   - Evaluate the allocation of the club building cost impact on individual unit pricing
   - Is this an opportunity for an enclosed pool?
     - Is this a common amenity provided by competitors in your market area?

5. **Service-Enriched Active Adult Community Options**
   - Figure 14-2 and 14-3 in Chapter 14 provide a detailed summary of core and optional services typically offered by active adult communities.

Moore Diversified Services, Inc.

You will also diversify your product mix and realize a more optimum resident profile. At the same time, you'll also extend the average length of stay on your campus. If you offer any form of life care, you will likely lower your future actuarial and financial risks. Remember, as Chapter 48 points out, entry fees (one active adult pricing option) are essentially *interest free loans* that you get to keep for an extended time – typically for as long as the resident lives on your campus.

Market Positioning for a Slightly Different Resident Profile

When adding active adult villas, you'll have some unique market positioning issues to address. Your current independent living or CCRC resident profile probably consists of 70 to 80 percent single/widowed females with a typical entry age of 80 years or more. Most of these residents have specific needs and have probably already experienced a health related "wake-up call." This type of situation has motivated them to make the senior living decision in the first place.

On the other hand, active adult villa residents are typically couples in the 75- to 80-year-old age range, active, and in relatively good health. Their average entry age will change slightly. Instead of residents moving in at 80 years or older, residents – primarily couples – will typically move in when they are 75 to 80 years old. They desire hassle-free living with the option of purchasing additional a la carte services such as meals, housekeeping, and possibly health care. Figure 13-2 provides a comparison of the resident profiles.

FIGURE 13-2
TYPICAL RESIDENT PROFILES FOR AGE RESTRICTED ACTIVE ADULT COTTAGES/VILLAS VS. SERVICE-ENRICHED INDEPENDENT LIVING APARTMENTS

	Cottages/Villas	Service-Enriched Independent Living Apartments
1. Typical Resident Services		
• Meals • Housekeeping • Social activities • Assistance with the activities of daily living	Services are typically accessed on optional, a la carte basis	Usually part of a defined service package for a fixed monthly service fee. The fee varies as a function of unit type/size
2. Likely Resident Profile		
• Marital status	Mostly couples	70% to 80% Single/widowed females
• Age upon move-in	Primarily 75 to 80 years old	Primarily 80+ years old
3. Relative Health/Lifestyle		
• Chronic conditions	Relatively good health	Probably experienced a modest health "wake-up call"
• Acuity	Lower acuity	Quasi need-driven, moderate acuity levels
• Need for some direct/indirect support	Moderately active lifestyle	Some residents may exhibit significant frailty
4. Primary Decision Motivator		
• Avoid hassles of home ownership	Access hassle-free living	Quasi need-driven
• Ease of access to high quality future services	Downsize and simplify their financial situation	Pre-planners anticipating future needs
	Options to access future services on an as-desired or as-needed basis	Current need for sheltered living and some bundled services

Note: The two types of living arrangements have somewhat unique resident profiles.

Moore Diversified Services, Inc.

The rules change slightly when developing a new CCRC campus that involves active adult housing. Market positioning must be concise and clearly segmented to avoid confusion and cannibalization between your cottages/villas and your independent living apartments. Each must be positioned as separate products for seniors who have different *short-term* wants and needs, but common *long-term* concerns.

Active adult housing provides seniors with a single family unit that is smaller and thus more manageable than their conventional house, yet is associated with an array of both packaged and optional services. These services can include lifetime interior and exterior maintenance. To many seniors, this represents the cure for the classical *"I'm not ready for retirement living"* sales objection. They can access senior living without a comprehensive array of mandatory services. To many CCRC owner/operators, it represents a whole new market. In the past, this niche market of senior housing was usually perceived as a site-specific, large-scale project involving hundreds of units. But today, a moderate-sized CCRC can boost its bottom line by developing its own brand of active adult housing at minimal cost. Chapter 14 will address active adult risk-hedged development strategies.

Typical Active Adult Services

Figure 13-3 outlines the typical services offered in an active adult community. Think of active adult housing this way: You're offering the senior no hassle, single-family living with lifetime home maintenance, landscaping, snow removal (if applicable), etc. These residents can have full access to all of your CCRC services on an a la carte basis or as part of your defined life care program.

FIGURE 13-3

TYPICAL COTTAGE/VILLA SERVICES AND AMENITIES PROVIDED

I. <u>Basic Services</u>

1. 24-hour security
2. Basic cable television service
3. Scheduled transportation
4. Access to main building public spaces, dining rooms, library, etc.
5. Housekeeping/maid service – upon request
6. Home handyman services
7. Gardening areas
8. Community newsletter/calendars
9. Hobby/craft facilities and instruction
10. Chapel and pastoral care services
11. Health care and community referral services
12. Concierge services
13. Volunteer opportunities
14. Social and recreational programs
15. Scheduled banking

(Items 9–15: Services offered in the main building/clubhouse)

II. <u>Hassle-Free Maintenance</u>

1. Interior maintenance of cottage:
   - Appliances/plumbing
   - Heating/air conditioning
   - Normal cosmetic enhancements
2. Exterior cottage maintenance:
   - Landscaping
   - Snow removal – if applicable
   - Scheduled window washing

III. <u>Other Main Building/Clubhouse Services and Amenities</u>

1. Dining
2. Computer access
3. Wellness center
4. Beauty/barber shop

Also refer to Figure 14-3 in Chapter 14

Moore Diversified Services, Inc.

Call to Action

Has this chapter piqued your interest in the active adult housing option? If so, read on. Chapter 14 provides more details, including pricing strategies vs. service package options. Before moving on, take a very close look at your specific situation and consider whether active adult housing is appropriate for your campus in terms of the location and availability of land. Also, consider "resident flow patterns" and how active adult housing expands your continuum of living options. These are important issues you and your team should consider. Don't forget the potential financial impact.

CHAPTER 14

THE ECONOMICS OF ACTIVE ADULT HOUSING

Pricing and Development Strategies

Chapter 13 outlined the synergistic opportunities associated with active adult senior housing. The *concept* appears simple enough, but the *execution* requires some complex decision making. You must develop specific strategies in two important areas: pricing and development.

Develop a Pricing Strategy

Before you take the plunge into active adult housing, the next challenge is to select a market-responsive, financially-viable pricing strategy. There are a number of options, but you need to make a core decision: Will you charge residents a straight monthly fee or an upfront fee with a more moderate monthly fee?

There are typically four basic pricing approaches:

1. **Conventional purchase.** Owners pay a one-time fee similar to the conventional home purchase. This approach is also known as fee simple ownership.
2. **Cooperative/condominium**. Residents either own their unit (condominium) or they "own" an undivided share of the entire complex. Typically, residents own a share of the active adult/independent living public/common areas of the campus.

3. **The life estate or master trust concept**. Residents pay an upfront fee sometimes classified as an entry fee which is similar to the amount paid for a fee simple home purchase; however, the resident does not technically own the unit. Instead, the resident has a "lifetime right" (non-transferable) to live in that particular unit (refer to Figure 14-4 for expanded details).
4. **Straight monthly service fee**. This pricing approach charges no large upfront fee. The senior pays a monthly fee to cover two primary costs:
    - The equivalent one time cost of capital to finance the unit and a share of the public spaces
    - The ongoing cost of core mandatory services provided

Figures 14-1 and 14-2 provide some guidelines for making the complex pricing decision.

Cost Recovery for Core/Mandatory Services

A fixed monthly service fee is usually assessed based on full cost recovery for certain core/mandatory services – much like a monthly condominium fee – sometimes called a "homeowner's fee". These services constitute the normal costs of hassle-free living that seniors receive when they choose active adult communities. The monthly service fee is individually adjusted for the relative size of the living unit. The owner/operator must typically recover costs in five major areas:

1. **High-value homeowner services.** Examples include security, real estate tax recovery (if applicable/necessary), and participation in selected community activities/social programs.

2. **Maintenance.** This usually includes lifetime interior and exterior maintenance of the structure, such as appliances and normal wear and tear (cosmetics).
3. **Landscaping and grounds maintenance.** This includes vegetation, roadway repairs, maintenance, and, in some areas, snow removal.
4. **Priority access to other living arrangements.** This includes access to assisted living, nursing, and other health-related services on the campus.
5. **Pro-rata share of the debt service.** This recoups the initial cost of the land, site development, hard construction costs for the living unit, and all relevant development soft costs if no upfront fee is charged.

Figure 14-3 provides a more detailed outline of these typical costs to be recovered.

Optional Services With A La Carte Charges

The resident could also pay a la carte fees for desired meal service, housekeeping, flat linen laundry, assistance in living services, wellness/preventive health program, full health care services, and home health services, etc. Access/use of your community's common areas (lounges, dining room, meeting/activity rooms, etc.) would be included as an active adult resident benefit. Figure 14-4 outlines typical a la carte services offered.

Hedging the Development Risk – Master Plan and Pre-Sales

As the saying goes, it takes money to make money. Fortunately, you can spread out your active adult investment risk by designing a master plan with multiple phases. One approach is to master plan the entire campus but pre-sell and release for construction seven to ten units at a time – a typical "phase." The senior consumer would select a specific lot (within an active phase) for a home; opting for one of four or five floor plans and building elevations. Although the consumer is offered certain upgrade options such as custom flooring, wall coverings, drapes, or minor changes to the interior configuration, the end product is architecturally controlled and carefully integrated within the overall campus plan.

In essence, you can help residents sort out different product/service benefits by identifying which option might be best for them. When approximately 80 percent of a particular "development phase" has been pre-sold, you can then begin construction. Figures 14-2 and 14-5 outline the necessary details for a typical risk-hedged active adult development plan.

Collect Progress Payments

If you charge an upfront fee vs. a market rate rental, you should establish a tiered progress payment policy. A series of progress payments might include:

- 10 percent upon signing a sales contract (sometimes refundable)
- 20 percent at ground breaking
- 40 percent at finish-out
- 30 percent upon move-in

This process allows you to cover most of your evolving cash flow needs. You can also use a short-term bridge loan to smooth cash flow needs and to fund the construction phase of your expansion project.

A Final Punch List

A well-conceived plan must initially consider ten important active adult planning issues:

1. **When marketing, make a clear distinction between active adult cottages/villas and service enriched independent living apartments (see Figure 13-2 in Chapter 13). Differentiate between:**
    - Resident services
    - Resident profile
    - Health/lifestyle
    - Motivating factor(s)
2. **Define mandatory costs (see Figure 14-3). These include:**
    - Pro rata share of the debt service
    - Lifetime interior and exterior maintenance
    - Landscaping/ground maintenance
    - Security
    - Real estate tax recovery – if applicable/necessary
    - Participation in selected community activities/social programs

- Priority access to other living arrangements on the senior living campus
- Access/use of the community's common areas (lounges, meeting/activity rooms, etc.)

3. **Define how a resident pays a la carte fees (see Figure 14-4). These could include:**
   - Meal service
   - Housekeeping
   - Flat linen laundry
   - Assistance in living services
   - Wellness/preventative health program
   - Full health care services
   - Home health services
4. **Define the final service plan.** For example, outline the typical cottage/villa service and amenities to be provided or offered for extra charges.
5. **Develop land resource and cost recovery strategies:**
   - Actual cost recovery:
     - Raw land
     - Site development
     - Overhead
     - Profit
   - Unit density vs. land cost scenarios:
     - Unit density vs. land cost recovery vs. profit

- Land as an asset:
    - Provides implied equity for the project
    - Include as a project cost even though currently owned

6. **Consider a broad menu of basic physical product options for active adult cottages/villas (see Figure 13-1 in Chapter 13):**
    - Single family – detached
    - Single family – attached (duplexes/quadraplexes, etc.)
    - Expected unit density (living units/acre)
    - Is there a need for a separate club building?
    - Service enriched active adult community options:
        - Basic
        - Extensive

7. **Develop distinctive price positioning for cottages/villas vs. service-enriched independent living apartments** (refer to Figure 14-1):
    - Straight/conventional monthly service fees

      vs. . .
    - Value-enhanced upfront fees with more moderate monthly service fees
    - The "homeowner's fee" concept

8. **Identify typical ownership/occupant options (see Figure 14-2):**
    - Conventional purchase – fee simple ownership of a specific unit

- Cooperative/condominium – also fee simple ownership
- Life estate/entry fee concept
- Straight monthly service fee
- Also define whether the sponsor or resident is responsible for re-selling the unit

9. Prepare a risk-hedged plan for developing active adult housing on your senior living campus (see Figure 14-5):

- Create a master plan
- Do work in phases
- Pre-sell villas by project phase

10. Putting it all together – the forward-looking active adult strategic master plan:

- The external competitive market is dynamic and changing in terms of:

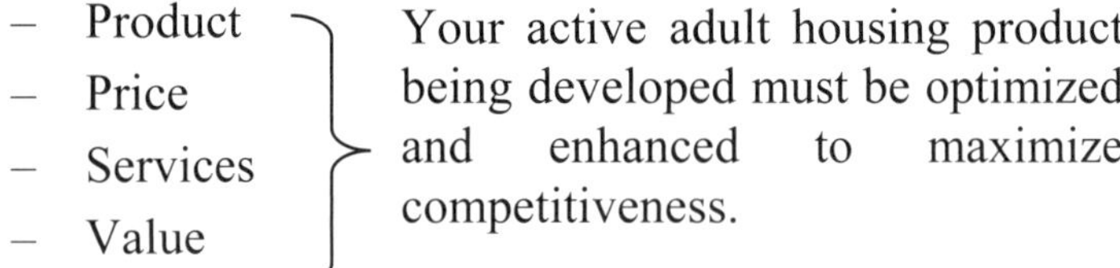

  - Product
  - Price
  - Services
  - Value

  Your active adult housing product being developed must be optimized and enhanced to maximize competitiveness.

  - Market-responsive pricing should offer:
    - Flexibility
    - Options
  - The current senior consumer prospect's mindset and expectations may favor the competitor (be aware of competitive advantages).

- Phasing plan:
  - Approximately 7 to 10 units per pre-sold phase

- Approach to the market:
  - Pre-sales approach
  - Final sell-out approach
- Deposit/tiered progress payment policy
- Selling price takes down construction costs/financing?
  - Partial
  - Total
- Full product cost recovery:
  - Hard costs
  - Soft costs
  - Land
  - Overhead
  - Profit

During the planning process you must develop practical, market-responsive approaches to each of these important issues.

Call to Action

Before making any active adult housing decisions, consider the following:

1. Evaluate which pricing strategy for active adult housing best suits your needs.
2. If active adult housing sounds interesting, use the figures in this chapter and Chapter 13 to develop issues to be addressed. This chapter also contains a final punch list. Highlight those issues that need a closer look.
3. Create a master plan that allows for growth.

Active adult housing is market-responsive and can materially improve your financial position. It just may be the right strategy at the right time to complete your continuum and optimize your CCRC.

FIGURE 14-1
ACTIVE ADULT PRICE POSITIONING
UPFRONT FEE VS. STRAIGHT MONTHLY SERVICE FEE
(For different senior consumer preferences & propensities)

Value-Enhanced Upfront Fees With Moderate Monthly Service Fees:[1]	**Vs. . .**	**Straight/Conventional Monthly Service Fees:**
1. Allows the senior to maintain the same stable savings portfolio they had prior to home sale: • Income qualified seniors can afford (and prefer) to pay lower monthly service fees with *current income*.		**1. Allows seniors to keep and invest their home equity proceeds:** • Seniors can manage their own portfolio, expanded by their home sale proceeds (plus receiving the increased earnings from their invested home sale proceeds).
2. Entry fees attract seniors who ideally desire future estate preservation and "no hassle" estate liquidity. Examples: • Family has no home to sell upon their death. • Seniors have predictable legacy/estate proceeds in the form of a guaranteed refundable entry fee.		**2. Attractive to seniors who prefer to manage all of their financial assets and who can easily afford the higher monthly service fees.**
3. Many would feel that the value-enhanced entry fee is a good tax-advantaged use of their money.		**3. Some seniors may desire to put some of their estate/capital assets to work *now* – in various personal ways:** • Gifts to children • Grandchildren's education • Charitable contributions, etc.
4. Fee simple ownership (condo) or a co-op arrangement allows a senior to realize potential market value appreciation.		**4. <u>CAUTION:</u> If the cost of your product drives the monthly service fee too high, the senior may go into sticker shock. Avoid this with an alternative upfront fee/lower monthly service fee strategy.**

A common approach to pricing involves an upfront fee which basically retires/takes down the construction loan and a monthly service fee to cover the cost of ongoing services rendered.

[1] Upfront fees could be life estate/entry fee, condo, cooperative or various hybrids such as master trusts.

Moore Diversified Services, Inc.

FIGURE 14-2
TYPICAL OWNERSHIP/OCCUPANT OPTIONS
(Active adult, master planned housing)

I. Conventional Purchase - Fee Simple Ownership of a Specific Unit

1. Buyer selects specific lot location (for project phase being sold).
2. Buyer also selects specific living unit type from approximately four or five floor plans.
3. Lot and unit may be separately priced. Total cost is a function of:
   - Location of lot
   - Unit floor plan selected
4. Resident (or their estate) is responsible for selling the unit upon death/move-out:
   - Sponsor to act as the selling agent
5. Monthly service fee for core/mandatory services outlined in Figure 14-3.

II. Co-operative/Condominium Ownership

1. Resident pays upfront fee similar to conventional purchase.
2. Unit selection process similar to above.
3. There are several resale options:
   - Resident/estate is responsible for resale
   - Sponsor could retain first right of refusal for purchase of the unit upon resident move-out or death
   - Sponsor could control the resale of the units as an agent:
     - Include a typical real estate sales commission

III. Life Estate/Entry Fee Concept

1. Resident pays upfront fee similar to purchase options I and II above.
2. Unit selection process similar to above.
3. Resident has "lifetime right" (non-transferable) to live in the unit
4. Life estate fee could have a defined refundable feature upon death/move-out of resident(s). (Obviously, there could be multiple pricing plans offered.)
5. Alternatively there could be a monthly service fee for core, congregate, and health care services outlined in Figure 14-3.
6. Sponsor is responsible for reselling unit:
   - Can sometimes delay refund to the estate until that specific unit is resold
     - Typical contractual terms for estate refund are within 30 days of closing of the resale or approximately 12 months after previous resident death/move-out, whichever comes first
   - Sponsor is likely to experience financial gain on unit resale (current appreciated market price less resident refund contractual obligation)
     - Sometimes a "shared appreciation" concept between the sponsor and the resident/estate is yet another pricing option

IV. Straight Monthly Service Fee (Covering the Cost of the Unit)

1. The monthly service fee is based on the cost of the unit and lot and is "priced" based on total capital cost and the sponsor's cost of capital (interest rate).
2. In addition, there would be add-on fees for core services.

V. The Fundamental Issues In Deciding Between The Various Pricing & Ownership Options Are

1. Marketability
2. Who takes resale risk:
   - Risk-taker also enjoys the potential gains on resale rewards
3. Are any prepaid benefits (health, etc.) offered in the plan?

Each alternative selected should be "financially neutral." Your financial/cost recovery should be essentially the same, regardless of pricing method. Any of the above plans could also offer a form of life care. Price accordingly.

Moore Diversified Services, Inc.

FIGURE 14-3
PRICING/COST RECOVERY FOR TYPICAL CORE/MANDATORY SERVICES PROVIDED TO ACTIVE ADULT COTTAGES/VILLAS

These core/mandatory services are part of an ongoing monthly service fee (like a homeowner's townhouse or condominium fee) that pays for the normal costs of hassle-free living services that active adult seniors desire.

1. Pro-rata share of the debt service that funded:
   - Initial land cost
   - Site development costs
   - Marketing budget
   - Other relevant soft costs:
     - Overhead
     - Profit
     - Etc.
   - All-in unit capital cost if straight monthly service is charged
2. Lifetime interior and exterior maintenance:
   - Structure
   - Appliances
   - Cosmetics - normal use/wear and tear
3. Landscaping/grounds maintenance:
   - Vegetation
   - Roadway repairs and maintenance
   - Snow removal - if applicable
4. Security
5. Real estate tax recovery - if applicable/necessary
6. Participation in selected community activities/social programs:
   - Coordinated by the project staff
   - Focal point: main/club building
7. Priority access to other living arrangements on the senior living campus:
   - Assisted living
   - Health-related services
8. Access to the community/common areas (lounges, meeting/activity rooms, etc.):
   - Usually located within the congregate/independent living building

A fixed monthly service fee or "homeowners fee" is typically assessed to realize full cost recovery for these types of services. Monthly fees are adjusted for the relative size of the living unit. Refer to Figure 14-4 for typical optional, a la carte, extra cost services available to residents.

Moore Diversified Services, Inc.

FIGURE 14-4
PRICING OPTIONS FOR TYPICAL COTTAGE/VILLAS A LA CARTE SERVICES, AMENITIES AND EXTRA CHARGES

Active adult residents pay a la carte fees (added to their base monthly service fee) for the following type of services:

1. Dining in main building
2. Housekeeping
3. Flat linen laundry
4. Assistance in living services[1]
5. Assisted living or nursing[1]
6. Home health services
7. Wellness/preventive health program[1]
8. Full health care services[1]
9. Beauty salon/barber shop
10. Unscheduled maintenance/"home handyman" assistance
11. Customized concierge services:
    - Mailing, fax and copier services
    - Telephone service and calls
    - Etc.
12. Activities/social events
13. Utilities and premium cable/satellite channels are typically not included and are paid separately by the resident
14. Guest accommodations
15. Bus/taxi transportation by appointment

A la carte fees are assessed on an actual cost plus modest mark-up as a contribution to overhead and profit.

Active adult villas should have a fixed monthly service fee which would cover both core/packaged components (Figure 14-3) and an a la carte service component fee schedule.

[1]Could be part of a comprehensive or modified lifecare program.

Moore Diversified Services, Inc.

FIGURE 14-5
A RISK-HEDGED PLAN FOR DEVELOPING ACTIVE ADULT HOUSING ON A SENIOR LIVING CAMPUS

I. The Big Picture

1. Available land should be worked into the master plan for orderly future growth.
2. A phased development plan should be implemented.

II. Adding Medium Density Cottages/Villas

1. Sequence of a prudent master plan:
   - Divide construction into three to four *"development blocks"* or phases
   - Prospects can select the lot and floor plan within the specific development block of the master plan being pre-sold
   - When approximately 80% of a particular "development block" is pre-sold (deposits received), a release for construction (of that block of units) is initiated
   - In this manner, the project will realize the benefits of both orderly master planning and the safety of prudent phasing
2. Unit density yield for single family attached housing is likely to be 6-8 units/acre
3. Establish competitive pricing that also makes your pro forma work
4. Pre-sell units from a phased master plan:
   - Pre-sell/release villas for construction in phases consisting of blocks of 7 to 10 living units
   - Pre-sell specific lots (locations) and specific floor plans
   - Require tiered progress payment/deposit policy. For example:
     - 10% upon signing sales contract
     - 20% upon ground breaking
     - 40% upon finish-out
     - 30% upon move-in

NOTE: ***In a new project, you must avoid confusion and cannibalization between active adult cottages/villas and congregate independent living apartment units. You must carefully position each as separate products for seniors with different wants and needs.***

Moore Diversified Services, Inc.

CHAPTER 15

SENIOR APARTMENTS

The Battle for Market Share Intensifies

For years, full-service independent living and CCRC owner/operators and sponsors have been trying to get inside the minds of seniors. They try to convince them that service enriched senior living is the optimum solution for their future planning. Many seniors are not buying their story. There are three basic reasons:

1. Seniors Frequently Complain About the Hassle of Current Homeownership and Ongoing Maintenance – While many are willing to explore alternative living arrangements, they seek their definition of successful downsizing.

2. Consumer Psychographics and Value Perceptions are Changing – Senior consumers have sharpened their definition of *value* which typically involves product, value, price, choice and service options.

3. The "I'm Not Ready Yet" Syndrome – This is today's biggest sales objection. For many seniors, they're not yet ready to accept service intensive independent living.

Market rate service free senior apartments are a relatively new product that offers *choice, flexibility* and is responding to the "*I'm not ready yet*" sales objection. The product looks a lot like independent living apartments except it does not offer an extensive mandatory service package such as meals and housekeeping. The product is for seniors who are relatively healthy (or think they are) and do not require assistance with cooking, cleaning or other typical supportive services that are usually offered at full-service independent living retirement communities. The public spaces are well done but on a much smaller scale.

This product captured more than a 46 percent share of new senior living construction in 2007 while offering both low/moderate income (with tax credits) and market rate pricing models. In 2008, senior apartments accounted for 27 percent of new senior living *properties* and expansions constructed. These properties may have central kitchen facilities but they generally do not provide programmed meal packages for residents. Many offer community rooms for social activities and other limited amenities.

The average community consists of approximately 120 to 150 units. Over the past 10 years, senior apartment communities have been built containing a total inventory of approximately 90,000 units. Tax credit financed senior apartments for low to moderate income seniors dominated the development in early years. The focus has now shifted towards conventionally financed, market rate communities.

Resident Characteristics

Typical resident profile characteristics can be summarized as follows:

- The average age upon move-in is 73.
- On average, females comprise approximately 75 percent of the total resident population. Approximately 10 percent are married couples.

- Death is reported to be the leading cause of turnover. Residents typically have access to licensed home health care services provided by an unaffiliated third-party provider. A small but growing percentage of residents report receiving home health care.

Typical Physical Design Characteristics

Obviously the physical design of a senior apartment community is influenced by many factors. However, here is a typical profile:

- The majority of developments are multi-story buildings (up to five floors with elevators and interior access to individual living units using double-loaded hallways). The properties are primarily located in suburban metropolitan areas.
- Typical size 150 unit project
- Approximately 130,000 to 150,000 gross square feet are under roof
- Approximately 15 to 20 percent of that area is public spaces and circulation (hallways, stairwells, etc.) The public space in service-enriched independent living communities usually involves approximately 30 to 35 percent.

Let's look at a real world senior apartment community on the market in the southwest in 2009 [1]:

[1] Age restriction is 55+

		Monthly Service Fee (2009 Dollars)	
Unit Type	**Living Area**	**Market Rate**	**Low-Moderate Income** [1]
• Efficiency	450- 500 s.f.	\$ 800- \$ 825/mo	\$530/mo
• One Bedroom, One Bath	700- 900 s.f.	\$ 900- \$1,200/mo	\$540- \$680/mo
• Two Bedroom, One Bath	925- 1,300 s.f.	\$1,020- \$1,500/mo	\$640- \$820/mo

Typical Service and Amenities

While services and amenities can vary from project to project, this particular community offered the following:

- Transportation service
- Elevators in all buildings
- Social and recreational programs
- Fitness center
- Arts and crafts room
- Swimming pool
- Restaurant-style dining room (meals optional)
- Beauty salon
- Coffee shop

---

[1] Typical low-moderate income limitations: annual income must be less than \$28,000 for one person and \$32,000 for a two person family. This income criteria varies from market-to-market based on prevailing median income.

Financial Performance

While there are not yet any extensive financial benchmarks established for senior apartments, here is a typical market rate financial profile for a 150-unit project at 93 percent occupancy with an average monthly service fee of $1,100 per occupied unit and 2 percent miscellaneous revenue:

• Revenue	$ 1,884,960	
• Expenses	(739,200)	40% Expense Ratio
• Net Operating Income	$ 1,145,760	60% EBITDA Margin [1]

Total, all-in cost per unit is typically in the range of $125,000 to $140,000 per unit.

Call to Action

Recognizing that senior apartments are here to stay, they are perhaps the best current example of how the senior living product life cycle is changing. The traditional definition of a CCRC is changing. Senior apartments can provide both new development opportunities and competitive heartburn. Some sponsors and owner/operators are adding senior apartments to their existing CCRC campus. Also, keep your eye on service free senior condominiums being offered for sale on a fee simple basis. See Chapter 46 for more new product details.

[1]EBITDA = Earnings Before Interest, Taxes, Depreciation and Amortization

You must also carefully monitor these emerging trends:

1. Some residents – upon move-in should really be opting for service-enriched independent living.

2. Other residents will inevitably age in place and need an increasing level of services (meals, housekeeping, assistance in living, etc.).

Will you ultimately provide some of these services or expect these residents to move out? Think about this situation now because it could influence your initial design (comprehensive commercial kitchen, etc.).

CHAPTER 16

CONVERSION/ADAPTIVE REUSE

Emotional Love Affair or Sound Business Strategy?

If I told you that I had an old hotel that would make a perfect independent living community, would you be somewhat skeptical? You should be.

Adaptive reuse and conversions is a trend I hear more and more about these days. But let me say upfront, that if your love for a property is so strong it causes you to forget what you learned in this book or in business school, fasten your seatbelt and prepare for the worst.

Developers are successfully converting old apartment buildings and moderately-sized hotels and motels into senior living communities. But many people dive into adaptive reuse without doing their homework. A reuse project must involve an objective evaluation of the community and a clear understanding of the marketplace risk. That evaluation process is the topic of this chapter.

Before we begin, however, I must stress that, in a reuse project, you must keep your emotions in check. Your love and vision for a property must not control your decisions, and it should not overshadow building and site limitations.

The property you're considering should, however, provide significant *benefit-driven* opportunities and upside potential.

Unfortunately, the underlying motivation of the developer or sponsor in many cases is, ***"I have this old property (that I'm in love with) – now what do I do with it?"*** A common, but frequently deadly, rationalization is that, ***"Surely the market will understand what I went through to pull off this difficult conversion!"*** It probably won't.

Conversion/adaptive reuse typically involves two types of "bricks and mortar:"

1. ***Existing senior living structures*** that require change/ improvement. An example might be converting older, small independent living units into assisted living on a campus.
2. ***Non purpose-built structures originally used for other purposes*** that are now considered candidates for senior living conversion.

I can cite dozens of examples of reuse projects that went well, and just as many that were disastrous. The successful conversions were based on sound rationale. Other projects were agony, not unlike that of a homeowner "fixing up that old house." Serious problems continue to emerge as you get deeper and deeper into the conversion. You can quickly pass the point of no return.

The Existing Owner-Operator's Perspective

Many owner-operators consider adaptive reuse. Typically the goal is one of the following:

- Expand, upgrade and renovate existing – probably aging – senior living structures on the campus.
- Add more cosmetically pleasing and expanded, functional public spaces.

- Convert a wing or floor of an independent living community into purpose-built assisted living space.
- Combine smaller studio units into one-bedroom independent living units. There is now an emerging trend of converting one-bedroom units to more market-responsive two-bedroom accommodations. Today's market is demanding more space.
- Convert portions of existing independent living or assisted living into an Alzheimer's/dementia neighborhood.

The fancy word for this type of effort is now called "repositioning," a term that was previously used to describe marketing strategies.

Even with laudable objectives, we frequently fail to initially ask the defining strategic question, **"Should this structure be saved in the first place?"**

Answering this question is often postponed – especially when the real estate market is hot. Why sink money into a building, even if it is substandard, when apartments still command *standard* and sometimes *premium* market rates? While we all know pricing bubbles don't last forever, there never seems to be a good time to bite the bullet and renovate. But when the bubble does burst – vacancies increase, remarketing efforts stall and then the inevitable crisis emerges. With less revenue coming in, now it's even harder to convince yourself to start a renovation project.

The Potential Buyer's Perspective

Risks aside, there are some economic and market realities which make adaptive reuse a very valid concept. From time to time, real estate markets become overbuilt or, as some say facetiously, under-demolished. Some properties become functionally or geographically obsolete for their originally intended usc. These properties are frequently sold by lenders and owners for deep discounts. It can be hard to turn down a bargain, and you might suddenly find an interesting adaptive reuse opportunity on your hands. But, along with this tempting opportunity comes significant risk.

The Rules of the Adaptive Reuse Game

I have five fundamental rules for successful conversion/ adaptive reuse communities. If these rules are broken or inappropriately applied, your project may fail.

1. ***The site characteristics*** of the adaptive reuse building should be appropriate and essentially irreplaceable in the immediate primary market area. If someone else can build a new, state-of-the-art independent living community on a similar nearby site with competitive pricing, the new project is likely to be far more competitive than your converted existing/older property.

2. ***The building structure*** should be truly unique – with innovative, practical and cost-effective adaptive reuse potential. It could be a historical landmark, or one with a past that is memorable for *positive* reasons.

3. ***The total turn-key cost*** of acquisition, renovation and conversion should be somewhat less than the all-in cost of a newly-designed and developed state-of-the-art senior living community. Keep in mind that the *real estate cost* – your debt service recovery - makes up only 30 to 36 percent of the resident's total required monthly service fee. (Refer to Chapter 44 for details.)

4. ***The consumer will give very little consideration*** to the necessary tradeoffs and compromises made in order to reuse the existing structure. The only thing that counts in the consumer marketplace is the perceived value and tangible benefits of the end product or service. Just as homeowners fall in love with the "quaint old home" that appears suitable for fix-up, some operators get involved in irrational love affairs with their newly acquired "bargain real estate."

5. ***Finally***, will your product be truly competitive in terms of product, price, service, and value?

You will always share a common nut to crack with your competitors; your ongoing operating costs. Saving on capital costs certainly helps, but be sure to totally quantify the real benefit in the competitive marketplace. And here's a key point:

With adaptive reuse, you must offer *very* competitive pricing. You can bet that consumers will focus on this important economic issue, so make sure you're competitive *before* you make another move. Poor pricing could highlight the undesirable tradeoffs you made rather than the benefits you offer.

The key to successful adaptive reuse is to make sure there is a match between the conversion opportunity and the benefits and needs of the marketplace.

The Scoreboard: Product, Price, Services and Value

I'm frequently asked whether a reuse project will be feasible. The acid test is whether the fully converted community can effectively compete in terms of product, price, services, and value.

The renovated community must be able to compete with new state-of-the-art competitors that are not stigmatized. To improve the odds of feasibility, there are three traps to watch out for.

Three Traps to Avoid

There are three major traps that tend to snare developers and owner/operators during an adaptive reuse community:

1. ***Inappropriate design configuration*** – Significant flaws frequently exist in the basic building footprint, floor layouts, lack of common areas, or the configuration of the existing living units. The units should be accessed off of interior loaded hallways.

2. ***Mediocre location*** – The community location was not really unique and ideally situated. For example, the surrounding area is non-residential; heavy commercial/ industrial (train tracks, highways, airports, etc.). Determining site location is very similar to site selection for a completely new building. The margin for error is very narrow – and major compromises will likely lead to a troubled community.

3. ***Undesirable perceptions or misconceptions of the past*** – Sometimes the building's history/reputation stirs a permanent negative perception on the new community. If this is the case, all the renovation in the world might not change negative perceptions.

Figure 16-1 summarizes the delicate tradeoff: Conversion dreams or economic nightmare!

Adaptive reuse is one way to deliver needed senior housing and health care while helping to balance an overbuilt real estate market. The strategy can also save classic structures from the wrecking ball.

FIGURE 16-1
ADAPTIVE REUSE OUTCOMES

REALIZED CONVERSION DREAMS? **OR . . .** **ECONOMIC NIGHTMARE?**

The Right Approach	***The Wrong Approach***
• The site is unique	• The site is really not unique
• Approvals were obtained with relative ease	• You paid too much for: – Acquisition – Renovation – Approvals
• You paid no more than 80% of alternative (new development) costs for: – Acquisition *Plus* – Renovation • There were no major design tradeoffs: – Suitable unit size and configuration – Appropriate building layout – Interior loaded hallways – No asbestos	• You rationalized away serious design flaws: – Bedrooms too small – Very narrow corridors – Long walk distances to insufficient common areas – Asbestos – Inadequate HVAC system – Very institutional – Etc.

Focus on the practical realization of a good end product and don't fall in love with your real estate!

Moore Diversified Services, Inc.

Putting It All Together

To be successful with adaptive reuse, **first** consider what the marketplace needs and wants. Then determine whether the conversion candidate really meets those needs. While apparently simple, the reverse of this process is frequently undertaken. Remember that adaptive reuse works best if the site is irreplaceable and the ultimate turn-key cost is approximately 20 percent less than a new building. This pricing advantage makes reasonable tradeoffs easier to accept in the marketplace.

This strategy can deliver a powerful product into the marketplace when it involves a unique location and excellent value at a surprisingly affordable cost for that particular market area. That is something that most consumers will notice. Without these advantages, adaptive reuse becomes much riskier. Chapter 17 presents some conversion success stories.

Call to Action

Before moving forward with your adaptive reuse project, evaluate whether:

- Your reuse project is really based on marketplace needs.
- The design, location, and perceptions of the building avoid the three traps explained in this chapter.

Run some detailed numbers. Can you really deliver financially superior end-results? Finally, will your adaptive reuse project really be competitive in terms of product, price, services, and value?

CHAPTER 17

CREATIVE CONVERSION SUCCESS STORIES

Some Real World Examples

The previous chapter summarized pitfalls and opportunities of adaptive reuse/conversion. Let's now look at some real world success stories.

Many different structures can be good conversion options, as long as the "footprint" and overall design configuration can compete with current state-of-the-art independent living communities. Schools, hotels/motels and apartments/condos are examples of structures that have been successfully converted (under the right conditions).

Schools

Many elementary schools in mature neighborhoods are now "demographically obsolete." The residents are aging. So the demand for large numbers of elementary classrooms has long since passed. From a strategic standpoint, adaptive reuse of these facilities frequently triggers less neighborhood opposition to planning and zoning approval requests than one hears when proposing a start-up senior housing development on a vacant piece of land adjacent to existing neighbors.

Some physical characteristics that make schools good candidates for conversion include:

1. Public spaces are adaptable:
    - Cafeteria converts into a dining room
    - Kitchen can be expanded/used as the commercial kitchen
2. The configuration of classrooms and hallways can generally be converted to double loaded corridors for independent living units:
    - Load-bearing walls and columns are frequently easy to deal with in the adaptive reuse process.
3. Many schools have a flexible "building shell." That means the basic exterior shell stays in place, while a number of substantial changes can be made inside the building with relative ease.
4. In many cases, the auditorium can be left largely in place and be converted into a "senior village mall or public meeting room (movie theaters, etc.)."

Each situation has unique opportunities as well as challenges.

Hotels and Motels

A number of hotels and motels across the United States have faced depressed occupancy or are geographically obsolete. Some markets may be permanently overbuilt. Many of these buildings make excellent adaptive reuse candidates, while others are beyond repair. In the right location, a hotel/motel makes an excellent conversion candidate. Many are located in traditional, well-established neighborhoods representing excellent in-fill locations in both suburban and urban areas. Some have both legitimate and nostalgic historical significance.

In terms of design, a number of unsuccessful attempts have been made to convert austere budget motels that do not have appropriate interior hallways, suitably configured sleeping rooms, or adequate public spaces. These attempts are clearly situation-driven, and miss the mark in the senior living marketplace. Conventional hotels with interior, double-loaded corridors and moderate-sized sleeping rooms might make a good conversion to assisted living, but it is highly unlikely they could properly serve the independent living market, which typically requires larger living areas and full-function kitchens (with complex plumbing requirements). An exception would be a suite hotel, which I'll discuss later.

Apartments and Condominiums

Condominium and apartment buildings can also make solid adaptive reuse buildings. As with hotels, these structures typically have living units with double loaded interior hallways. A typical shortcoming is likely to be inadequate common/public spaces, the absence of elevators and narrow, tunnel-like hallways. The public and circulation space requirements can represent 30 to 35 percent of the total area under roof for a well conceived, purpose-built independent living community.

The portion of the total area devoted to common space in a typical apartment or condo is frequently only 15 percent or less. However, there are ways to compensate:

- Sometimes an added building appropriately connected to the apartment complex can satisfy the new common space requirements.
- The space between a footprint with two parallel wings of living units offers the opportunity to provide room to add a "commons building." This new space would include a dining room, commercial kitchen, and space for other services in the center of the footprint, which provides another connection to the two wings of the building.
- Alternatively, those structures with only modest common space can be considered for limited service senior apartments. This senior living option is growing in market share across the U.S. (refer to Chapter 15).

Apartments and condos can make good conversion candidates for independent living because they typically have the following characteristics:

- Separate sleeping rooms
- Full-function kitchens
- Adequate living areas
- Interior double loaded hallways (in many geographical areas)
- Frequently located in a residential neighborhood setting

Smaller condos and apartments, however, are better suited for assisted living since assisted living requires less space than independent living.

Specific Conversion Considerations

Living units that enter into the interior double loaded hallways, and communities that have adequate common space and public areas, are key requirements when evaluating the overall suitability of a potential adaptive reuse structure. Obviously, the building's exterior elevations, roof lines and "external look" are also very important. Some characteristics to look for include:

- What is the first impression and "curb appeal" of the building's exterior?
  - Does it look residential versus institutional?
- Are there patios and balconies?
- Are there aesthetically pleasing "breaks" in the contour of the vertical surfaces?
- Are there interesting roof lines?

In other words, how appealing does the building look when one first observes it? Many facilities are functionally adequate, but appear to be far too institutional from a consumer perspective.

Design features such as the ability to meet current fire and life safety codes and other licensing requirements must be carefully considered. It is amazing how often experienced operators overlook building codes and requirements that suddenly come into play when previous variances that were grandfathered no longer apply to the new owner. Some even overlook the troublesome presence of asbestos.

Conversion Economic Yield

As I said in Chapter 16, it's very important to have a minimum favorable all-in cost differential of at least 20 percent.[1] That's because the majority of the costs to be recovered in independent

[1] All-in costs include all land, site development, hard construction and soft costs as detailed in Figure 23-1 in Chapter 23.

living involve ongoing and unavoidable operating expenses. New construction versus adaptive reuse cost sensitivity is summarized in Figure 17-1.

FIGURE 17-1
THE COST SENSITIVITY OF NEW CONSTRUCTION VS. ADAPTIVE REUSE

	New Construction	**Vs.**	**Adaptive Reuse**[1]
Total **all-in** capital costs/unit (See Chapter 23)	$180,000/unit		$144,000/unit (20 percent lower costs)
Weighted average cost of capital @ 8% debt constant (principal plus interest for a 70% loan to cost)[2]			
• Annual	$ 10,800		$ 8,065
• Monthly	$ 900		$ 672
• Monthly debt service recovery difference (potential reduction in monthly service fee)		$228/month	

[1] Includes value/acquisition cost and retrofit of an existing structure.
[2] Refer to Appendix B for debt constant.

Moore Diversified Services, Inc.

What They See Is What They Pay For

The paramount consideration is your customer. Consumers really do not care what it took to convert the building, or why some of the obvious tradeoffs or compromises are still highly visible. If there are competitors nearby, people will comparison shop – and you may get even less credit for your conversion compromises.

Conversion Success Stories

In spite of all of these cautions, there are numerous success stories. Some examples include:

1. ***A relatively new suite hotel*** with full-function kitchens and separate living and sleeping areas became a troubled property in an overbuilt hospitality market. It was easily converted to independent retirement living because of its original configuration. The location was ideal, and the property offered the opportunity to convert one floor to assisted living. A new nursing section was added to one end of the property. Everything was integrated with the original building.

2. ***An aging hotel and convention center*** was donated by the city to the local housing authority in order to serve modest gap-income seniors. The gap group typically has annual incomes between $12,000 to $25,000, and is extremely difficult to serve in a private pay situation. This donation helped the local housing authority avoid excessive capital costs and instead offer reasonable congregate services at a modest fee.

3. ***An office building*** without serious load bearing wall limitations was gutted and converted to relatively upscale independent living. The exterior elevations, roof lines and window treatments were creatively enhanced. It is now difficult to tell that the structure was once a commercial office building.

4. ***A company in Paris*** has taken a different approach to adaptive reuse. Paris is the epitome of urban density, yet one company finds urban sites of varying shapes and sizes and determines how many of their standard state-of-the-art living units can fit on the site. If the size is acceptable, they save the original building elevations/facades, demolish the existing structure, create a state-of-the-art structure – and then put the original Parisian facade back in place. The end result has the flavor of traditional Paris – with a state-of-the-art interior and a highly desirable location.

Each of these successful examples was the result of careful consideration of the ultimate end product design. Development teams carefully considered the location of the community and how the product would be perceived in the future by the senior consumer marketplace. Most importantly, none of the communities broke my five fundamental rules of adaptive reuse, first addressed in Chapter 16.

Call to Action

Before moving on with your conversion project, consider the key points of this chapter:

- When looking for a conversion community, look for certain critical design elements.
- To ensure a successful community, correctly answer the five key questions outlined in Figure 17-2.

Ideally, the site should be irreplaceable. Also review Chapter 16 as you finalize your plans.

FIGURE 17-2
ADAPTIVE REUSE – THE FIVE CRITICAL QUESTIONS TO ANSWER

1. **Is the site truly irreplaceable in the primary market area?**
2. **Is the building really unique, with practical and cost-effective adaptive reuse potential?**
3. **Is the total turn-key acquisition and conversion cost moderately less (approximately 20 percent) than the replacement cost of a newly-developed, state-of-the-art independent living facility?**
4. **Will the consumer understand and give appropriate consideration for the inevitable tradeoffs and compromises in the end product that typically result from adaptive reuse process?**
5. **Finally, will the community be truly competitive in terms of product, price, service and value?**

Objective answers to these questions will consistently separate the winners from the losers.

CHAPTER 18

COMMUNITIES ALSO AGE IN PLACE

Product, Price, Value, & Services Are What Really Count

While most of us are aware that our *residents* age in place, we frequently overlook or ignore another chronic aging trend - the gradual deterioration of our *physical plants*. As the senior living industry matures and we learn more about changing consumer preferences and needs, significant and innovative improvements are being made in the design and ambience of new senior living communities. This new trend is good, but it also represents a major challenge to older communities forced to compete with new state-of-the-art projects.

Strategic Focus

Let's sharpen our focus on this huge challenge by reviewing a "reality punch list." Here are five very relevant issues and questions that must be ***consistently*** addressed:

1. How market-responsive is your campus? Do you compete effectively on **product, price, value,** and **services?** Will you really be able to compete in the future? (See Chapters 10 and 11.)

2. Have you responded to the emerging trend of today's senior consumers rejecting the "status quo?" (See Chapter 4.)

3. Do you understand the dynamics of the senior living product life cycle and is your progression through this life cycle appropriate? (See Chapters 9, 11 and 46.)

4. Are any of your competitors converting independent living studios to one-bedroom units, or one-bedroom units to two-bedroom units? (See Chapters 10 and 11.)

5. Are you striving to become a unique **community of choice** - in terms of both programming and the physical plant? (See Chapters 47 and 48.)

Finally, are you charging *Buick/Cadillac* prices for a *Chevrolet/Pontiac* quality physical plant? Some feel compelled to do it in order to pay their escalating expenses, sustain break-even cash flow, and avoid financial distress. Read on.

Charging for Buicks But Delivering Chevrolets

Your response to the inevitable aging of a community must focus on two important issues:

1. The mindset and value perceptions of *future* residents and their families

2. The reaction of your *existing* residents

The two issues are very complex, and inevitably interrelated. Existing residents express reasonable levels of satisfaction. However, the future marketplace is heavily focused on four key attributes: **product, price, value,** and **services**. Over the next five years, the status of many of the existing physical plant aging problems will evolve from *serious* to *critical.*

For example, when an automobile ages, we still expect essentially the same performance as when it was new. Eventually, we buy a newer, better car. The same obsolescence factor is true with our facilities, except the solutions are far more complex. Many sponsors of aging communities feel trapped because the solution is not as simple as trading up to a better automobile.

Staff members will usually start to recognize subtle changes in the viability of their community. Long waiting lists become shorter, resulting in a smaller inventory of serious, qualified prospects. Stabilized occupancy begins to decline and marketing momentum eventually stalls.

Basic Design Flaws

Typical shortcomings in many older senior living communities include:

1. Very small studio or alcove units
2. Not enough two bedroom units
3. Small Pullman kitchens or no kitchens at all
4. Dated appliances, plumbing fixtures, lighting fixtures and cabinetry

5. Obvious wear and tear in public spaces, coupled with outdated interior designs
6. The community scores low on the ambience scale

Combined, these flaws result in negative value perceptions.

Space is Always at a Premium

There is frequently inadequate space in community common areas; space that is now desperately needed. Aging residents have more needs and staff frequently require more space to serve those needs. Dining areas are often small or lack ambience. Some communities opened only self-service buffet lines, but with aging residents and competitive threats, full wait staff service and a menu offering multiple entrees is becoming imperative. The problems are exacerbated by the overall cosmetic deterioration of the public areas and serious deferred maintenance issues, which, in turn, can have a costly impact on efficient operations.

Six Warning Signs

As I said earlier, a community ages, just like its residents. People wear down, and so do buildings. Both gradually decline in a highly predictable manner. Planning for appropriate physical plant capital investment is critical, and must be executed in a pragmatic manner. There are six warning signs to look for which signal that some capital investment is necessary:

1. Cosmetic wear and tear. Frayed or soiled upholstery, worn carpets, out of style drapes and faded wall coverings are common examples of cosmetic wear and tear. Wear and tear can also include cosmetic defects in the floor, wall surfaces and finishes in your public areas. Even if you offer outstanding quality of life and programming for residents, small but obvious blemishes on furniture or other amenities may give the opposite impression.

2. Physical plant deterioration. Leaky roofs or chronic heating, ventilating and air conditioning (HVAC) failures are tell-tale signs of ignored or deferred maintenance. You can probably avoid higher repair costs later by tending to smaller, inexpensive problems as they occur, before the situation becomes worse.

3. Functional obsolescence. The most obvious examples of outdated décor are kitchen and bathroom cabinets, plumbing fixtures and lighting in the individual living units. Dated furniture styles and electrical fixtures in the public areas are other common examples. Outdated and drab interiors in public spaces create negative first impressions for potential residents and their families.

4. Increased operations costs. Higher utility bills and a hampered work flow are often signs that various types of capital improvement are necessary. Again, it may be a matter of tending to small challenges before they turn into major problems. Chapter 24 addresses operating expenses and Appendix C deals with project valuation and capitalization rates. Every $1 in increased operations costs that could be corrected decreases the value of your community by at least $10.

5. Competitors are making capital improvements. It's one thing to keep your original physical plant functioning, and another to remain competitive. If the "other guy" upgrades his facilities and you don't, you're handing him a marketing advantage. This doesn't mean abandoning cost-effective common sense, of course. Some sponsors become so obsessed with adding additional bells and whistles that they price themselves out of the market just to pay for all the extras. It's always wise to keep track of what your competitors are doing and, when possible, beat them to the punch.

6. Obsolete locations. Many communities are now asking the strategic question, ***"Will our current senior 'living' campus and community be an acceptable, appropriate, and competitive location option for seniors in five to ten years?"***

Some sponsors are relocating their campuses from changing, demographically obsolete and sometimes deteriorating neighborhoods to locations that will better serve their future needs. Others are studying the viability of adding an additional satellite campus to serve the expanding needs in their primary market area. This additional campus strategy typically takes one of two approaches:

1. A new campus including the full continuum of living arrangements.
2. A well-conceived satellite location usually specializing in one or more living arrangements or medical service delivery systems.

In some cases, the sponsors or owner/operators are responding to a changing, split market. The seniors are clustered in one geographical area but the growing neighborhoods of adult children (decision influencers) are located across town.

Remember, you're trying to be in a position to respond to a dual threat – first, the inevitable aging of your plant, and second, efforts by competitors to offer newer amenities with more attractive environments in better locations.

At this point you may be thinking, ***"All this sounds great, but where's the specific financial or business plan?"*** Read on . . . I cover these important details in Chapters 19 and 23 through 26.

Top Five Areas for Potential Capital Improvements

Just as there are five signals that it is time to consider capital improvements, there are five areas to consider, in particular, when planning these improvements:

1. **Make a good first impression.** That old adage, ***"You never get a second chance at a good first impression"*** is truer than ever in today's highly competitive business environment. Consider how the outside of your campus looks to visitors. Review signs, pavement, landscaping and lighting, for example.

2. **Improve the look of the building exterior.** This includes fresh paint, new color combinations, window treatments, and interesting elevation facades and roof lines. Use the entrance to create a good

first impression. These tricks of the trade have proven effective for many communities.

3. Rejuvenation of interior public spaces. This generally means using new materials, finishes and renovation to improve and update the interior design of each community.

4. Back-of-the-house details. Expand and improve kitchen equipment, laundry facilities, and provide energy-efficient HVAC systems.

5. Improvements to individual living units. Update or replace appliances, plumbing fixtures, cabinetry, carpeting, and vertical and horizontal surfaces.

Figure 18-1 summarizes the top five areas of improvement.

FIGURE 18-1
THE TOP FIVE AREAS OF
PHYSICAL PLANT IMPROVEMENTS

1. **Enhanced first impressions of the community:**
    - Strong "sense of entrance"
    - Landscaping
    - Signage
    - Roadways
2. **Improved impressions of the building exterior:**
    - Elevations
    - Roof lines
    - Window treatments (exterior)
3. **Rejuvenation of the interior public spaces:**
    - Lounges
    - Furniture
    - Dining room
    - Vertical surfaces/floor coverings
    - Lighting fixtures
4. **Back-of-the-house improvements:**
    - Commercial kitchen
    - Laundry
    - HVAC
    - Elevators
    - Life safety equipment
5. **Individual living unit enhancement:**
    - Cabinets
    - Appliances
    - Wall/floor coverings
    - Plumbing fixtures
    - Window treatments (interior)

<u>Expected Outcome</u>: Enhance value without runaway costs!

Moore Diversified Services, Inc.

Exploit Market Niche Opportunities

Market niches should be carefully considered during a comprehensive renovation and/or expansion effort. This would include purpose-built applications such as special Alzheimer's/dementia units, space for a home health agency or fresh approaches to rehabilitation and adult day care. If land is available, the addition of active adult cottages/villas and possibly senior apartments with limited services can enhance the value of a CCRC campus and cash flow. Chapter 46 addresses the concept of market niches in detail.

Your Existing Residents May Deceive You

Many sponsors judge the severity of their physical plant problems by monitoring the relative degree of *existing* resident satisfaction. This approach can be dangerously misleading, because the mindset of existing residents in these outdated facilities can represent a good news/bad news situation.

The good news is that many existing residents living in sub-par living units (by today's competitive standards) are generally quite content. Formal resident panels indicate a surprisingly high degree of resident satisfaction. While many residents are aware of – and have visited – the newer competitors, they still prefer their "home," and are either willing to accept or are not sensitive to their sub-par conditions. Some residents are even paying premium prices for a community lacking ambience and modern amenities.

The bad news is that the positive attitudes of such residents frequently mask the true reaction of the broader replacement market, which is the lifeblood of any senior living community. New prospects and their loved ones visiting these communities are generally much more critical in terms of their first impressions. They see an aging facility serving an older, frailer community of residents. This can represent an immediate turn-off.

A Master Plan to Retrofit as Units are Vacated

Many sponsors find that with these capital improvements, they must change their pricing and service delivery policies. Naturally, they are concerned about how existing residents will react. To defer such changes indefinitely is not viable. An attrition strategy – upgrading rooms as residents move out – is an alternative. The attrition strategy clears the way for reasonable changes in pricing and service delivery policies. The future viability of the community is gradually re-established. This approach involves a number of challenges. Still, it should prove very effective in the long-run.

One of the most effective ways to gradually make changes on an existing campus is to have a master plan that addresses the *total concept,* but implements the necessary changes in *phases*. The plan could include a unit-by-unit upgrade or retrofit by attrition, as individual units become vacant. This approach minimizes the impact on existing residents, and even provides a rationale for a two-tiered pricing strategy as the newer, more state-of-the-art living units become available to future residents.

Upgraded living units can also be offered to existing residents for a modest increase in monthly service fees. There are obviously serious financial implications to consider. Chapter 19 shows you how to compute a modest increase in a unit's monthly service fee in order to break-even on the capital cost of the improvement.

Don't Procrastinate – The Time to Act is Now!

Many owner/operators and boards of directors are reluctant to make relatively expensive, progressive capital improvement investments. Instead, they hope for a miracle – that the downward occupancy spiral will level off to a plateau of acceptable performance.

The physical plant problem is not going away. Capital improvement efforts should be implemented as a consolidated, proactive strategic initiative. Capital improvements should not be a fragmented, reactive, band-aid approach.

Chapter 19 provides quantitative guidance on how to make financially viable improvements. Chapters 20 and 21 provide a broader, long-term strategic view of capital investment.

Call to Action

Before moving on to the next chapter, consider the following:

- It's now time to observe any aging physical plant capital improvement warning signs that are occurring in your community.

and . . .

- Determine which improvements should receive the highest priorities.

Remember, if the situation will gradually become critical in five years, now may be right time to start taking action.

SECTION THREE

Capital Improvement

Strategies

CHAPTER 19

COST RECOVERY FOR CAMPUS IMPROVEMENTS

Creating a Financially Viable Improvement Plan

Chapter 18 addressed one of the most significant challenges of senior living today – the physical plant aging process. The problems that come with aging buildings are relentless and every year issues become more serious. In Chapter 18, we discussed ***what*** needed to be accomplished. Now let's discuss ***how*** to pay for these campus improvements.

Determining the Cost-Effectiveness of Capital Improvements

In Chapter 18, we identified the need for improvements to both individual units and common/public spaces. Some of your capital investments will require difficult value judgments to determine whether they are really worth the dollars you would have to commit. I like to use a quantitative approach that reduces the decision to the lowest common denominator. This decision process should be viewed from two perspectives:

1. **How much will I have to raise monthly fees** in order to cover (i.e., break-even on) the added capital costs – assuming the necessary funds were borrowed at market interest rates?

2. How will the value of my community be enhanced with the new capital improvement investment? Try to be very specific in your value assessment.

To answer the above questions, let's look at the two major areas where improvements would be made:

- Individual living units
- Common/public areas

Improvements To Individual Living Units

First, let's evaluate the cost recovery of investing money in your individual living units by determining how many *additional dollars* Mrs. Barker – an existing resident – will have to pay each month in order for you to break-even on the additional debt service needed to fund those improvements. This analysis involves a four step common-sense process:

1. Dollars invested. Determine the amount that will be invested to enhance each individual living unit. Let's use $10,000 as an average per unit cost as an example.

2. Cost of capital. Determine the interest rate to be paid on the newly borrowed funds. This could be approximately 7 to 8 percent for a for-profit, or as low as 5 to 6 percent for a not-for-profit community.

3. Debt payment. Use the debt constant concept described in Appendix B. This allows you to easily determine the annual increase in debt (for both principal and interest payments). This figure includes the annual money needed to recover the cost for the improvements to each *individual* unit.

4. Adjust for debt service coverage ratio (DSCR). This ratio simply states that your friendly lender wants you to have about $1.30 in available cash (after operating expenses) for every dollar you owe in debt payments.

A Real World Example

Let's assume a $10,000 investment per unit financed at an 8 percent interest rate for 30 years and a 1.30x debt service coverage ratio yields the following calculations:

- $10,000 times a debt service *constant* of 8.81 percent (see Appendix B) = **$881 per year**[1]

Now we need to increase that amount by 1.30 times or $264 in order to satisfy our lenders' required cash safety margin. That yields a total annual debt service obligation per unit of approximately **$1,145 per year**. If you already have a favorable debt service coverage ratio, you may not have to include the $264. That would lower your needed cost recovery requirements. Finally, let's determine what it will cost Mrs. Barker on a *monthly* basis. So, we will divide the $1,145 per year by 12 months, yielding approximately **$95 per month**.

By following the above steps, you can now judge whether the perceived value of those investments are worth the increase passed on to residents. It's likely that Mrs. Barker will already be paying a monthly service fee of approximately $2,100 per month for existing (not new) independent living. So the $10,000 investment will increase what she pays per month by $95 or $3.12 per resident-day; about a 5 percent increase in her monthly service fee.

[1]A debt service constant takes into consideration both interest rate and loan amortization to compute total principal and interest payments.

Mrs. Barker might experience mild sticker shock, primarily due to habit, not necessarily affordability. However, a *new* prospect viewing an improved ***vacant*** unit might see considerable value and give a deposit without flinching at the price.

Note that $10,000 can usually fund significant capital improvements for a single living unit. Figure 19-1 provides a matrix of different levels of ***individual living unit*** capital improvement investments vs. borrowed money interest rates.

Improvements to Common Areas

In a similar manner, Figure 19-2 provides us with a summary of what the individual cost increase or allocation for each resident's occupied unit would be when substantial dollars are invested in ***common areas*** or the physical plant in general. The analysis is the same as the one for improvements in a typical ***unit*** with one big difference. In this case, we allocate or spread these new debt service costs across *all* of the total *occupied* units. For example, approximately 140 occupied living units in a typical 150-unit independent living community at 93 percent occupancy.

FIGURE 19-1
COST RECOVERY FOR CAPITAL INVESTMENT IMPROVEMENTS TO *INDIVIDUAL LIVING UNITS*

Individual Living Unit Capital Improvement	Break-Even Increase in Resident's Monthly Service Fee to Cover Incremental Increase in Debt Service on Borrowed/Invested Funds to Pay for Improvement[1]				
	7.0%	**7.5%**	**8.0%**	**8.5%**	**9.0%**
$ 3,000/unit	$25.95	$27.27	$28.62	$29.99	$31.38
5,000	43.24	45.45	47.69	49.98	52.30
7,500	64.87	68.17	71.54	74.97	78.45
10,000	86.49	90.90	95.39	99.96	104.60
15,000	129.73	136.35	143.08	149.94	156.90
20,000	172.98	181.80	190.78	199.92	209.20
25,000	216.22	227.24	238.47	249.90	261.50
30,000	259.47	272.69	286.17	299.88	313.80

[1]Indicates annual interest rate @ 30 years and a 1.30x debt service coverage ratio.

Moore Diversified Services, Inc.

Figure 19-2 indicates that a $200,000 investment in improving the public/common spaces, staff areas, and "back of the house" resources of your senior living community will require each resident's monthly service fee to be increased by less than $14 per month or about $0.43 per resident-day. That's less than a 1 percent increase. The ***leverage*** of investing in common spaces is very significant, because we are spreading the new debt service cost for common/public space improvements across *all occupied* units. That's a tremendous bang for the buck!

FIGURE 19-2
COST RECOVERY FOR CAPITAL INVESTMENT
IMPROVEMENTS TO *COMMON AREA/PHYSICAL PLANT*

Common Area/ Physical Plant Capital Improvement	Break-Even Increase in Resident's Monthly Service Fee to Cover Incremental Increase in Debt Service on Borrowed/Invested Funds to Pay for Improvement[1]				
	7.0%	7.5%	8.0%	8.5%	9.0%
$ 25,000	$1.55	$1.63	$1.71	$1.79	$1.87
50,000	$3.10	3.26	3.42	3.58	3.75
75,000	$4.65	4.89	5.13	5.37	5.62
100,000	$6.20	6.52	6.84	7.17	7.50
125,000	$7.75	8.14	8.55	8.96	9.37
150,000	$9.30	9.77	10.26	10.75	11.25
175,000	$10.85	11.40	11.97	12.54	13.12
200,000	$12.40	13.03	13.68	14.33	15.00
300,000	$18.60	19.55	20.51	21.50	22.49
400,000	$24.80	26.06	27.35	28.66	29.99
500,000	$31.00	32.58	34.19	35.83	37.49

[1] Indicates annual interest rate @ 30 years and a 1.30x debt service coverage ratio.

Moore Diversified Services, Inc.

Figure 19-3 summarizes the typical monthly impact on service fees for a ***combination*** of improvements to both individual independent living units and common/public spaces. This combined investment would increase the typical monthly service fees by approximately $108 per month or about $3.56 per resident-day. That's approximately a five percent increase over an average monthly service fee of $2,100 per month.

FIGURE 19-3
COST RECOVERY FOR CAPITAL INVESTMENT IMPROVEMENTS FOR BOTH COMMON AREA/PHYSICAL PLANT AND INDIVIDUAL LIVING UNITS

← *Common Area Costs*
Investment in Individual Living Units →

8.0% *Debt Interest Scenario*

Common Area Capital Costs	Break-Even Increase in Future *Resident's Monthly Service* Fee to Cover Incremental Increase in Debt Service At Various Interest Rates On Borrowed/Invested Funds To Pay for Improvement[1]				
	$5,000	$7,500	$10,000	$15,000	$20,000
$75,000	$52.46	$76.31	$100.16	$147.85	$195.55
$100,000	$54.05	$77.90	$101.75	$149.44	$197.14
$150,000	$57.23	$81.08	*$104.93*	$152.62	$198.73
$200,000	$60.41	$84.26	$108.11	$155.80	$200.32
$300,000	$66.77	$90.62	$114.47	$162.16	$201.91
$400,000	$73.13	$96.98	$120.83	$168.52	$203.50
$500,000	$79.49	$103.34	$127.19	$174.88	$209.86

[1]Indicates annual interest rate @ 30 years and a 1.30x debt service coverage ratio.

Moore Diversified Services, Inc.

Surprisingly, the cost recovery sensitivity for a CCRC campus is frequently favorable. In other words, you can invest significant amounts of capital and pass the cost recovery on to the residents in an effective, affordable manner – at least on an attrition basis as units are vacated due to resident turnover. Properly planned, incremental campus improvements may present *short-run* challenges, but they will result in substantial *long-run* benefits.

Call to Action

Using the formulas and tables in this chapter, determine how much you will have to raise fees in order to fund capital improvements of both independent living units and common/public spaces. Next determine how much the value of your community will increase once capital improvements are made.

Finally, consider implementing an improvement plan in two phases:

1. **First, the common/public spaces** – This offers the biggest bang for the buck at a very nominal cost per resident.

   Then . . .

2. **Upgrade the living units** – At least on an attrition basis as units turn over.

You may be pleasantly surprised at what you can accomplish.

CHAPTER 20

GETTING CREATIVE WITH NEW APPROACHES TO CAPITAL INVESTMENT

Four Simple Strategies That Can Produce Dramatic Results

Chapters 18 and 19 addressed capital investment strategies for renovating and renewing an aging physical plant in an existing community. Chapter 23 will address the development of an initial independent living capital budget for a new 150-unit independent living community. This chapter deals with some subtle, but still important, strategies and how capital investment, on an ongoing basis, are crucial to keeping your senior living community in a competitive condition.

Three Capital Investment Traps

In planning a capital investment strategy, many owners and sponsors frequently commit three tactical errors. They:

1. Spend money on the wrong things

2. Lose sight of their overall strategic objectives

3. Pay too much for less-than-optimum value

Consider Two Important Time Frames

In developing a new senior living community or improving an existing one, capital expenditure decisions must consider two distinct time frames:

- ***Short-Run*** – The *initial* (one time) costs of the capital investment
- ***Long-Run*** – The ongoing (perpetual) *operating* costs of ownership

Cost of Ownership Considerations

To plan effectively, you must carefully weigh the short run capital cost expenditures (immediate capital costs, such as new heating, ventilation, and air conditioning systems) against the long run costs of ownership (ongoing operating costs such as maintenance, utilities, and insurance). Investing less in capital improvements in the short run can sometimes be very expensive over your total ownership period. These cost considerations become very important if you plan to hold your property for more than five years. Even if you plan to be a short term property owner, realize that your ultimate sale value can be adversely affected by your earlier "short run" capital investment mentality. The buyer's sophisticated due diligence efforts will likely detect flaws in your original capital investment planning.

These four simple steps should help you make important cost of ownership trade-off decisions:

1. ***When considering two alternative capital investments evaluate the payback period and calculate the impact on total community value.*** How many years of operation are required for the operational savings/benefits to result in financial break-even or recovery of each of your alternative initial cash investment options? This can be a simple arithmetic calculation (dividing the initial cost of the capital investment by the estimated annual financial benefit or savings) or a more sophisticated discounted cash flow analysis that takes into consideration the time-value of money invested. Ideally, your payback period should be between three and five years. From that point forward, there should be an ongoing positive incremental financial impact.

For example, let's assume that a combination of capital expenditure decisions costing a total of $50,000 could actually save you $1,000 a month in total operating expenses. Using the simplified approach, this $12,000 per year in additional net operating income can pay back your initial investment in about four years. Keep in mind that these annual operating expense savings will likely be realized far beyond the initial payback period – possibly – over the entire useful life of the community.

2. *Estimate the total impact on community value.* To determine the increased intrinsic value of your community, you should *capitalize* the incremental increase in your net operating income resulting from the capital investment[1]. The *capitalization rate* is the cash return (percentage) that reasonable buyers or investors would expect to realize on their cash investment. This would obviously be influenced by their perception of relative risk. Appendix C briefly describes the capitalization rate concept.

[1]Net operating income equals revenue minus operating expenses (before depreciation, amortization, interest payments, and applicable taxes).

Continuing with the example from Item 1, that same $12,000 annual savings would also increase the economic value of your community. An investor expecting an 8.5 percent return on a cash investment should, therefore, be willing to pay or invest about an additional $141,000 for your community (12,000/.085 = $141,177). Simply stated, with that $50,000 investment, the value of your community is likely to be increased by approximately $141,000.

3. ***Value engineer your capital investments.*** This means lowering or controlling capital costs without significantly detracting from the look, operational efficiency, or marketplace acceptance of your community. The results of this effort should be largely invisible to the consumer marketplace.

4. ***Let the "flash value" concept influence capital investment.*** Flash value is a fairly obscure, but surprisingly simple, way of quantifying, and thereby maximizing, perceived value in the eyes of the consumer. This concept is defined as follows:

$$\textbf{Flash Value Index} = \frac{\textbf{What Consumer } \textbf{\textit{Thinks}} \textbf{ an Item Costs}}{\textbf{Your } \textbf{\textit{Actual}} \textbf{ Cost}}$$

Through consumer testing (focus groups, etc.), you can identify a menu of design features and amenities that exhibit a positive "flash value index" of greater than two to one. This means that the consumer thinks the item is worth at least twice as much as your actual cost. You should incorporate a number of highly favorable flash value items into your community. Typical high flash value items in senior housing include high-quality wood molding or millwork, walk-in closets, unusual (but attractive) public spaces, recessed solid-core living unit entry doors, incandescent or new LED lighting vs. traditional, older fluorescent lighting, wall coverings and artwork, interesting roof lines, and "breaks" in exterior elevations. The list could go on, but the ideal outcome is for a senior prospect and their family to comment, ***"This place sure seems to offer a lot for the money!"***

Call to Action

Before you move on, remember you can get very creative with your capital investments by taking four basic steps:

1. Evaluate the investment payback period.
2. Estimate the total impact on existing operation and long-run community value.
3. Value engineer for cost investment savings.
4. Invest in *flash value* to enhance perceived value.

Finally, address the key question, ***"Is now the appropriate time to take action?"***

CHAPTER 21

LONG-RANGE CAPITAL INVESTMENT PLANNING

Creating an Orderly Seven-Step Plan Now Saves Money in the Future

Capital budgeting sounds complex and something only very large, sophisticated organizations can really implement. But, by executing some basic fundamentals, long-range capital budgeting for senior living can be one of your most important strategies for the future.

Up to 20 percent of older communities across the United States may no longer be able to effectively serve their future residents while being truly competitive in the marketplace. This is especially true in market areas that compete with newer, state-of-the-art buildings. The term "older, functionally obsolete community" does not necessarily mean a facility that has been operating for 15 to 20 years. Some five-year-old communities have serious obsolescence and deferred maintenance problems.

How Did We Get There?

Faced with an aging physical plant, most operators can't help but wonder, ***"How did we get in this position in the first place?"*** Part of the answer is related to the elusive concept of depreciation as a generally accepted accounting practice. Depreciation is a non-cash (accrual) accounting expense. That means you don't write someone a check for "depreciation" each month. Most buildings are depreciated annually over at least a 25- to 35-year period; using a conservative definition of the building's useful life. If you are a for-profit, writing off depreciation allows you to save taxes and satisfy your CPA or auditor on paper, but the real issue is, ***"Are you actually investing any real cash in your aging community?"***

The Unfunded Depreciation Trap and the Cap 'X' Solution

The problem with writing off depreciation is that you are not actually investing any real cash in your aging community. This "*unfunded depreciation trap*" is a recipe for trouble and it is creating major problems for many older senior living and health care communities.

Owner/operators and lenders are also using a capital budgeting concept called Cap 'X' (for "capital expenditure" or "reserve for replacement"). This is an imputed operations expense line item of approximately $250 to $350 per unit per year. For an older property with serious deferred maintenance, this assessment can be as high as $600 to $700 per unit per year. These funds are allocated, expensed, and reserved as real cash for future capital needs of a routine, generally predictable nature (wear and tear, cosmetic refurbishment, etc.). This allocation does not cover the more serious capital needs, such as roof repair or a major HVAC overhaul, etc.

Buyers and appraisers will also impute a Cap 'X' factor into your income statement that reduces their estimate of your community's value. This can suddenly become troublesome for the owner/operator because Cap 'X' is an expense line item and every dollar is subject to the capitalization rate of approximately 8.5 to 9.5 percent (for independent living with some assisted living) in the 2009 time frame. As described above, Cap 'X' is a partial solution to the unfunded depreciation trap.

Most progressive new communities now deploy a Cap 'X' strategy along with a pragmatic, more extensive forward-looking annual capital investment plan like the one we'll discuss in this chapter.

The Capital Budgeting Process – A Seven Step Process

A relevant question to ask is, ***"Now that we recognize the problem, how do we properly plan for the future?"*** The answer is to deploy a pragmatic annual capital investment plan and strategy. A good technique is to combine your actual facility experience with available industry standards and guidelines. Here are seven key capital budgeting issues to address:

1. **What major points need to be considered when establishing a capital budgeting plan?** Three important issues need to be addressed:
   - Set capital budgeting priorities
   - Determine payback or return on capital investment
   - Evaluate your relative cost of ongoing ownership

   Prioritizing involves categorizing capital budget line items in a manner similar to those summarized in Figure 21-1.

FIGURE 21-1
PRIORITIZING CAPITAL INVESTMENTS

Priority Code	Approximate Time Frame For Execution
• Urgent	Next 90 Days
• Very Important	Next 6 Months
• Important	Next 12 Months
• Routine	Part of Multi-Year Capital Plan
• Discretionary (Wish List Item)	Build Into Multi-Year Capital Plan

The types of capital items listed in Figures 21-2 and 21-3 should be assigned these appropriate priority codes.

Moore Diversified Services, Inc.

Wherever possible, you should target a minimum criteria of 6 to 8 percent cash return on your invested capital. Hopefully, every capital investment initiative will have a favorable return, either in the short-run or long-run. This is where the cost of ownership concept comes in. Estimate how a capital investment will affect your *ongoing* operations costs. For example, a $3,000 annual expense savings in an energy-efficient heating, ventilation, and air conditioning system may increase the value of your community by over $33,000 using a 9.0 percent valuation capitalization rate. The *capitalization rate* is the cash return (percentage) that reasonable buyers or investors would expect to realize on their cash investment. This would obviously be influenced by their perception of relative risk. Appendix C briefly describes the capitalization rate concept.

FIGURE 21-2

TOP FIVE CAPITAL INVESTMENT WARNING SIGNS

Assigned Priority Code

1. **Cosmetic Wear and Tear:**
   - Public Spaces
   - Individual Living Units
2. **Physical Plant Deterioration:**
   - HVAC
   - Elevators
   - Commercial Kitchen
   - Roof
   - Etc.

   (Assign appropriate ***Priority Codes*** as suggested in Figure 21-1)
3. **Functional Obsolescence:**
   - Office Equipment
   - Security System
   - Business Equipment
4. **Increased Operations Costs:**
   - Optimize Energy Efficiency
   - Repairs and Maintenance
5. **Capital Improvements by Competitors:**
   - Enhanced Public Spaces
   - First Impression Improvements
   - Landscaping
   - Front Entrance (Exterior)
   - Building Elevations
   - Window Treatments

FIGURE 21-3
SUMMARY OF A TYPICAL REVOLVING 5-YEAR CAPITAL BUDGETING PLAN

Capital Investment Item/Priority *Urgent/Very Important*[1]	Estimate of Capital Investment Required 2009	2010	2011	2012	2013
1.	$______	$______	$______	$______	$______
2.	______	______	______	______	______
3.	______	______	______	______	______
4.	______	______	______	______	______
5.	______	______	______	______	______
6.	______	______	______	______	______
7.	______	______	______	______	______
8.	______	______	______	______	______
9.	______	______	______	______	______
10.	______	______	______	______	______
Total Dollars Required	$	$	$	$	$

Complete this matrix and you'll be well on your way towards developing a proactive capital budget plan. At year-end, add a new year to replace the one that is now history – resulting in a revolving 5-year plan.

[1]Create similar spreadsheets of other priority categories summarized in Figure 21-1.

Moore Diversified Services, Inc.

2. **Create a detailed punch list of possible capital investment items.** Here is a suggested start of that punch list:
   - **Machinery and Equipment:**
     - Kitchen
     - HVAC
     - Plumbing – Sanitary – Mechanical

  - Electrical
  - Laundry
  - Security
  - Emergency Call Systems
  - Fire Protection
  - Landscaping – Snow Removal Equipment
  - Tools and Housekeeping Equipment
- **Furniture and Fixtures:**
  - Furniture
  - Window Treatments
  - Artwork and Decorations
  - Audio-Visual Equipment
  - Entertainment
- **Office Equipment:**
  - Telephone Equipment
  - Radios and Building Intercoms
  - Photocopier/Fax
  - Camera Equipment
- **Computers and Computer Software:**
  - Computer Hardware
  - Computer Software
- **Building Improvements:**
  - Flooring – Common/Public Spaces
  - Flooring – Unit Interiors
  - Lighting Fixtures
  - Roofing

  - Exterior Siding and Trim
  - Entry/Main Entrance
  - Elevators
  - Interior Doors and Locks
  - Exterior Doors and Locks
  - Sprinkler System
  - Insulation and Moisture Protection
  - Renovations – Common Areas
  - Renovations – Living Units
- **Vehicle:**
  - Van/Bus Maintenance
  - Auto Maintenance
  - New Vehicle Purchase or Lease
- **Site Improvements:**
  - Parking Lot – Paving
  - Parking Lot – Sealing and Striping
  - Drainage
  - Exterior Site Lighting
  - Sidewalks and Stairs
  - Fencing – Gates – Enclosures
  - Landscaping
  - Irrigation
  - Signage
  - Site Utilities and Sanitary

Your list of capital investment needs should be prioritized similar to that illustrated in Figure 21-1.

3. **Develop a pragmatic step-by-step capital budgeting process.** Sound capital investment planning can be a five-step process:

- **List potential needs.** Make a detailed list of potential capital investment needs - all of the components, subsystems, and materials that make up your community. The list should be extensive, certainly including those items within those broad categories shown in Figure 21-2 and those appropriate punch list items outlined in Item #2 discussed earlier in this chapter.

- **Estimate each item's life expectancy.** Now, identify each item's life expectancy and warranty expiration dates. Let's take the roof, for example. First, determine its current age and then project the expected remaining life. When this is done to all the items on your list, you're now in a position to estimate the likely need, cost, scope, and timing for future repairs and replacement costs at your community.

- **Create a working spreadsheet.** Insert all this information into a spreadsheet, like Figure 21-3, listing potential repair and maintenance details vertically, with five-year planning columns spread horizontally.

- **Consider a revolving five-year plan.** Create a revolving five-year plan, updating your plan by adding an additional 12 months with every year that passes (see Figure 21-3).

- **Estimate costs.** Insert budgetary cost estimates into the spreadsheet. You now have the basis for a simple, pragmatic and prioritized five-year revolving capital investment program. There are also more comprehensive computer-based software systems available to accomplish this task.

4. **How much time should you allocate for decision-making, budgeting and actual execution?** Whatever it takes. This effort will likely have a very high return on your time investment.

5. **What time of year should the process be initiated?** The capital budgeting activity should be synchronized with your annual operations budgeting process. That's because the annual financial budgeting process yields an estimate of next year's cash flow. Revenues less expenses equals net operating income. Net operating income less debt service hopefully results in a positive cash flow. Your annual capital investment expenditures should typically come out of available cash flow proceeds generated in that year of operations.

6. **What other ways can I plan for future capital investment?** Some organizations and lenders establish a previously discussed Cap 'X' concept. These funds are allocated, expensed, and reserved for future capital needs of a more routine, generally predictable nature (wear and tear, cosmetic refurbishment, etc.).

7. **Which administrative team members and department heads should be involved in the budgeting process?** All of them. From an operations' perspective, every major department (healthcare, dietary, housekeeping, plant maintenance, etc.) should be a stand-alone cost and contribution to profit center. The capital budget plan should evolve from these same cost centers. Department heads should develop a reasonable rationale for each line requested. Management and administration (CEO, COO, CFO, etc.) should then negotiate and modify these budget numbers, resulting in a cohesive,

achievable, value-engineered budget. This compels all the players to take ownership and implement the finalized capital budgeting plan.

Remember, capital investment is not just to spend money for obvious needs. ***It involves spending the right amount of money for the right items at the right time.*** This requires prudent capital investment planning that optimizes financial returns to the sponsor or owner/operator while delivering positive impressions and tangible benefits to current and future residents. Both of these lofty goals can be accomplished with the help of the basic capital investment principles that were outlined in this chapter.

Call to Action

In an old TV commercial for the FRAM automobile oil filter, a cagey auto mechanic stood by a smoking engine and held up a filthy oil filter as he said, ***"You can pay me now, or you can pay me later."*** Like skimping on an oil filter change, deferring needed repairs or replacements can be penny-wise and pound foolish for senior housing sponsors. "Later" can be synonymous with "very, very expensive."

CHAPTER 22

CAPITAL FORMATION INITIATIVES

Successful Debt and Equity Strategies

In the late 1990s, lenders introduced a new industry catch phrase. Lenders informed senior housing and health care professionals that they were embarking on a "flight to quality." Properly decoded, this meant lenders were going to focus more on safe, high-quality loan transactions. This "flight to quality" represented a dramatic change in how lenders approached for-profit owner/operators. In the early-to-mid 1990s, most lenders had aggressively pursued almost any and all senior living opportunities.

In the late 1990s, many for-profits, flush with Initial Public Offering (IPO) cash after going public, had little trouble finding lenders to take the risk behind the first 25 to 30 percent of cash equity exposure provided by investors. Back then, senior living was considered a hot development opportunity. *Refinancing* was almost a slam dunk. There were significant debt and equity dollars chasing the senior housing and health care sectors. However, financing *new* communities was always more complex and frequently more difficult.

In 2009, the slam dunk opportunities are very limited and lenders are hustling for the "right deal." Many credit markets are frozen, refinancing has slowed considerably and many new development pipelines have been shut down. There are, of course, exceptions, but now lenders focus almost exclusively on experienced sponsors and owner/operators who have assembled impressive professional teams and, ideally, operate a *portfolio* of properties. As a potential borrower, you must also have a sound, current market feasibility study, and a comprehensive financial plan/pro forma. There are several important issues and initiatives to consider:

1. Develop a sound business plan. You must have a well-conceived, pragmatic strategic business plan. This is the central theme of this entire book! (But pay particular attention to the first 21 chapters.) Figure 22-1 also provides some helpful benchmarks.

FIGURE 22-1
INDEPENDENT LIVING INDICES & BENCHMARKS[1]

	Range Covering Approx. 75% of the Market	
	Low	High
I. Lender Criteria		
1. Debt Service Coverage Ratio	1.25	1.35
2. Loan to Value	70%	75%
3. Implied Equity	25%	30%
4. Capital Reserve (Cap 'X') for Replacement (per unit)	$250	$350
II. Operations/Pricing Criteria		
1. Operating Expense Ratio	55%	70%
2. Operating Expenses PRD	$40-$50	$55-$65
3. Management Fee as a Percent of Gross Revenues	4.5%	7.0%
4. Percent of Senior's Cash Flow Disposable Income Used for Monthly Service Fees	60%	80%
5. Operating Margin (EBITDAR)	30%	45%
III. Capital Budget Criteria		
1. All-in Cost/Unit	$180,000	$250,000+
2. Land Cost/Unit	12,000	16,000+
3. Marketing Cost/Unit	9,000	13,000+

Industry Benchmarks Can Be Both Helpful And Dangerous - Use With Caution

[1]These benchmarks refer to "stand-alone" **independent living**, not comprehensive CCRCs.

Moore Diversified Services, Inc.

2. Assemble the right team. Assemble an impressive, experienced professional team. Don't hire the naïve "never-say-no feasibility consultant," or the inexperienced architect who wants to learn the business at your expense. Most importantly, assemble a team that can help you decide how you can most cost-effectively develop and operate your community. Review Chapter 32 which deals with third-party developers and property managers.

3. Accurately determine borrowing amount. Lenders are tightening loan criteria on borrowers' terms sheets. The important ratios of "loan to value" and "loan to cost" have taken on new definitions. In today's market, you can probably borrow about 70 to 75 percent of your new community's total estimated cost or indicated value. You must provide the other 25 to 30 percent in hard cash for a new community, and tangible equity or very strong collateral to refinance an existing senior living community.

Chapter 23 provides more details on determining the realistic capital cost for your existing or planned community. Your borrowing power will also be affected by your debt service coverage ratio, which we'll discuss later in this chapter. If you are a not-for-profit organization, it is possible to obtain 100 percent financing using tax-exempt bonds. But you must spend considerable cash *before* you qualify for that financing. Start-up CCRCs collecting substantial entrance fees frequently use a portion of that fee to pay off short-term construction financing or short-term bonds.

4. Estimate the cash burn rate. The cash burn rate during fill-up is massive. Lenders particularly want to see several capital budget items frequently overlooked by the borrower. These are indicated in Issues #5 and #6.

5. Plan for a comprehensive working capital reserve fund. There will be significant negative cash flow in the early months of initial fill-up for your new community. That's because most of your operating costs are fixed, or at best, only semi-variable. In fact, only about 20 to 25 percent of your operating expenses are truly variable (raw food, some utilities, housekeeping, etc.). A typical independent living community takes at least 18 to 24 months after opening to reach break-even cash flow (after debt service). On larger communities, break-even cash flow might not occur until the 30th month after opening. During that critical fill-up period, your community may experience cumulative negative cash flows of at least several hundred thousand dollars. This shortfall must be initially funded by the working capital reserve fund.

6. Fund a full scope sales and marketing initiative. Another area frequently overlooked by borrowers is the cost of early *comprehensive* sales and marketing activities needed to initially reach a stabilized occupancy. Start-up marketing and sales costs will probably add at least $6,000 to $8,000 per unit for assisted living, and frequently in excess of $15,000 per unit for a pricey CCRC. This budget allocation includes all collateral/brochure design and production, marketing, program development, sales office design, and overhead expenses. The budget also includes base salaries and sales-based incentives for sales and marketing staff.

7. Accurately estimate construction costs. Obviously, the accuracy of your hard construction cost estimate is very critical, and will undergo significant scrutiny by lenders. Currently, hard construction costs average from a low of $115 to a high of $150 per square foot in most areas of the United States. But depending upon how tight your local labor market is, very high contractor and subcontractor bids may give you financial heartburn! **Always** factor in local market costs rather than relying on generic regional or national figures. The fact that you took this extra step should impress potential lenders. Consider adding a 5 to 10 percent construction cost contingency factor.

8. Develop a seamless relationship between capital budgeting and emerging operations. From a lender's perspective, the basic strategy of capital budgeting for a CCRC or independent living community is to identify and fund *all* costs associated with designing, developing, financing, marketing, and bringing the community to a stabilized occupancy of approximately 93 percent. At that point, the annual ongoing operating budget kicks in, and sufficient operating revenues to cover both ongoing operating expenses and debt service should be available. See Chapter 23 for the development of a detailed capital budget. Chapters 26 and 27 provide inputs for a stabilized occupancy income statement.

9. Have a foreclosure contingency plan. Lenders must always consider the unpleasant prospect of foreclosure. As a result, lenders require that borrowers have an orderly contingency plan before they will approve your loan.

10. Allocate costs of management fees and Cap 'X'. Along with a carefully conceived, comprehensive capital budget, you must develop an income statement with at least two important financial safeguards. Lenders want to see a management fee of approximately 5 percent of revenues, along with a reserve for repair and replacement of approximately $250 to $350 per unit, annually. The concept is called Cap 'X' (for future capital expenditures). The management fee allows the lender to hire another manager (if necessary because of foreclosure) and the Cap 'X' allowance is intended to keep the property in "like new" condition.

Chapters 21 and 32 address the details of Cap 'X' and management fees, respectively. Factoring in the Cap 'X' allocation and the 5 percent management fee represents a good news/bad news situation. The good news is that these safeguards certainly help ensure the success of your community. The bad news is that these factors are considered normal operating expense line items, which lower your community's net operating income, indicated value, and debt service coverage ratio (discussed later in this chapter). That, in turn, reduces how much money one can borrow.

11. Develop a solid, comprehensive financial pro forma. A detailed pro forma outline is available in Appendix A. Simply stated, the pro forma should detail both initial capital needs and realistic community operating results showing how your community will perform over the long run. Lenders will probably also want an additional safety margin in the form of an overall operating expense contingency factor of at least 5 percent.

Detailed market feasibility studies and comprehensive financial pro formas must be closely integrated. The market feasibility study's findings – *outputs* – must drive the financial pro forma *inputs*. In addition, your pro forma must accurately reflect:

- Community development costs
- Estimated operating expenses
- Expected revenues
- The financial dynamics of initial unit absorption/fill-up

As your community progresses, any cost increases or other significant financial changes must be factored in. If the revised pro forma indicates that increased revenues are needed, then obviously service fees must be increased. But first, the market feasibility study must be reworked to determine whether the necessary service fee increases are, in fact, acceptable in the competitive marketplace.

12. Plan for an appropriate debt service coverage ratio. This critical financial ratio is the lender's "acid test". Debt service coverage ratio is defined as available annual net operating income (revenue minus operating expenses) divided by the peak annual debt service (principal and interest) to be paid. Simply stated, lenders want $1.25 to $1.35 in available cash (net operating income) for every $1.00 owed in annual debt payments. This is the cash available after deducting ***all*** operating expenses, except depreciation, and includes the previously discussed management fee and Cap 'X' assessment. Some lenders also key in on "liquidity" of cash resources. In some tax-exempt bond financing situation, a 30 to 35 percent cash to debt liquidity covenant is required. Frequently, there is also a current ratio loan covenant. [1]

Tax-exempt bond financing for a not-for-profit organization usually has an additional requirement. Underwriters routinely require you to reserve an amount of cash equal to one year's maximum total debt service payments (this is allocated as a *debt service reserve fund*). This cash must usually be placed in a restricted reserve account.

[1] Current ratio = current assets divided by current liabilities (on your balance sheet).

13. Determine how much the loan will cost. Not-for-profit organizations enjoy the lowest interest rates being charged. These involve variable rate, credit enhanced tax-exempt bonds, which currently average 5 to 6 percent in the 2009 time frame. Creditworthy, for-profit borrowers closing on *construction loans* typically receive interest rates from .5 to 1.5 percent over the prime rate.

Conventional *long-term financing* rates are likely to be 1.5 to 2.5 percent over the yield on similar term treasury bonds. **Caution: These rates are constantly changing. Always be certain you have the most current rate information available!**

Six Pitfalls Facing the Borrower

Securing a loan means more than just meeting your lender's requirements. The lender-borrower relationship should generally reflect a level playing field - balanced and equitable. In drafting the final loan agreement or "term sheet," you should take care to avoid, or at least be aware of, six potential problem areas:

1. Excessive loan cross-collateralization. Lenders may ask you to pledge other existing assets on your campus for a long period of time as additional security for your new or refinanced senior living community. If initially necessary, request that this cross-collateralization be eliminated or "burned off" after a relatively short period of demonstrated success with servicing the debt on the newly-financed community.

2. Requiring too much cash equity. Prudent borrowing or leveraging will optimize your financial returns. Currently, the acceptable debt-to-equity ratios range from 70 percent debt and 30 percent equity to a higher ratio of 75 percent debt and 25 percent equity. In 2009, the credit crunch made these ratios difficult to realize for many borrowers.

3. Excessive loan pre-payment penalties. Many lenders charge a significant financial penalty if you attempt to pay off your debt sooner than the agreed-upon term. This concept is identified by a fancy term called "yield maintenance". Try to negotiate a declining scale prepayment penalty clause, in which the penalty decreases or "burns off" with time, allowing you to pay off or refinance your loan without significant penalty before the end of the original contractual loan term.

4. Personal liability. Most loans are "non-recourse", meaning lenders look only to the property being financed for security. Other loans attempt to secure other collateral, including personal assets. Avoid personal liability if at all possible. Reluctantly pledge other unrelated assets only if necessary.

5. Loans that mature or come due before the end of the amortization period. Some lenders will provide a loan with a *10-year term* containing structured payments with a *25-year amortization*. This means the loan *looks like* a 25-year pay-off, but actually becomes due in 10 years. While this can be a good financial arrangement from a cash flow perspective, make sure you plan for the payment of the 10-year "balloon loan."

6. Upfront balancing costs versus fixed interest rates. Lower permanent interest rates frequently require higher, one-time, upfront financing costs, frequently called "points." A point is a one-time charge that equals 1 percent of the total loan amount.

This trade-off consideration between lower rates vs. higher financing costs is usually more sensitive for loans of less than $10 million.

Another variation of capital formation involves taking equity out of your existing community by a sale/manage-back or sale/lease-back strategy that is addressed in Chapter 32.

Some Sobering Realties

The days of simply assuring your lender, ***"If we build it, they will surely come,"*** are over. Lenders want to see a definitive plan that identifies and funds all costs associated with developing, financing, and marketing your senior living community. That means bringing your community to a stabilized occupancy of approximately 93 percent in a reasonable time frame. Once you approach stabilization, your operating budget kicks in and there should be sufficient revenues to cover ongoing operating expenses, debt service, cash flow and entrepreneurial profit.

And remember this: lenders are in the business of making successful loans involving acceptable risk. If you present them with a proposal that is obviously well-thought out, you will impress them that you are a pragmatic professional who is obviously a much better risk than a disorganized dreamer with big plans and a limited strategy. Lenders realize it is to their benefit to associate with borrowers who have realistic goals and sensible ways to achieve them. Additional planning **before** you approach lenders will pay off!

Call to Action

Regardless of the type of financing you're after, remember that things always get more complex as you approach the loan closing. Knowing ahead of time what your lender is likely to ask can make the process much easier.

Use the rules and fundamentals contained throughout this book as a "pre-flight checklist" for your important loan. Why? There are three important reasons: 1) You will increase the probability of getting your loan; 2) You will likely have a smooth launch and a safe landing; and, 3) Most leading lenders buy my books!

SECTION FOUR

Capital Costs,

Operating Expenses And

Financial Strategies

CHAPTER 23

THE CAPITAL BUDGET

Realistic Cost Estimates For Developing A New Community Are Critical

Some new independent living and CCRC owners and sponsors are headed for a financial wake-up call. The problem? Flawed or very high ***total, all-in*** cost projections for development of a new community. Owner/operators who want to attract equity investors, achieve favorable start-up financing and pay off long-term debt must start by taking a long, hard look at their basic numbers.

Credible financial guidelines and benchmarks are helpful, but some people go too far. Relying solely on benchmarks to estimate the capital cost of a specific new CCRC or independent living community can be dangerous. Remember, a new community's cost will vary from community to community, region to region.

Important Note – The Current Cost Dilemma – ***As this book goes to press (August, 2009) the U.S. is experiencing:***

1. ***A credit crisis***
2. ***Economic recession***
3. ***Stock market crash***
4. ***A housing market meltdown***

Economists and analysts currently define the senior housing industry as "experiencing strong headwinds!" The total all-in cost for new independent living and CCRC development is experiencing very significant construction cost volatility resulting in a very wide range of a planned project's total, all-in cost projections. Refer to Figure 23-1 for a definition of the major cost elements contained within the all-in cost per unit metric.

Here are a couple of real world examples that demonstrate the volatility of all-in costs of new independent living and CCRC development:

1. **A not-for-profit CCRC** – An average cost per unit is frequently well in excess of $200,000 per unit-bed.

   Vs. . .

2. **An experienced for-profit owner/operator** – This company is developing a quality independent living and assisted living community with all-in costs budgeted at approximately $160,000 per unit (2009 dollars).

Developing realistic cost benchmarks in Figure 23-1 was the most difficult part of writing this book. Some experienced owner/operators say that conceiving a new independent living community whose all-in costs exceed $200,000 per unit is ridiculous and irresponsible. Others say coming in with all-in costs less than $200,000 per unit is impossible.

Sure, there are regional differences and some are developing *Cadillacs* rather than *Pontiacs*. So use the metrics in Figure 23-1 with extreme caution. Get second and even third cost estimate opinions wherever possible and don't let your emotions override facts and common sense.

Projecting the development costs and ongoing financial performance of your new community has become increasingly difficult and requires a detailed evaluation of two elements:

1. The initial capital budget (addressed in this chapter).
2. Ongoing operating expenses (covered in Chapters 24 and 25).

> **THE CARDINAL RULE**
> **OF CAPITAL BUDGETING**
>
> **Your initial capital budget should include all of the significant expenditures necessary to design, develop, and construct your community. The budget must also include all other costs to bring your community to a stabilized occupancy of at least 93 percent in a reasonable timeframe. Figure 23-3 illustrates this concept.**

The Capital Budget Contains Two Major Components

A complete, realistic capital budget includes more than just the *"hard costs"* - the bricks and mortar cost of your community. *"Soft costs"* will also play a critical role in the total development cost of your community.

Hard costs are typically identified as those tangible items such as land, construction, bricks and mortar, furniture, fixtures and equipment. These costs typically represent up to 70 percent of a community's total *all-in cost.*

Soft costs are very important, yet sometimes elusive. These costs include development fees, design and engineering fees, working capital, and financing fees. These costs represent approximately 20 percent of total *all-in costs.*

Total all-in costs per unit are calculated by dividing the sum of all the hard and soft costs by the total number of living units and, if applicable, nursing beds. The all-in cost per unit is very important for strategic planning purposes. Here's why. Of all the cash generated through revenues of an independent living community, approximately 50 to 65 percent of that cash is used to pay operating expenses. CCRCs typically have a higher expense ratio in the 75 to 85 percent range, due primarily to the lower operating margins experienced in nursing and assisted living. If entry fee pricing is used, much of the initial entry fee cash proceeds are typically used to pay down all or part of the construction loan – resulting in a reasonable and acceptable ongoing debt burden. Simply stated, we must know all of our initial cash needs with a high degree of accuracy.

Here are two examples using figures from the 2009 cost envelope for a 150-unit independent living community as outlined in Figure 23-1. These examples essentially reflect the *Pontiac* and *Buick* type communities described in Chapter 11.

Cost Element	***Pontiac***		***Buick***	
• Hard costs	$25.0	million	$30.4	million
• Soft costs	7.5		9.7	
• Total costs	$32.5	million	$40.1	million
• Total average all-in cost/unit	$216,550	per unit[1]	$267,300	per unit[1]

[1]Caution: In 2009 and beyond, these all-in project costs can vary significantly.

<u>**Important Note**</u> – ***These costs reflect actual experience in 2008 and expected costs in the 2009 time frame. Due to the highly unusual volatile economic environment currently being experienced, these costs must be very carefully reviewed and evaluated during 2009 and beyond.***

In order to demonstrate *sound* capital budgeting, this chapter contains specific dollar figures for a typical 150-unit independent living community. The same concepts would apply to a more complex CCRC with a comprehensive product mix of independent living, assisted living, Alzheimer's/dementia and nursing. Capital costs for assisted living and Alzheimer's/dementia can be found in the second printing of my book ***"Assisted Living Strategies for Changing Markets."*** [1]

Top 12 Elements of a Capital Budget

Figure 23-1 summarizes a typical range of costs for the top 12 elements of independent living capital costs. (Costs for an 80-unit *assisted living* community are shown for comparison purposes.) A newly developed independent living community typically has an all-inclusive community cost ranging from a low of $180,000 to a high of $250,000 or more per unit.[2] Note that the capital budget could also include a debt service reserve fund. This added cost may be required for not-for-profit tax-exempt bond financing.

[1] For information go to www.m-d-s.com

[2] In 2009, as Figure 23-1 indicates, many all-in project costs for independent living will typically be in excess of $200,000 per unit.

FIGURE 23-1
SENIOR LIVING CAPITAL COST INDICES AND BENCHMARKS[1, 2]
(In 2009 Dollars)

Element of Capital Cost	150 Units Independent Living	80 Units Assisted Living
1. Raw Land	$12,000 -$16,000/Unit	$8,000 -$12,000/Unit
2. Site Development	5,000 - 8,000	1,000 - 3,000
3. Hard Construction (Bricks & Mortar)	143,000 - 170,000	98,500 - 115,000
4. Design & Engineering	5,000 - 7,500	5,500 - 6,600
5. Furniture Fixtures & Equipment	6,500 - 8,500	4,600 - 5,500
6. Development Fee	7,300 - 9,000	5,000 - 6,000
7. Accrued Construction Interest	8,750 - 9,800	5,100 - 6,200
8. Working Capital/Fill-up Reserve Fund	8,500 - 11,000	7,500 - 8,500
9. Sales & Marketing	9,000 - 13,000	6,000 - 8,000
10. Financing/Underwriting	3,000 - 3,500	2,500 - 3,500
11. Community Contingency	8,500 - 11,000	5,000 - 5,500
Average Total (All-In) Cost Per Unit *Before* Debt Service Reserve Fund[3]	$216,550 - $267,300	$148,700-$179,800
12. Debt Service Reserve Fund[4]	10,800 - 13,300	7,400 - 9,000

Moore Diversified Services, Inc.
Moore Institute Data Base

[1]Indices and benchmarks reflect approximately 75% of current industry comparables; the remaining 25% can either be above or below ranges indicated herein.
[2]Costs can vary significantly as a function of area of the country, urban vs. suburban, and unit design density (number of units per acre).
[3]From 2003 to 2009 there have been huge swings and escalation in both hard construction and soft costs. Use these benchmarks with caution. Value engineering can still produce dramatic variance in total all-in costs.
[4]Typically required for tax-exempt bond financing (12 months of debt service).

To many, these per unit costs may seem surprisingly high – until you realistically consider *all* of the necessary hard, soft, and intangible costs of bringing your community to at least 93 percent stabilized occupancy. There are some new communities – primarily CCRCs – that are approaching an all-in cost of over $300,000 per unit! Key cost variables are often location-sensitive, such as developed land values and hard construction costs.

What follows is a brief description of each element of capital cost that is shown in Figure 23-1. The numbered line items in Figure 23-1 match the following numbered items of capital cost descriptions:

1. Land costs – Typically range from between $12,000 to $16,000 per unit for raw land. Obviously, the cost of land is sensitive to development density (number of units per acre) and prevailing real estate values. Some land costs per unit can approach and even exceed $25,000 per unit.

Typical densities for senior housing range from 15 to 20 units per acre for *independent living* and 18 to 22 units per acre for *assisted living*. These densities generally include roads, site infrastructure, building setbacks, and parking. Obviously, higher densities can be achieved through multi-storied buildings in excess of the typical three to five stories – coupled with underground parking.

2. Site development and infrastructure – Costs vary as a function of topography, wetlands, and other unique site characteristics. A typical cost is approximately $5,000 to $8,000 per unit for site development.

Parking Ratios – Factors for visitor and employee parking space requirements are typically about 0.75 spaces per unit and slightly lower for assisted living. Local planning and zoning departments may have unique building codes.

Land cost sensitivity – Land-related cost variables obviously impact your debt service and pricing. At a 7 percent interest rate, your debt service per occupied unit per month for land and site development should match up approximately with the costs summarized in Figure 23-2. Land cost recovery can represent 5 to 8 percent of a typical independent living monthly service fee.

FIGURE 23-2
THE FINANCIAL SENSITIVITY OF LAND COSTS
(For 150 Independent Living Units)

Raw Land Cost		Site Development		Total Land Related Costs		Monthly Debt Service Impact
Per Unit	Total[1]	Per Unit	Total[1]	Per Unit	Total[1]	Per Unit[2]
$ 7,000	$1.1 Mil	$4,000	$600,000	$11,000	$1.7 Mil	$102/Month
12,000	1.8	6,000	900,000	18,000	2.7	160
18,000	2.7	7,500	1.1 Mil	25,500	3.8	236

[1]For 150 independent living units.
[2]Assumes 7%, 30-year mortgage and a 1.30 debt service coverage ratio for a community experiencing 93% occupancy.

Moore Diversified Services, Inc.

3. **Hard construction costs** – These costs typically range from $125 to $150 per square foot, or approximately $140,000 to over $170,000 per unit (depending upon living unit size, quality, and ambience). Overall building efficiency is also a critical design factor. This includes efficient resident living units, high value common/public spaces, "back of the house" space (commercial kitchen, laundry, etc.) and appropriate "circulation" (hallways, stairwells and elevator shafts, etc.). Building efficiency is discussed in detail in Chapters 10 and 11.

Hard costs also include a cost element called "general conditions" such as builders' overhead, bond insurance, and possibly other factors. You should get qualified professional opinions to insure these project costs are equitable and included in your pro forma.

4. Design and engineering fees – Typically range from $5,000 to $7,500 per unit and include the cost of an architect, owner's representative, civil engineer, structural engineer, and other professionals necessary to implement the design. Fees are obviously negotiable and typically represent about 4 to 5 percent of hard construction costs – unless there are some very unusual design, engineering, or structural challenges.

5. Furniture, Fixtures & Equipment (FF&E) – Usually includes all *movable* items, such as furniture for the dining room and public spaces, artwork, office equipment, and other equipment. Residents typically furnish their own living units. Commercial kitchen equipment costs are sometimes either erroneously double-counted or inadvertently omitted because it's a toss-up as to whether it should be included in FF&E or as part of the hard cost construction budget. One way or the other, make sure it's properly accounted for in your capital budget because we could be talking about $250,000 or more. On a per unit basis, overall FF&E costs typically range from $6,500 to $8,500. This is excluding the commercial kitchen costs.

6. Development fees – These fees are earned by those individuals who essentially make the community happen. They coordinate the process from community inception to Certificate Of Occupancy (CO). Development fees are negotiable, but are typically 5 percent of the total all-in community cost. There are also some significant reimbursable/pass-through expenses which must be negotiated and paid by the owner.

7. Accrued construction interest – This money is needed to pay the month-to-month interest that is accrued on the construction loan. This obligation accumulates during the construction period and prior to opening. This loan interest accrual is typically included as part of permanent financing and planned debt service payments that are initiated upon opening of the new community.

8. Working capital/fill-up reserve funds – Working capital is needed because independent living and CCRCs have such high fixed initial operating costs. This results in substantial cash operating losses during the early fill-up period. You may have an in-rush of initial unit absorption upon opening, but after that, the typical fill-up rate for independent living ranges between five to seven units per month *net.* The operative word is "net," because some units turn over even in the initial stages of occupancy. Though it's easy to overlook, don't forget: You've got to pay your lender even *before* your community generates sufficient revenue and a positive cash flow for break-even operations.

A 150-unit independent living community could have a cumulative negative cash flow (after paying debt service) averaging approximately $8,500 to $11,000 per unit until the community reaches a break-even cash flow occupancy of approximately 80 to 85 percent. Break-even cash flow is defined as covering *both* operating expenses and debt service.

9. Initial sales and marketing budget – Covers the cost of all of the sales and marketing activities needed to bring your community to stabilized occupancy. This used to add up to about $4,000 to $7,000 per unit. Today, this figure can be considerably higher with sophisticated Type 'A' life care CCRCs or in markets with heavy competition or expensive advertising costs. Some are budgeting $9,000 to $13,000 per unit or more. Before setting a figure, you must create a detailed sales and marketing budget. The budget should be supported by a detailed sales and marketing plan. This budget includes all collateral/brochures, program development, media costs, sales office set-up, frequently full-scale models and ongoing overhead expenses. It also includes base compensation and performance incentives for the sales and marketing staff during the initial fill-up period.

10. Financing and underwriting costs – Includes the lender's permanent financing fees and the cost of other professional services (legal, accounting, etc.). These services are used to formalize the organization's borrowing plan, establish the lender relationship, and to successfully "close" on the community's financing. The process and the resulting fees vary and can become complex. See Chapter 22 for details.

11. Contingency funds – In your capital budget, contingency funds should be provided in two areas:

- *Construction contingency* of at least 5 percent and sometimes up to 10 percent of the initial hard construction cost budget.
- *Overall project cost contingency* of at least 5 percent of your total, all-in (bottom line) capital budget.

The size of the community's contingency depends on what stage the community is in, as well as the perceived risk. If there's bad news in the future, you want to be covered. The good news is you may end up with surplus cash!

12. Debt service reserve fund – Usually this is a unique requirement for not-for-profit organizations seeking tax-exempt bond financing. Underwriters typically require a restricted reserve (cash) account totaling one year's maximum required debt service payments.

Put Capital Costs in Perspective

It is important to put these broad categories of capital costs into perspective. When reviewing the total community cost, consider that:

- Land and site development costs typically represent approximately 8 to 10 percent.
- Hard construction costs represent approximately 70 percent.
- Other soft costs represent approximately 20 percent.

Remember, these are broad benchmarks. Your unique, detailed capital budget could reveal more appropriate metrics.

Interest Income During Construction

Depending on how you receive and take down your development construction loan, you may have some idle cash as you make construction payments based on periodic draw requests. Put this cash to work! It should be earning interest income.

Remember: The basic strategy of sound independent living and CCRC capital budgeting is to identify and fund all costs associated with developing, financing, marketing, and bringing your community to a stabilized occupancy of approximately 93 percent. At that point, your annual operating budget "kicks in" and funds ongoing operational expenses. This concept is depicted in Figure 23-3.

FIGURE 23-3
THE FINANCIAL INTER-RELATIONSHIP BETWEEN CAPITAL & OPERATING RESOURCES

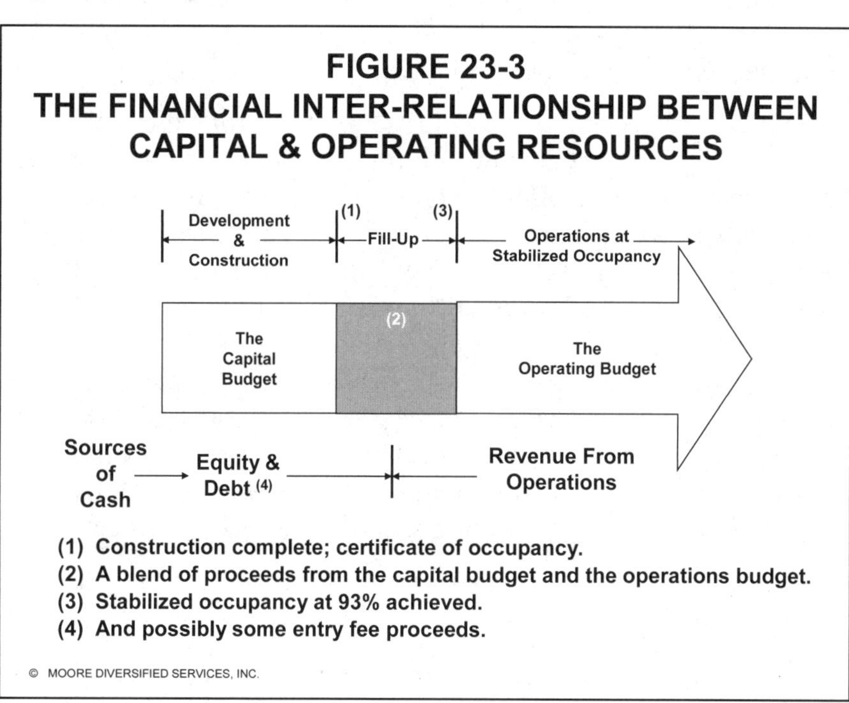

(1) Construction complete; certificate of occupancy.
(2) A blend of proceeds from the capital budget and the operations budget.
(3) Stabilized occupancy at 93% achieved.
(4) And possibly some entry fee proceeds.

It is essential to accurately determine your total community cost. Since we're only human, let's talk about what to do when the cost of the community unpredictably increases. Merely increasing your pricing could be dangerous. A community must not become totally cost-driven, pricing itself out of the market or offering consumers too little value for their money.

Value Engineering Your Community

In most instances, your goal should be to deliver comfortable yet reasonably affordable *Pontiacs* or *Buicks* – not extravagant *Cadillacs*. A concept called *value engineering* can help control costs and actually increase a consumer's perceived value.

Value engineering is the reduction (or control) of capital costs without significantly changing the final "look" of your community. The results of this effort should not negatively impact your competitive position and should be largely invisible to the consumer marketplace. Value engineering starts with an exhaustive review of essentially every line item of capital cost. Through this process, it is not unusual to realize a reduction in total capital costs of between 3 and 7 percent. Sometimes the value engineering exercise actually *increases* costs – but only when the increase is reasonable, necessary, and competitive. Hopefully, the result is an obvious increase in value, a reduction of ongoing operations expense, or providing specific benefits to residents.

Value engineering capital costs is best implemented using a two-tier process:

- ***Tier 1 – Architect/contractor driven.*** If you are still in the preliminary design phase, ask your development team what it would take to reduce overall costs by 10 percent. If your design and development process is further along, a cost reduction goal of 5 percent is probably more realistic. Your professional team may not reach your total value engineering goals, but more often than not, you'll be pleasantly surprised with the overall results.

- ***Tier 2 – Owner/sponsor driven.*** With the help of your professional design team and staff, next determine what reasonable tradeoffs you are willing to make in an effort to reduce costs. If a 150-unit independent living portion of a CCRC community with a preliminary cost of $30.0 million (or $200,000 per unit) could be value engineered by just 5 percent, the savings would be about $1.5 million. Residents would save approximately $75 on their monthly service fee. If your pricing strategy involves entry fees, those fees might also be reduced modestly to become more competitive.

Let's take a close look at this calculation:

- Preliminary community cost of $30.0 million, or $200,000 per unit, with a cost of capital (interest rate) of 7.5 percent.
- A 5 percent cost savings realized through the value engineering exercise, or $1.5 million.
- Multiplying the $1,500,000 savings by an 8.39 percent *loan constant* results in a reduction in annual debt service of $125,850; $900 per *occupied* unit, or approximately $75 per unit per month.[1] Remember, debt service can only be paid by revenues from *occupied* units.

---

[1] *Loan constant* – A convenient analysis factor which provides a single arithmetic calculation for computing the combination of a specific interest rate (7.5%), principal, and loan term (30 years). See Appendix B for additional loan constant details.

Consider the Big Picture

This savings may not seem like much until you consider the possibility of putting that money to work. You can invest some or all of the savings in other areas to reduce ongoing operating expenses or to realize a much higher impact on value. I call this concept "flash value." See Chapter 20 for details on this beneficial strategy. You might also consider lowering the monthly service fee or entry fee so that it is slightly more affordable and competitive.

Call to Action

Spend considerable time developing your capital budget. First, consider ***everything*** and then ***value engineer*** with a passion!

Establishing a sound capital budget is literally the financial foundation of your new independent living community or CCRC. Like the original cost of your personal home, you'll be living with (and paying for) any mistakes made during its creation for years to come.

CHAPTER 24

PROJECTING AND EVALUATING REALISTIC OPERATING EXPENSES

Start by Laying a Solid Foundation

Sponsors and owner/operators frequently miss the mark when it comes to projecting their true operating expenses. This results in all sorts of bad things: inappropriate pricing, unacceptable operating profit margins, inadequate cash flow after debt service, and, ultimately failed communities. Eventually, many residents receive an unpleasant surprise as monthly service fees reflect hefty, but necessary, increases. You can avoid many of these problems by focusing on several important factors that define the financial envelope of acceptable senior living operations.

Three Key Operating Ratios

Three important ratios can provide guidance when evaluating independent living and CCRC operating expenses. These ratios define the "envelope" of acceptable independent living and CCRC operations:

1. ***Operating expense ratio*** – This ratio represents total *cash* operating expenses paid divided by net revenues collected. In computing this ratio, depreciation, debt payments (principal and interest) and major capital investments are not included. Typical expense ratio ranges are as follows:

- **Independent living:** Approximately 55 to 70 percent.
- **Assisted living:** Approximately 65 to 75 percent.
- **Alzheimer's/dementia:** Similar to assisted living if properly managed and priced.
- **Nursing:** A range from approximately 88 to 94 percent. Nursing expense ratios are largely a function of actual payor mix; private pay, Medicare and Medicaid.
- **CCRCs:** CCRCs represent a more complex situation because the product mix is usually a combination of independent living, assisted living, nursing and frequently Alzheimer's/ dementia. The blended operating expense ratio can typically range from approximately 67 to 89 percent.

2. ***Operating profit margin*** **-** Operating profit margin is the inverse of the operating expense ratio. This is commonly referred to as net operating income (NOI) or EBITDAR (earnings before interest, taxes, depreciation, amortization and rent). Typical ranges include:

- **Independent living:** Approximately 30 to 45 percent.
- **Assisted living:** Approximately 25 to 35 percent.
- **Alzheimer's/dementia:** 25 to 35 percent.
- **Nursing:** 6 to 12 percent.
- **CCRCs:** Approximately 11 to 33 percent.[1]

[1] Depends upon product mix.

If these margins shock you, recognize that they are being achieved by astute owner/operators. If you're not part of that group, you may want to "drill down" a little deeper to identify your problems as well as evaluating your possible upside potential. Chapter 25 addresses operating margins and financial ratios in more detail.

NOTE: Earnings Before Interest, Taxes, Depreciation, Amortization and Rent (EBITDAR), as well as cash flow per share, and earnings per share have become the critical industry bottom line performance benchmarks for publicly traded senior living companies. Meanwhile, not-for-profits are adopting a net operating margin-adjusted (NOM-adjusted) concept. NOM-adjusted is similar to EBITDAR but excludes investment earnings, contributions and amortization of entry fees. NOM-adjusted includes net entry fee cash (unit entry fee resale dollars less resident/estate refunds).

Be careful when you look at published operating profit margins. Some operators put management fees, real estate taxes and liability insurance below the line. One rationale is that real estate taxes and liability insurance are largely "noncontrollable expenses". But the sobering fact is they are still operating expenses consuming cash.

3. ***Operating Expenses Per Resident-Day (PRD).*** Defined as total annual operating expenses divided by total annual occupied resident-days (the average number of residents x 365 days). While it is appropriate to spread certain fixed costs and overhead across a number of departments, it is also very productive initially to separately analyze each cost center or department and attempt to equitably allocate fixed costs (such as appropriate direct labor, fringe benefits and materials) to that department.

With rare exceptions, each department should stand alone financially. Resident-day expense ratios can provide an excellent, detailed evaluation of each line item of expense, especially when compared with frequently relied upon industry benchmarks. The per resident-day (PRD) concept is the lowest common denominator for benchmark evaluation.

In many market areas, total operating expenses per resident-day typically range from $42 to $63 for independent living and approximately $80 to $108 for assisted living (2009 dollars). Median operating expense benchmarks are shown in Figure 24-1 for a typical 150-unit independent living community. These costs include basic shelter services and a value-enhanced package of services that are desirable to age and income qualified seniors in both local and national markets.

For a very detailed financial analysis of assisted living, refer to my recently updated book, ***"Assisted Living Strategies for Changing Markets – Second Edition, 2009".***[1]

The rather broad range of this index reflects different quality and ambience levels and other significant variables that can exist from project to project and market to market. These variables typically include labor costs, real estate taxes, utilities, liability insurance, sophistication of dining services and other services offered.

[1]Available at www.m-d-s.com.

Some Special Operating Expense Considerations

There are four operating expense categories that require special consideration. These include:

- Management fees
- Reserve for replacement
- Dealing with uncontrollable expenses
- Annual expense escalation

Figure 24-1 provides detailed benchmarks of each expense category.

Management Fees

Management fees reflect both an important expense line item and a financial and operations strategy. Even though you may not be using a third-party management company, management fees should still be in your budget. That's because your lender wants to see at least a 5 percent management fee allocated as a normal expense line item. This serves as a safeguard for the lender in case there is a foreclosure, making it necessary to bring in a third-party manager. The management fee pays for up-to-date resources and appropriate systems and procedures that will provide adequate operation and oversight of your community. The management fee typically ranges from 4 to 8 percent of gross revenues.

FIGURE 24 -1
150-UNIT INDEPENDENT LIVING COMMUNITY
OPERATING EXPENSE BENCHMARKS

Major Department/ Cost Center	Typical Annual Operating Expense Budget (2009 $)	Range of Expenses Per Resident-Day (PRD) Lower Parameter	Median[1]	Upper Parameter
1. Administration	$319,375	$5.00 PRD	$6.25 PRD	$7.49 PRD
2. Activities	63,875	1.10	1.25	1.50
3. Plant Maint./Security	222,285	3.48	4.35	5.23
4. Food/Dietary	800,737	12.41	15.67	19.59
5. Housekeeping/ Laundry	135,926	2.13	2.66	3.20
6. Transportation	44,968	0.70	0.88	1.06
7. Property	540,127	8.45	10.57	12.68
8. Sales & Marketing	193,158	3.03	3.78	4.54
9. Management Fees	191,114	2.99	3.74	4.48
10. Reserve for Replacement	151,767	2.38	2.97	3.56
TOTAL	**$2,663,332**[1,2]	**$41.67PRD**	**$52.12PRD**[1]	**$63.24PRD**

Cautions:

1. Annual operating expense is computed as follows: 150 units @ 93% occupancy x 365 days per year = 140 units x 365 days = 51,100 resident-days x $52.12 PRD (the median) = $2,663,332.
2. Some communities add an expense contingency of approximately 5% to 10%t of total expense.

Each community and market area will have a unique operating expense profile. Accounting systems and chart of account formats vary and could impact these benchmarks. Source: Moore Diversified Services, Inc.

The management fee provides for the overall management and oversight of the community, but does not include many direct costs of the management operation which reflect additional operating expenses. These are passed on to the owner/operator for payment. Management fees are covered in detail in Chapter 32. If you don't include management fees as a *direct cash expense,* appraisers, lenders and buyers will certainly impute them in their analysis of your community.

Reserve for Replacement

This cash line item of expense replaces depreciation (a non-cash accounting expense line item). Cash reserve for replacement is a way to technically fund a portion of depreciation, placing a specific dollar amount per unit each year in a restricted reserve account. This concept, discussed in Chapter 21, is commonly called the Cap 'X' factor, an easy-to-remember abbreviation for ***capital expenditures***.

For a new community, the replacement reserve is funded by directly expensing approximately $250 to $350 per unit per year. (Older communities would have a higher assessment.) This cash is typically used to fund future "wear and tear" items and cosmetic replacement. You should also have a more comprehensive capital investment program like that described in Chapters 20 and 21. This allocation is in addition to the normal operations and maintenance department budget, which pays for the community's routine and scheduled maintenance.

Depreciation (as a non-cash expense) is usually not included in a typical senior living operating statement. That's because the income statement is generally prepared and evaluated on a *cash basis,* less depreciation. Amortization, interest and tax payments are also excluded. That's because we're typically trying to communicate net operating income or the previously discussed EBITDAR.

Dealing With "Uncontrollable" Expenses

For several years, rapidly escalating liability insurance premiums have been considered by many operators as an uncontrollable expense. Some even put this expense, as well as real estate taxes, below the operating profit line. But like it or not, these are still operating expenses that impact profit and cash flow. Appraisers, lenders, investors and buyers factor in all ongoing expenses when developing their quantitative calculation of value.

Annual Expense Escalation

Independent living and CCRC financial pro formas typically assume escalation factors for both revenue and expenses. The actual inflation rate in the senior housing industry over the past 10 years has been approximately 3 to 4 percent annually. That is essentially the same rate at which owner/operators have increased monthly service fees to their residents. Frequently, a positive one-point spread is used between *rate increases* (4 percent) and actual *expense inflation* (hopefully around 3 percent). If this spread is successfully implemented, your out-year profits will grow at an even faster pace.

Operating Cost Sensitivity - Good News and Bad News

Most experienced operators consider themselves successful if they can hold direct and indirect operating expenses between $1,245 and $1,915 per unit per month. This translates into operating expenses of about $41 to $63 per resident-day for independent living.

If you conduct a detailed operating cost vs. occupancy *sensitivity analysis,* you will discover another challenge - a large percentage of independent living operating costs are largely fixed when the doors open. That's the bad news. The good news is these fixed costs do not vary significantly when occupancy is between 80 and 95 percent. So, at those high occupancy levels, there will be a huge swing in operating profit margins. That's because these margins will vary largely as a direct function of increasing revenues collected.

This leads to what I call the "75/25 rule" for independent living operating expenses. Approximately 75 percent of your independent living operating costs are fixed or only semi-variable, while just 25 percent are truly variable as a function of increasing occupancy (raw food, some staffing, etc.). What this means at the end of the day is that there is only a modest increase in the cost to operate a 150-unit community at 85 percent occupancy versus one that is 93 percent occupied. Obviously, the lower occupancy results in a significant loss of potential cash flow. However, as Chapter 31 points out, incremental increases in occupancy above 85 percent results in significant amounts of cash flowing right to your bottom line.

Similar occupancy vs. fixed cost relationships exist for other living arrangements within a CCRC (Assisted Living, Alzheimer's and Nursing).

Suppressed Revenues or Excessive Expenses?

Let's suppose your operating profit margins are unacceptable - is it a revenue or expense problem? This is a common dilemma many sponsors face. As a helpful indicator, consider that the *operating expense ratio* shows the relationship between both revenues and expenses, while the *expenses per resident-day index* is based solely on operating expenses.

If your operating expense ratio appears high or out of line with industry guidelines (55 to 70 percent), the expenses per resident-day index can direct you to the source of your problem. There are two possibilities: Either your revenues are too low or your expenses are too high. For example, if your independent living operating expense ratio is 75 percent (high), but your operating expenses are $50 per resident-day (about normal), it is likely that your revenues are suppressed.

Financial Windfall or Lost Opportunity Cost?

For every independent living unit occupied above breakeven, about 75 percent of the monthly service fees collected go right to your bottom line. But let's say you have excessive vacancies in your moderately priced independent living unit. At $2,000 per month, occupying one more unit will typically increase your operating costs by about 30 percent or $600. The rest is profit or dollars flowing to your bottom line. What this means is that every vacant unit costs you about $1,400 per month in real profit. So, perhaps, you should be investing more in sales and marketing, one-time move-in incentives or other occupancy enhancement strategies.

Call to Action

Carefully evaluate your actual or projected expenses. How do they compare with the benchmarks and operating ratios in this chapter? It may be OK to have a variance . . . as long as you can specifically identify and explain the differences. Review the next chapter for some additional expense evaluation and reduction strategies.

CHAPTER 25

OPERATING EXPENSE STRATEGIES

Creative Initiatives to Reduce and Control Expenses

Chapter 24 addressed part of the foundation of a solid senior living financial model: appropriate operating expense benchmarks and ratios. Now, let's start putting the expense statement together as a very important component of the independent living income statement that will be covered in Chapters 26 and 27. To do this properly, we need to explore some additional concepts and strategies.

Operating Expense Benchmark Budget

Figure 24-1 in Chapter 24 provided a summary of a typical *operating expense budget* in terms of both total dollars and per resident-day financial benchmarks. The operative word is "summary," because behind this one page of numbers could be 50 pages of financial pro forma computer spreadsheets and voluminous work papers. Looking ahead, Figure 26-1 in Chapter 26 inserts this operating expense budget into an overall *income statement.* The income statement shows how all the financial ratios and operating profit margins combine for a financially viable independent living community.

<u>Caution</u>: Don't just force changes in your operating expense budget to look like my benchmark numbers. Each community and market area will have a unique operating expense profile. In addition, accounting systems and chart of account formats vary and could impact these benchmarks. What you should do

is explain <u>why</u> your numbers are substantially different . . . and be totally objective and comfortable with your rationale.

The Concept of Financial Break-Even for a New Community

Before you dream about future positive cash flow, it is wise to completely evaluate the agony and the ecstasy of project *lift-off.* Like our space program, the most critical phase of your mission is staffing and initially launching your project – *without* any catastrophic events!

Figure 25-1 depicts the classic break-even chart applied to independent living. You may have been required to study this theoretical concept in college, but this is how a practical application actually works in the real world of senior living.

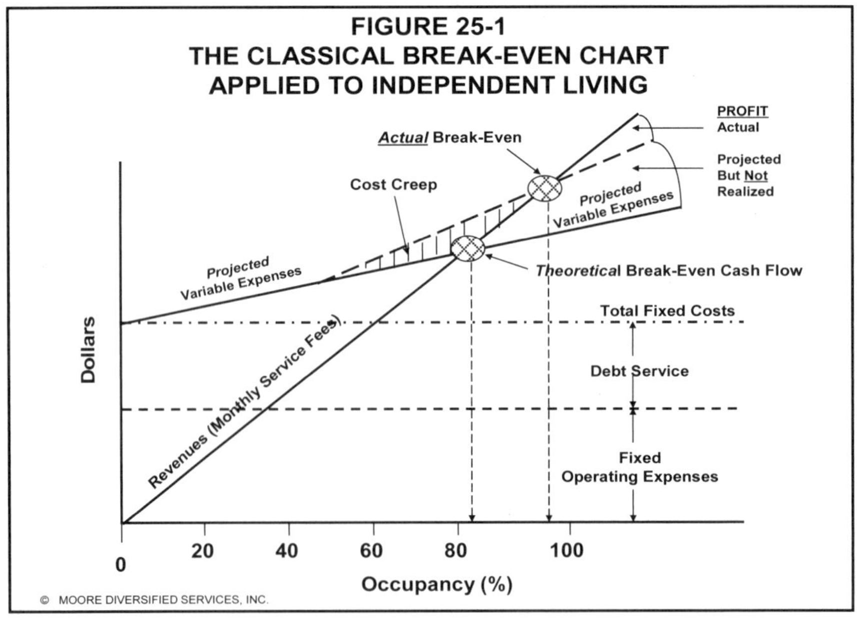

FIGURE 25-1
THE CLASSICAL BREAK-EVEN CHART
APPLIED TO INDEPENDENT LIVING

The break-even chart graphically depicts the following important points:

1. ***Total fixed costs*** – Certain operating expenses and debt service are fixed. These expenses face you every day after opening for business.

2. ***Variable costs*** – Expenses that "ride" on top of fixed costs and make up your total dollar outlay for operating expenses at various levels of occupancy.

3. ***Revenues*** – These gradually increase as a function of increasing occupancy (as do variable expenses).

4. ***The break-even point*** – This magic milestone (frequently a moving target) occurs when revenues equal the sum of both fixed and variable costs and debt service. This is the point where you make the happy transition from *loss* (negative cash flow) to *profit* (positive cash flow).

5. ***Cost creep*** – The culprit that *shifts* the actual break-even point. Cost creep extends losses, requires more time and higher occupancy before you experience profits and positive cash flow. Some troubled communities *chase* this elusive break-even point relentlessly – but never even come close to catching it! Cost creep is very common in assisted living, but it can also be a serious problem in CCRCs and independent living.

The break-even concept is not just a dry academic theory. It is the essence of your independent living and CCRC financial and operational dynamics!

Ben Franklin once said, ***"A penny saved is a penny earned."*** In the case of valuing independent living, I say, ***"A dollar (of your operating expenses) saved annually is worth about $12 in imputed value" (based on an 8.5 percent cap rate).*** In other words, it's obvious that the potential payoff is well worth the cost reduction effort. As this book goes to press, typical independent living cap rates (excluding an assisted living component) are about 8.0 to 8.5 percent. A detailed discussion of the cap rate concept is contained in Appendix C.

Eight Operating Cost Control Initiatives

How are astute operators keeping costs in check? There's no surefire solution, but here are eight strategies that have proven effective:

1. ***Reduce initial capital cost*** – For example, a $10,000 per unit capital cost reduction will lower a resident's monthly service fee by about $60. This would represent about a 5 percent value engineering cost reduction on a community with an average total, all-in capital cost of $190,000 per unit.

2. ***Closely watching operating expenses*** – An operating expense savings of just $1.50 per resident-day could be worth at least $901,765 in value! This is a pretty provocative statement, but it's true. Consider the following:

- An operating expense savings of $1.50 per resident-day represents a decrease of less than 3 percent on total independent living expenses of $51 per resident-day.

- Multiplying this savings by 51,100 resident-days (for a 150-unit community at 93 percent occupancy) equals a reduction in expenses of $76,650 per year, and a corresponding increase in net operating income and cash flow. This increase in cash flow should make both your investors and lenders happy as it could increase their returns or debt service coverage ratio.
- The increased net operating income of $76,650 would be capitalized at approximately 8.5 percent by an appraiser or potential buyer (see Appendix C). This results in an increase of approximately $901,765 in the imputed value of your community.
- Alternatively, this modest expense reduction could reduce the typical monthly service fee for *each* resident by about $45.

3. ***Build a community big enough to optimize operational efficiencies*** – That allows you to *spread* your fixed and semi-variable costs across more revenue-producing units. But take care not to build more units than your marketplace can absorb. Refer to Chapter 12 for more details. This involves a classic trade-off analysis between optimum operational efficiencies and excessive marketplace risk. The optimum size range for independent living in most markets is approximately 150 to 180 units. If you have a CCRC, your assisted living, Alzheimer's and nursing operations also represent additional revenue producing units to better spread both some fixed and semi-variable costs.

4. ***Where possible, avoid direct labor cost growth*** – This could involve cross-training some of your staff in key areas, such as food service, housekeeping and possibly direct care. Reducing your payroll by just two entry level FTEs with a loaded hourly rate of $20.00 per hour can lower labor costs by approximately $80,000 annually[1]. And this could reduce a resident's monthly service fee by about $45 per unit per month in a 150-unit community.

The $80,000 savings would also increase net operating income by the same amount which, when capitalized at 8.5 percent, would increase your community's imputed value by over $940,000.

5. ***Make capital expenditure decisions that will stand the test of time*** – "Poor-boying" one-time capital costs in the wrong areas can raise operating expenses for the life of the community. This decision involves a classic capital investment versus payback period analysis (see Chapter 21).

6. ***Make sure the community stands alone financially and is fully self-supportive*** – Then, and only then, factor in supplementary, non-operating income from private subsidies, charitable donations, interest/investment income and other mission initiatives. Many not-for-profit board members assume their charitable mission of the past can automatically be projected into the future with their new independent living community or CCRC. Remember, independent and assisted living is basically a competitive, private-pay business.

---

[1]Loaded hourly rate = base salary, fringe benefits and modest overhead allocation.

7. ***Consider a multi-tier AIL pricing strategy*** – Delivering increased assistance-in-living services into independent living is a viable strategy if executed with both care and caution (see Chapter 8). But be sure to recover additional costs with a fair and definitive cost measurement, recovery and pricing strategy.

8. ***Develop a comprehensive, but flexible, initial financial pro forma*** – Make sure that your pro forma design can quickly execute a sensitivity analysis and answer a number of *"what if"* questions:

- ***What if*** your actual expenses are two dollars higher than expected per resident-day?
- ***What if*** occupancy is 3 percent lower than the hoped-for stabilized rate of 93 percent?
- ***What if*** the new project fills up more slowly than expected?

Plan your operating expenses using a realistic estimate of the costs you are likely to encounter. Don't ever stop looking for ways to operate more efficiently and moderately increase monthly service fees, even if it's unpleasant. It's still far better than procrastinating, which usually results in steep future increases to existing residents.

Call to Action

Going the extra mile – you can control a portion of your operating expenses. Remember that the last 10 percent of expenses you reduce is clearly the most profitable – the cost saving dollars usually fall right to the bottom line increasing both profits and cash flow. It's the "sweet spot" of your income statement. Conversely, failing to optimize that final 10 percent can be very expensive. Chapters 28 and 29 can assist you in your expense reduction initiatives. These chapters deal with benchmarking and operations analysis.

CHAPTER 26

THE SIMPLIFIED INCOME STATEMENT

It's the Financial Engine of Your Community

The independent living or CCRC business model is frequently described by owner/operators, investors and lenders as a cash-producing black box. But in recent years, the term "black box" has developed a bad reputation in the eyes of many investors and Wall Street analysts because it also implies questionable off balance sheet transactions like those of Enron. Black box accounting practices are obscure, as if developed in darkness. That doesn't mean these practices are always inaccurate or illegal, of course. But, some companies take advantage of loose accounting rules to massage their numbers and make their results look better. In senior living, we have a rather simple financial barometer – the income statement.

The Income Statement as Your Financial Engine

There is a very sensitive barometer of revenues and expenses. This barometer is so important I consider it the *financial engine* of your community. Accountants call this engine your income statement.

Revenues comprise the fuel for your financial engine. *Expenses* represent the energy consumed or how much fuel it takes to run your engine. *Net operating income (NOI)* is a measure of your financial engine's efficiency – just like the miles per gallon performance index for your car.

I also compare the performance of a senior living income statement to a high performance aircraft. As the pilot, you'd like to experience at least three favorable outcomes:

1. Operating your flying machine in an efficient manner.
2. Not constantly flying at the edge of the envelope.

And . . .

3. Always having a soft landing.

The same is true when managing senior living operations.

What Are Efficient Operations?

Operating in an efficient manner means striking a delicate balance between the revenues you collect and the expenses you must pay – resulting in a reasonable operating profit margin. What is reasonable? Well, that depends on who you ask. Many industry experts can't seem to agree on a consistent set of benchmarks. The operating expense ratio for independent living typically ranges from 55 to 70 percent – depending heavily upon the overall quality of the community and the spectrum of services offered. The ratio is also influenced by pricing strategies that attempt to cover all expenses and deliver a debt service ratio (as defined later in this chapter) of at least 1.3x.

Typical independent living operating profit margins range from 30 to 45 percent. This margin is the inverse relationship to the previously mentioned operating expense ratio and is calculated by dividing operating profits by net revenues collected. It is commonly expressed as *net operating income (NOI)* or, for public companies, the fancy term of *(EBITDAR)* – *earnings before interest, taxes, depreciation, amortization and rent.*

The 30 to 45 percent operating profit margin is seen as an elusive, moving target – primarily because sponsors must consistently struggle to keep operating expenses under control and within reasonable budgets. But, whether you're a for-profit or not-for-profit operation, your independent living operating profit margin should come close to 35 to 40 percent. If not, you may find yourself flying at the edge of the envelope with an unstable aircraft – and you will not have a soft landing!

A Pre-Flight Checklist for Your Financial Engine

Check to see if you have all of these necessary components before you start your financial engine:

1. A cost-effective **design concept** – Chapters 10 and 11.
2. A realistic **capital budget** – Chapter 23.
3. An accurate estimate of **operating expenses** – Chapter 24.
4. A detailed **financial operations and sensitivity analysis** – Chapters 28 and 29.
5. A realistic and competitive **pricing strategy** covering normal operating expenses and reasonable safety margins – Chapters 40 through 43.
6. A mutually acceptable (borrower/lender) **project financing plan** – Chapter 22.

Also, look over your shoulder and see if you have an acceptable **exit strategy** as outlined in Chapter 49. That's the equivalent of checking out your parachute!

The Typical Income Statement

Figure 26-1 presents an income statement for a typical **newly developed** 150-unit independent living community **for the first full year of stabilized operations** (all-in cost per unit assumption of $180,000) I've shown a baseline scenario which represents a well-conceived community whose concept has been subject to value engineering and scrutinizing all costs from day one. Geographic location, specific product and service characteristics, labor rates and construction costs can explain some of the differences between Figure 26-1 and those you see in your community. (Figure 26-2 shows the same scenario, but with the all-in cost per unit assumption of $200,000.)

Income statements associated with CCRCs that charge entry fees are different and typically more complex. Some of these unique issues are addressed in Chapter 42.

The basic income statement has three major sections: I) key input variables, II) financial performance and III) key financial ratios. We'll look closer at each of these three sections in the pages that follow. **Note:** The numbered items we'll discuss cross reference to those in Figure 26-1.

I. Key Input Variables – When developing an income statement for a typical independent living community, there are a number of critical input variables[1]:

(1) ***Number of units*** is the total number of revenue-producing units in your community.

(2) ***Occupancy*** is usually considered stabilized at approximately 93 percent.

[1]Keep in mind that the numbers in parenthesis (1, 2, etc.) cross-reference those numbered line items in Figures 26-1 and 26-2.

FIGURE 26-1
INDEPENDENT LIVING'S FINANCIAL ENGINE
Income Statement For A 150-Unit Community - $180,000 Cost Per Unit

I. KEY INPUT VARIABLES:

1.	Number of Units:	150	Total Cost:	$27.0 Mil
2.	Stabilized Occupancy:	93%	Equity @ 30% =	$8.1 Mil
3.	Average Mo. Service Fee:	$2,650	Debt @ 70% =	$18.9 Mil
4.	Operating Expenses PRD:	$53.00	Loan Interest Rate:	7.0%
5.	Double Occupancy:	25%	Amortization (Yrs.)	30
6.	Second Person Charge:	$650		
7.	Average Cost Per Unit:	$180,000		

II. FINANCIAL PERFORMANCE:

8.	Gross Annual Income	$4,770,000	/yr
9.	Vacancy Factor @ 7.0%	(333,900)	
10.	Double Occupancy Revenue	136,013	
11.	Net Rental Revenues	$4,572,113	
12.	Other Miscellaneous Revenues	91,442	
13.	Total Net Revenues	$4,663,555	
14.	Operating Expenses	(2,708,300)	
15.	NET OPERATING INCOME	$1,955,255	/yr
16.	Debt Service	(1,508,906)	
17.	CASH FLOW	$446,349	/yr

III. KEY FINANCIAL RATIOS:

18.	Debt Service Coverage Ratio (DSCR)	1.30x
19.	EBITDAR	41.9%
20.	Operating Expense Ratio	58.1%
21.	Operating Expenses Per Unit	$18,055
22.	Cash Flow/Unit (Unleveraged)	$13,035
23.	Cash Flow/Unit (Leveraged)	$2,976
24.	Cash Return on Total Cash (Unleveraged)	7.2%
25.	Cash-on-Cash Return on Invested Equity (1st Stabilized Year)	5.5%
26.	Internal Rate of Return (IRR)	13.8% to 17.1%

Moore Diversified Services, Inc.

FIGURE 26-2

INDEPENDENT LIVING'S FINANCIAL ENGINE

Income Statement For A 150-Unit Community - $200,000 Cost Per Unit

I. KEY INPUT VARIABLES:

1. Number of Units:	150		Total Cost:	$30.0 Mil
2. Stabilized Occupancy:	93%		Equity @ 30% =	$9.0 Mil
3. Average Mo. Service Fee:	$2,780		Debt @ 70% =	$21.0 Mil
4. Operating Expenses PRD:	$53.00		Loan Interest Rate:	7.0%
5. Double Occupancy:	25%		Amortization (Yrs.)	30
6. Second Person Charge:	$650			
7. Average Cost Per Unit:	$200,000			

II. FINANCIAL PERFORMANCE:

8. Gross Annual Income	$5,004,000	/yr
9. Vacancy Factor @ 7.0%	(350,280)	
10. Double Occupancy Revenue	136,013	
11. Net Rental Revenues	$4,789,733	
12. Other Miscellaneous Revenues	95,795	
13. Total Net Revenues	$4,885,528	
14. Operating Expenses	(2,708,300)	
15. NET OPERATING INCOME	$2,177,228	/yr
16. Debt Service	(1,676,562)	
17. CASH FLOW	$500,666	/yr

III. KEY FINANCIAL RATIOS:

18. Debt Service Coverage Ratio (DSCR)	1.30x
19. EBITDAR	44.6%
20. Operating Expense Ratio	55.4%
21. Operating Expenses Per Unit	$18,055
22. Cash Flow/Unit (Unleveraged)	$14,515
23. Cash Flow/Unit (Leveraged)	$3,338
24. Cash Return on Total Cash (Unleveraged)	7.3%
25. Cash-on-Cash Return on Invested Equity (1st Stabilized Year)	5.6%
26. Internal Rate of Return (IRR)	19.0% to 19.2%

Moore Diversified Services, Inc.

(3) ***Base monthly service fees*** are the fees charged for each particular unit type for a "value-enriched" package of services. This includes all basic shelter components (real estate, utilities, taxes, maintenance, for example) and a package of services (such as food, housekeeping and activities). There is frequently "other income" in the form of extra/guest meals, beauty shop charges and a la carte options offered to residents.

The above description applies to what we typically call a "market rate rental". This is a common pricing model. Another pricing model includes both recurring monthly service fees and a one-time payment of an entry fee. This pricing model is addressed in some detail in Chapters 40 and 42. Frequently, monthly income for a community is impacted by the financial dynamics of these entry fees. These impacts fall into two categories; unfavorable and favorable:

- **Unfavorable Impact** – Entry fees are properly *amortized* into income when using Generally Accepted Accounting Principles (GAAP). While an appropriate GAAP accounting procedure, the numbers are frequently misinterpreted. *Amortized* entry fees into income is not cash income to pay monthly expenses. Chapter 27 describes this dilemma.

- **Favorable Impact** – Chapter 42 describes an income statement concept called **"Net Operating Margin-Adjusted"**. NOM-A defines the *net cash* actually realized from the resale of an entry fee. Net cash is defined as the net of unit re-sales cash collected less paying any refund obligation to the previous resident's estate. See Chapter 42 for more details.

(4) ***Operating expenses per resident-day*** for independent living typically range from approximately $42 to $63 in most market areas. You should always evaluate your financials in terms of *dollars per resident-day*. It's the most useful common denominator. Operating expenses per resident-day in independent living are defined as total annual operating expenses (or expenses by each major department) divided by the number of occupied units multiplied by 365 days. This operating expense input variable (actual or estimated) represents the most sensitive performance risk metric which frequently leads to eroding profit margins. For more details, see Figure 24-1 in Chapter 24.

(5) ***Double occupancy factor*** enhances revenue. Couples, however, can eventually be an additional lifecare cost burden for a CCRC that offers Type A (comprehensive lifecare) health care benefits. This is discussed in Chapter 42. The double occupancy ratio (two related or unrelated seniors sharing a unit) is typically as high as 1.35 for a new community, gradually declining to about 1.2 persons per unit as residents age in place in an older independent, stand-alone community or one within a CCRC.

(6) ***Second person charge*** is driven by the previously discussed double occupancy factor and the additional monthly service fee for the second person (usually a spouse) in a living unit. It primarily covers the extra cost of meals.

(7) ***Total average cost per unit*** is the total all-in project cost divided by the number of units. Don't confuse this with just hard construction cost per unit, which does not include everything. Figure 26-1 reflects an average all-in cost per new

unit of *$180,000*, while Figure 26-2 addresses an average all-in cost per new unit of *$200,000*.

Note: This all-in cost per unit can vary over a wide spectrum as discussed in Chapter 23.

II. Financial Performance – This is the sparkplug of the income statement. I call it the community's financial engine. It contains the following key elements:

(8) ***Gross annual income*** is the total number of units multiplied by the average base monthly service fee. In Figure 26-1, we use an *average* monthly service fee of $2,650 per month multiplied by 150 *total* units x 12 months. This fee could have a wide variation depending upon the unique capital costs to be covered (equity returns and debt service, etc.) and the ongoing operating expense budget. This monthly service fee in Figure 26-1 is designed to support a newly developed project at today's construction costs. Existing communities could be financially viable at modestly lower monthly service fees. Remember, you must always strike a delicate balance between pricing to cover your costs while being market-responsive and competitive.

(9) ***Vacancy factor at 7 percent*** is typically the conservative industry standard for stabilized independent living. Many operators find that operating an independent living community *consistently* above 93 percent occupancy is difficult due to the competitive market and resident turnover. But remember, your profit margin and cash flow will generally soar if you can reach higher occupancy. Refer to the break-even chart (Figure 25-1 in Chapter 25) and the opportunity costs of a vacant unit

addressed in Chapter 31 which shows how most of the incremental revenue of an additional occupied unit at high occupancies falls right to your bottom line.

(10) ***Double occupancy revenue*** is the second person net revenue discounted by approximately 50 percent to cover the additional incremental expenses such as additional meals.

(11) ***Net rental revenues*** represent the end result of all the factors listed above. It is the gross annual income and net double occupancy revenue reduced by the vacancy factor.

(12) ***Other miscellaneous revenues*** include ancillary charges such as guest meals, beauty shop and other revenue from a la carte services provided.

(13) ***Total net revenues*** is the sum of all sources of revenue.

(14) ***Operating expenses*** in Figure 26-1 can be computed as expenses per resident-day (PRD) multiplied by the number of occupied resident-days. As an example, expenses can be calculated as follows:

- 150 units x 93 percent occupancy = 140 units x 365 days a year = **51,100 resident-days per year**
- Total operating expenses @ $53.00 PRD x 51,100 resident-days = **$2,708,300 per year** [1]

(15) ***Net operating income (NOI) before debt service*** is frequently expressed as "EBITDAR" – earnings before interest, taxes, depreciation, amortization and rent.[2] In Figure 26-1, the NOI is $1,955,255 per year.

---

[1] Adjusted for rounding.

[2] "Rent" is usually attributed to lease payments since leasing is essentially an equivalent form of financing.

(16) ***Debt service*** (in Figure 26-1) consists of a financing plan that is 70 percent debt and 30 percent invested equity, with a 7.0 percent interest rate and a 30-year loan amortization period. The actual amount financed depends on the all-in cost per unit and the amount of initial equity invested. The debt component is 70 percent of the total project cost of $27 million, or $18.9 million. Note that a not-for-profit could probably execute 100 percent financing with approximately a 6 percent interest rate, using tax-exempt bonds, and dramatically improve its cash return.

(17) ***Total annual cash flow after debt service*** is cash left over after paying all the operating expenses and the mortgage. In Figure 26-1, annual cash flow at the end of the first stabilized year is $446,349 or $2,976 per unit.

III. Key Financial Ratios – These ratios represent the financial engine performance gauges on your dashboard indicating whether your community is healthy, marginally performing or seriously troubled:

(18) ***Debt service coverage ratio*** is the key lender loan covenant or safety margin. Lenders typically require $1.25 to $1.30 of uncommitted, unrestricted available cash for every dollar of maximum annual mortgage payment you owe. The ratio is defined as net operating income (available cash) divided by the maximum annual debt service (mortgage payment).

(19) ***Operating profit margin*** is sometimes called "EBITDAR margin" and is the net operating income (operating profit) divided by net revenues. Independent living operating margins should come in somewhere between 30 and 45 percent.

(20) ***Operating expense ratio*** is the inverse of the operating profit margin, and is defined as operating expenses divided by net revenues. For independent living, the operating expense ratio should be in a range from 55 to 70 percent.

(21) ***Operating expenses per unit*** is total operating expenses divided by total units.

(22) ***Cash flow per unit unleveraged*** is the average amount of annual cash produced by each unit. Sometimes NOI or EBITDAR is viewed as the average *unleveraged* (before debt payments) cash flow per unit or bed. In this case, unleveraged average cash flow per unit is $13,035 (before debt service). It's defined as net operating income (before debt service) divided by the total number of units.

(23) ***Cash flow per unit leveraged*** is the cash that's available after all expenses are covered *and* debt payments are made.

(24) ***Cash return on total investment unleveraged*** (*before* debt service) typically ranges from 7 to 11 percent in the early years and is heavily influenced by the *total cost per unit.*

(25) ***Cash-on-cash return on invested equity*** (*after* debt service) typically ranges from approximately 5 to 8 percent in the very early years of a new project.

(26) ***Internal rate of return (IRR)*** is a fancy financial term which takes into consideration the *time value* of your invested (not borrowed) cash. This financial ratio, expressed as a percentage, answers the question: **"What is my average annual return on my invested cash – from the *first day* I**

invested it until some defined point in the future when I expect to get it back?" Internal rate of return also takes into consideration all dividends or profits distributed and assumes the net cash proceeds of a future sale. A 5-year holding period with an assumed future sale are typical assumptions used when computing IRR.

Planning for a "Soft Landing"

A "soft landing" can also be described as a graceful exit strategy. Happiness is not just positive cash flow – it is *sufficient* positive cash flow. Let's say you want to either sell or refinance your senior living community. A potential buyer or lender will evaluate the performance of your income statement (your financial engine) by focusing on it as an income-producing black box. In 2009, he or she will pay you about 12 times your net operating income (reflecting a capitalization rate of 8.5 percent). That, of course, assumes that you have properly allocated all of the appropriate expenses and your property is in very good condition.

Are You Headed for a Hard, Wheels Up Landing?

All this "theory" is great, but what if your community's financial performance is inconsistent thanks to circumstances that appear to be beyond your control? Read on. Chapters 28, 29 and 30 address the real world of dealing with adverse income statement variations and how to realize upside potential.

Call to Action

Whether you are operating an existing community or planning a new one, make sure your financial engine does not need a tune-up. That means making sure your bottom line financial ratios are similar to those outlined in Figure 26-1.

This was the easy income statement chapter. Chapter 27 deals with the more complex entry fee type projects.

CHAPTER 27

COMPLEX INCOME STATEMENT ISSUES

Entry Fee Pricing, Life Care Programs and Not-For-Profits Face Some Unique Challenges

Chapter 26 addressed a *simplified* but realistic income statement primarily focused on independent living. But life is not so simple for CCRCs that charge entry fees or offer life care services. Both for-profit owner/operators and not-for-profit sponsors face some very complex and multi-dimensional issues involving their income statement. More details on the specifics of entry fees and lifecare plans can be found in Chapters 41 through 43.

I think one of the more effective ways to address the complexities of the income statement is to tell you about a situation I encountered in a senior living boardroom. Actually, it is a story that applies to a large number of real world situations that exist today. Here it is:

The boardroom was silent. Finally, the board president broke the ice, "***Bob, how could we possibly get in such a serious financial situation? You're a talented, seasoned professional, and you've recruited an excellent staff. We have good accountants and auditors. I don't understand how this could happen.***"

Other board members carefully avoided making eye contact with each other. Everyone focused on Bob, the community's

Executive Director. Bob cleared his throat. At past board meetings, he had brought up the problems facing The Gardens at Westridge, a 25-year-old not-for-profit CCRC (the actual community's name and certain facts have been changed). Bob, however, had failed to communicate through effective financial reporting just how gloomy things were. Some critical CCRC issues combined to threaten the entire organization and its mission to serve its senior clients. Bob had considerable bad news for the board.

Carefully, Bob focused on the community's four most pressing challenges:

1. *Excessive deaths triggered unexpected cash demands* – An earlier actuarial study had projected an average of eight deaths annually, but death rates had risen sharply along with the average entry age. By June, the community had already experienced seven deaths that year. In addition, four units vacated in January were proving difficult to re-sell. And because of all the recent deaths, The Gardens at Westridge had a refund obligation of nearly $1,260,000 in entry fees.[1]

2. *Phantom income* – The Gardens at Westridge properly amortized past entry fees into income. Entry fees were amortized based on the expected life of the resident (for non-refundable entry fees) or the useful life of the community (for refundable fees). This was consistent with Generally Accepted Accounting Principles (GAAP). However, this common accounting practice artificially inflated the current income statement. This practice added several hundred thousand dollars in accrued entry fees (not real cash). The cash had been spent years earlier when the entry fees were initially collected.

[1] $200,000 entry fees, 90% refundable = $180,000 x 7 = $1,260,000.

The complication doesn't end here. Inadvertent misinterpretation of income statements led a number of organizations like The Gardens of Westridge to become involved in what I call an *"accidental faith-based Ponzi"* situation. Years ago, a disingenuous entrepreneur named Mr. Ponzi developed a pyramid scheme whereby money contributed by investors was used to pay artificially high distributions to earlier investors. As long as new money flowed in, everyone was happy. Eventually, the new money dried up and the scheme collapsed like a house of cards. CCRCs that become used to a certain level of deaths, turnover and immediate re-sales are at risk for creating a Ponzi-type situation if they're not careful. Essentially, they rob Peter to pay Paul. This high risk practice is described in much more detail in Chapter 42.

3. *Excessive costs* – Food and beverage costs exceeded $20 per resident day, compared to the industry benchmark average of approximately $18 for a similar level of service. Multiply this excessive food cost by the CCRC's 70,800 resident days per year, and that additional $2 PRD adds an extra $141,600 in annual expenses.[1] Other departments also had costs higher than industry benchmarks, but the professional staff and board had always agreed not to "cut corners like some of those for-profits."

[1] The Gardens at Westridge had 192 occupied independent living, assisted living, Alzheimer's and nursing units-beds x 365 days/yr = 70,080 resident-days.

4. ***Declining fundraising proceeds*** – Fundraising proceeds had declined steadily. The board had relied heavily on this *non-operating income* to pay *routine* operating expenses and debt payments. But today, most donors now prefer to help fund specific campus improvements or other investments with tangible long-range benefits. As one donor stated, ***"We're no longer going to fund your administrative black hole!"*** In addition, the organization's investment portfolio had been hammered since 2000 because of poor performance in the equities market and the lowest interest rates in over 40 years.

The board was stunned. One relatively new member, a self-made millionaire, had been a quiet observer at meetings for the past year. Now he said, ***"I always questioned some things in the financials that were inconsistent with my business experience. I thought I just didn't understand the different world of senior living and not-for-profits. But I now realize the differences in business fundamentals are not that significant and we should have focused more on cash flow. Unfortunately, we envisioned our roles as board members as largely ceremonial, when we should have rolled up our sleeves and helped Bob, using our professional talents and experience."***

The board president said, ***"Let's not panic. Bob and his staff are very capable. Bob, can you come back to us in 30 days with a plan that clearly identifies strategies and tactics along with short-run and long-run expected outcomes?"*** Bob agreed to do so.

One Month Later . . .

The board president opened the next board meeting by saying, ***"As you recall, last month Bob summarized four critical items about our community's income statement which, frankly, are of great concern. We asked Bob to come back this month with a definitive and practical action plan. Bob, are you ready?"***

"I am," Bob answered. ***"Let me tell you about the progress we've made in the last 30 days on those four problem areas."***

1. ***Excessive deaths triggering unexpected cash demands*** – Bob noted that the average entry age of new residents was one and half years higher than planned, contributing to a higher-than-anticipated death rate. To address the problem, Bob had transformed a largely passive "admissions" function into an aggressive and proactive sales and marketing program. In addition, Bob explained that the community's maintenance crews now go into 'red alert' mode when there is a move-out and can turn around a vacated unit within 72 hours.

2. ***Phantom income*** – Board members had been misled by entry fees that were booked as income, in accordance with generally accepted accounting protocol, even though the cash had been spent a long time ago. Bob said, ***"From now on I'll submit detailed cash flow statements at every board meeting indicating our real cash position, along with the current status of accounts receivable and accounts payable accruals. We've also intensified our focus on our entry fee refund obligations. "***

3. ***Excessive operating costs*** – Bob continued his briefing to the board. ***"For years, we've justified annual budget increases by***

building off last year's numbers. After last month's board meeting, I asked every department head to go back to square one and objectively budget their costs from a zero-based perspective.

After I got their initial inputs, I then got all department heads together, complimented them on their efforts, and asked how they could cut operating expenses by an additional 5 to 7 percent in ways that would have minimal impact on resident standards of care or quality of life.

After some grumbling, we achieved a savings of 5 percent in operating expenses. Most of that came in small increments: an FTE here, some minor operating supplies there. Some savings was achieved by more tightly integrating the "back of the house," in terms of how we deliver and serve food to each of our three satellite dining rooms."

4. *Declining fundraising proceeds* - Bob's solution to this problem startled some board members. Bob made eye contact with each board member and said, ***"After a six month period of adjustment, we will no longer use fundraising proceeds to subsidize our monthly operations deficits. Instead, all donations will pay for either tangible and permanent long-run improvements, or fund new and innovative programs in areas such as wellness or dementia. After we demonstrate complete financial viability, we may choose to buy down the rate on a selected number of units to provide scholarships for needy residents as part of the necessary charitable content of our mission."*** Bob added he had already tested this new philosophy on several donors, and received a favorable response.

Although not part of his original list of problems, Bob then commented on yet another problem, the challenges of lifecare.

"As a CCRC offering Type 'A' lifecare, we recognize that, as residents move into either our assisted living or nursing operations, our revenues are suppressed, while expenses continue to escalate. That's because we've promised our residents assisted living and nursing services for essentially the same fees that they paid in their original independent living unit. We didn't fully recognize the magnitude of this problem until we noticed that a very high percentage of our health center residents are from our lifecare contracts, as opposed to those from the outside market who are paying prevailing market rates. We're making further adjustments to our financial forecasts, in general, and the cash flow planning impacts, in particular."

Bob concluded: ***"Ladies and gentlemen, we're not out of the woods yet, but I truly believe we have a workable recovery plan. And nothing that I'm recommending in any way impairs our tradition, mission or our commitment to our residents. We still recognize, and will always honor, the commitment this non-profit makes to the well-being of this town. Any questions?"*** The plan was enthusiastically approved, and the meeting adjourned.

Call to Action

Is Bob's situation really that rare? What do you think? Is your community's income statement suffering from any of the type of problems Bob had at The Gardens of Westridge? If so, what are you doing about it? Do you think the timing of any corrective action is critical? Don't go to the next chapter until you answer these questions.

CHAPTER 28

BENCHMARKING & OPERATIONS ANALYSIS

Translating Benchmarking From a Theoretical Concept to a Practical Strategy

More and more board members, CEOs, and Executive Directors are asking their Chief Financial Officer two penetrating questions:

1. ***Since our operating profit margins are shrinking, won't we be in violation of our debt service coverage covenant?***

2. ***Why are our operating expenses substantially different than recently published benchmarks?***

Many not-for-profits face two additional very troublesome questions:

1. ***Why do we have to spend a large percentage of our annual donations or endowment portfolio principal to cover monthly operating expenses? And why are we not really helping some low-income seniors by offering reduced rates?***

2. ***Should we really be spending most of our entry fee cash, collected from the net gain on unit re-sales, to fund routine operating expenses?***

Perhaps it's time for a pragmatic benchmarking operations analysis. Chapters 24 and 25 addressed two important benchmarking ratios that can help you lay the foundation for a solid operations analysis. They are the operating expense ratio and operating expenses per resident-day (PRD).

Management buzzwords, such as "management by objectives" (MBO) and "total quality management" (TQM), come and go. Often perceived as vague, complex, or confusing, they fade into the past before most of us really understand or appreciate their true benefit.

But benchmarking is one recently popularized concept that deserves serious consideration. The concept involves a comparative analysis of industry operating factors, financial ratios, and business practices that answer the question: ***"How does my community really stack up?"*** Benchmarking has seen limited application in senior housing, but the concept will eventually become a management imperative for many senior housing organizations.

Benchmarking – comparing your community against regional and national organizations – can be an early warning system. Benchmarking can identify impending problems and also provide a good way to demonstrate the sound performance of your operation.

Not-for-profits will find benchmarking especially beneficial. Too many not-for-profits rationalize operational inefficiencies as being inevitable – a byproduct of fulfilling their mission. In fact, non-profits can implement change and realize *substantial financial improvements.* Failure to do so is compromising their effectiveness and seriously impairing their long run mission objectives. As a result, many boards of directors are asking increasingly pragmatic and penetrating questions, such as the ones at the beginning of this chapter. Bond underwriters, rating agencies, and accreditation organizations are also looking for increasingly sophisticated measures of success. Benchmarking may be the answer. Let's look at two vital indicators – the financial pulse of your operation.

The ***operating expense ratio*** shows the relationship between revenues and expenses. The operating expense ratio represents total cash operating expenses divided by net revenues. It generally *excludes* depreciation, interest, taxes, principal payments, and property leasing expenses. It should include a management fee and a modest allocation into a capital reserve fund for future building improvements. See Chapter 25 for more details.

The ***expense per resident-day index*** is based solely on operating expenses. It is your total annual operating expenses (as defined above) divided by your total resident population times 365 days.

Always look for symptoms. Typically there are two possible problems:

1. Revenues may be too low;

   or . . .

2. Expenses may be too high.

Say, for example, your operating expense ratio appears high. By computing your expenses per resident-day index, you can usually identify the source of the problem. For example, if your operating expenses per resident-day are also high, it is likely that your primary problem is excessive expenses and not suppressed revenues.

You Need Isolated Cost/Profit Centers

Let's drill down and try to isolate the potential operating expense problems on a typical campus. If you have a CCRC with multiple living arrangements (independent living, assisted living, nursing, etc.), try this exercise:

- Compute the operating expense ratio and the expenses per resident-day index for both your ***consolidated*** campus and for ***each*** of your living arrangements – treating them as individual cost/profit centers.
- Once you spot a potentially troublesome living arrangement (independent living, assisted living, etc.), compute the operating expenses per resident-day for each operating department *within* that isolated cost/profit center (dietary, housekeeping, direct care, administration, etc.) to further isolate the problem.

Does this analysis sound difficult? If so, it's not surprising. This is usually where sponsors and owner/operators "hit the wall". Their existing financial reporting structure does not always allow them to isolate *individual cost/profit centers*, much less allocate their direct labor (cooks, housekeepers, CNAs) and other costs to each appropriate department. That's important because each cost center (and each department) has a unique set of generally acceptable operating expense benchmarks (see Figure 24-1 and Chapter 24 for more details). Some sponsors may have serious operational problems, but these flaws are frequently masked by having one large consolidated "black hole of operations" rather than distinct, stand-alone cost/profit centers. Chapter 29 provides a detailed outline of a good operations analysis.

Big Dollars Are At Stake

At the lowest level of cost containment, there are three departments that frequently surface as problem areas. They are:

1. Administration
2. Dietary
3. Assisted living/direct care

Staffing is often a source of inefficiency. Let's look, for example, at the direct cost of just one additional entry level, direct care full-time equivalent employee (FTE) on each of the day and evening shifts in independent living. At $10.00 per hour, that's $20,800 per year. Add payroll taxes and fringe benefits of 25 percent and we're now at $26,000.

So for a 40-hour week, two-shift coverage, that's $52,000 per year. Add weekend coverage and the total annual direct cost is $72,800. And if you must also provide direct coverage for 20 percent employee downtime (frequently employee absenteeism and inefficiency) that cost will grow to over $91,000. For a 150-unit independent living community, this $91,000 cost could represent a typical resident's monthly service fee impact of about $54 per month ($91,000 divided by 140 occupied units divided by 12 months).[1] Could that money be better spent on enhancing resident quality of life and/or solidifying your market position as the high value community of choice?

[1] A 150-unit independent living section within a CCRC at 93 percent occupancy = 140 occupied units.

When conducting an operations analysis on medium-to-large CCRC campuses, I frequently find at least three or more excess FTEs. It is not unusual to find up to $500,000 per year of potential savings within a large CCRC. The return on the cost of the operations analysis – I consider it an investment – is high. The typical one time cost of an operations analysis by a qualified consultant should range between $18,000 to $25,000; depending upon the size of the CCRC.

A comprehensive benchmarking and operations analysis should address two strategic cost reduction questions:

1. What's reasonable?
2. Will a particular cost reduction change being considered really impair quality of life or standards of care?

The benchmarks shown in Figure 28-1 represent quality, successful operations reflecting a majority of communities nationally. Obviously, any benchmark must be used with caution, but you can no longer afford to rationalize your expensive operation by simply saying "we're different."

From a strategic and philosophical perspective, sponsors must strike a delicate balance between standards of care, quality of life, and reasonable costs. Today, hitting specific operational performance targets is a critical imperative for every for-profit operator and not-for-profit sponsor. Instead of "cost reduction," I prefer to use the phrase "value engineering." In the end, cutting costs is really about adding value for your residents.

FIGURE 28-1
KEY SENIOR HOUSING OPERATING RATIOS

Key Criteria/Benchmark	Independent Living Low	Independent Living High	Assisted Living Low	Assisted Living High	Nursing Low	Nursing High
Operating Expense Ratio	50%	60%	65%	72%	85%	93%
Operating Expenses Per Resident-Day	$42	$63	$79	$105	$115	$125
Average FTE's Per Unit/Bed	0.30	0.40	----	----	----	----
• Assisted Living[1]	----	----	0.45	0.55	----	----
• Dementia[1]	----	----	0.50	0.60	----	----
• Nursing	----	----	-----	----	0.70	0.85
Direct Care Minutes Per Resident Per 24 Hours[1]	N/A	N/A	65	80	210	250
Total FTEs/Occupied Unit-Bed	0.30	0.40	0.45	0.55	0.70	0.85

Benchmarks represent approximately 75% of market experience.

[1]For baseline level of care; benchmarks will increase with increased acuity.

Nine Major Benefits of Benchmarking

Still not sold on benchmarks? Here are nine major benefits. Benchmarks will:

1. Improve your financial position.
2. Increase operational efficiency.
3. Develop competitive and creative pricing strategies.
4. Better position your products and services in the competitive marketplace.
5. Assist in developing new ways to increase resident satisfaction.

6. Introduce new quality of life initiatives.
7. Enhance the perceived value of your services.
8. Increase community value; your exit equity or your refinancing potential.
9. Generate increased, ongoing cash flow.

Other specialty areas of your operation that could benefit from benchmarking include accounting, housekeeping, routine and preventive maintenance, sales and marketing, and overall capital investment planning. Perhaps the best targets for benchmarking are the things that cost you the most money, particularly those that directly affect the perceived value of your community. Staffing, for instance, represents over 60 percent of total operating costs in senior living – and adequate staffing ratios are important to residents and their families. Benchmarking can help you define realistic staffing patterns that strike a balance between high operational efficiency and optimum resident satisfaction.

Benchmarking also benefits food and beverage operations. Not only does meal service account for up to one-third of a community's operating costs (food and beverage costs range from approximately $16.00 to $19.00 per resident-day), but it is usually perceived by residents and their families as one of the most important services offered - and it's the one mentioned most critically in resident satisfaction surveys. For a 150-unit community, a savings of just 70 cents per resident-day in food services improves annual financial performance by approximately $36,000 (about a 4 percent reduction) and increases the value of your community by over $400,000, assuming a value capitalization rate of 8.5 percent ($36,000 ÷ .085 = $423,530). Certainly, food service is an area in which it doesn't pay to cut corners. Yet, finding a way to improve efficiency could really pay off, if it can be done without hurting quality or resident satisfaction.

Benchmarking can sharpen your focus and provide a bridge that links your strategic goals and objectives with desired expected outcomes. Finally, the process will force you to position, operate and price your community more effectively. Chapter 29 provides a detailed outline for conducting a comprehensive operations analysis.

Call to Action

The return on the cost of a benchmarking operations analysis investment is a no brainer. The significant return on investment makes operations analysis and benchmarking one of the most beneficial initiatives you could possibly execute. It's true that our primary mission is to consistently deliver high standards of care and quality of life to our residents. But in doing so, we can't let this noble objective either mask or oversimplify a rationale for grossly inefficient operations. For your community, it may be time to bite the bullet.

I've not yet conducted an operations analysis that did not result in a permanent, ongoing savings of at least $50,000 per year. A comprehensive third-party analysis typically involves a one time cost typically ranging from $18,000 to $25,000 depending upon the size of the community.

CHAPTER 29

THE RIGHT APPROACH TO FINANCIAL/OPERATIONS ANALYSIS

Seven Key Tasks for Every Operator

This chapter describes an important initiative that can help you develop practical and prudent ways to enhance revenue and reduce costs. You can accomplish this by comparing your operations with relevant industry benchmarks. Benchmarks can help identify places to reduce operating expenses as well as highlight variances – differences between accepted financial ratios and your typical results.

What is a Detailed Operations Analysis?

A benchmarking and operations analysis sounds great, but how does one go about it in a logical, sequential manner? Over the years, I've developed seven key tasks for evaluating operations. Here is a summary/outline of the seven major tasks:

I. Establish the foundation for a detailed financial operations and benchmarking analysis.

This initial task looks at the "Big Picture". It evaluates your overall financial envelope.

1. **Analyze your overall consolidated financials. Take an initial look at your basic income statement:**
    - Sources of revenue:
        - Market rate

- Private pay
- Medicaid - if applicable
- Medicare – if applicable
- Non-operating revenue

- Less operating expenses
- Equals net operating income (NOI)
- Less debt service (if applicable)
- Less capital expenditures
- Equals cash flow

2. Evaluate key operating ratios. These include:

- Operating expense ratio
- Operating profit margins:
  - NOI – Net Operating Income
  - EBITDAR – Earnings Before Interest, Taxes, Depreciation, Amortization, and Rent/Lease Payment
  - NOM-Adjusted – Net Operating Margin – Adjusted[1]
- Expenses per patient/resident-day:
  - Overall
  - By individual department/cost center [2]

[1] Considers the cash flow impact of net cash gain on entry fee re-sales (refer to Chapter 42).

[2] The analysis should evaluate each operating department as a relevant cost/profit center. These detailed operational evaluations could offer very significant and potentially favorable financial improvement.

3. **Analyze the budgeting process:**

   - Compare actual year-to-date financial performance vs. budget

     - Analyze and explain significant variances

4. **Evaluate current General and Administrative (G&A) expense allocation philosophy:**

   - What indirect costs are (or should be) allocated to each individual operation or departmental cost/profit center?

     - Evaluate the rationale for each allocation

     - Review special allocations

   - Identify specific services and benefits delivered from the "Corporate/Central Office" (if applicable) or from the general administrative department to the various cost/profit centers:

     - Investigate the real economies of scale

     - Review the rationale behind central control and allocation

     - Evaluate the synergy of G&A operations with other cost/profit centers

   - Is the G&A or corporate office function really providing cost-effective financial synergy?

- Critique the philosophy of "earning" management fees (if applicable)
  - Rationale for fees vs. specific services provided

Expected outcomes ***- My experience is that this exercise frequently shows where there is potential for significant financial improvement. These improvements should not unfavorably impact:***

- ***Resident/patient standards of care or quality of life***
- ***The amount existing residents/patients currently pay for services rendered***
- ***The favorable aspects and potential problems related to the current business plan or mission objectives***

II. Conduct a detailed evaluation of the objectives and expected outcomes for each specific department or other cost/profit centers.

True operations analysis and value engineering efforts must deal with the "lowest common denominator" – dollars per patient/resident-day of each cost/profit center. This ensures that no financial improvement areas are inadvertently overlooked.

1. Evaluate each living arrangement as a stand-alone cost/profit center:

- Independent living
- Assistance-in-Living
- Assisted living

- Alzheimer's care
- Skilled nursing
- Other ancillary services

2. **Identify labor costs; direct and indirect:**
    - Direct labor costs (direct payroll to employees)
    - Indirect labor costs (employee fringe benefits cost and organization's payroll taxes)
3. **Tabulate non-labor costs. This includes:**
    - Consumables
    - Equipment repairs and replacement costs
    - Supply costs
    - Raw food costs
    - Administrative supplies and associated costs
    - Etc.
4. **Provide an analysis of other relevant operating expenses. For example:**
    - General and administrative costs
    - Management fees and other cost impacts on operations
    - Fundraising/endowment activity costs (if applicable)

Expected outcomes ***- This type of detailed financial fact-finding analysis will likely help identify areas where operations could be improved.***

III. Conduct a detailed staffing analysis.

This includes a detailed analysis of the rationale for each staffing position. Analyze each individual FTE.[1] Staffing ratios (overall, hours per patient/resident-day, etc.) should be calculated and evaluated. Overall operating efficiency should also be evaluated - striking a delicate and necessary balance between operational efficiency and resident quality of life/standards of care. Factors to evaluate include:

1. **Staffing ratios (FTEs per unit-bed)**
2. **Staffing levels and shift patterns**
3. **Wage rates**
4. **Fringe benefits**
5. **Employee turnover trends (by position)**

***Expected outcomes* - Labor is *the* major expense category for senior housing and health care. This important analysis can identify areas where staffing patterns can be cost-effectively improved. These improvements can either be implemented immediately or on an employee turn-over/attrition basis.**

[1]FTE = Full time equivalent employee

IV. Develop an appropriate financial structure for each cost/profit center. Use absolute dollars, dollars per resident-day, and other appropriate ratios.

Based on the previous analyses defined in this chapter, you could develop a modified financial/operations structure. This new model might look something like this:

1. **Revenue; include revenue that is:**
   - *Operating Revenue – Earned* directly from operations. Do not include *non-operating revenue* here such as:[1, 2]
     - Donations
     - Interest income
     - Other
   - From third-party payors (as applicable)
2. **Expenses include:**
   - Direct costs incurred from operations
   - Appropriate overhead and G&A expense allocation
   - Exclude depreciation, interest expense, amortization, taxes, etc.
   - Compare expenses with appropriate benchmarks

---

[1] Net cash - exclude any endowment proceeds, fundraising proceeds, and other non-operating revenue.

[2] These resources should be considered below the operating cash flow line.

3. **Net operating income. Be sure to:**
   - Establish realistic and achievable operating profit objectives
   - Evaluate operating profit margin versus industry benchmarks
4. **Debt service allocation (if applicable). Review:**
   - Interest
   - Principal
   - Escrow/reserve accounts
5. **Cash flow.**
6. **Debt service coverage ratio (if applicable).**
7. **Average debt per unit (if applicable).**
8. **Other relevant operating ratios.**

Expected outcomes ***– After following the steps in Section IV, an optimized income statement now exists. The new income statement shows the financial improvement that could result from implementing the changes identified in the operations analysis. Refer to Chapter 26 for additional details on income statement formats.***

V. **Identify the (eventual) financial expectations that result from implementing cost/profit center objectives.**

This task involves a philosophical evaluation of how your operation should perform in the future. You should ask the question, *"Should additional and more extensive cost reductions and value engineering be implemented?"* In addition, ask yourself *should a particular cost/profit center's stabilized financial operations:*

- Permanently operate at a loss?
  - What's the rationale?
- Operate at approximately break-even:
  - Before *any* debt service allocation?
  - At the cash flow level *after* debt service?
- Be consistent with reasonable industry profitability benchmarks?
- Deliver targeted operating margins based on:
  - Reasonable and achievable *objectives?*
  - Reasonable industry *benchmarks?*

***<u>Expected outcomes</u>* - This task will compare the overall financial/operations improvements that you have made with your long-run business plan, operating philosophy, and mission.**

VI. Pricing policies and strategies.

Based on the previous operations analysis – including the challenges that were identified and the suggested improvements – you should carefully evaluate your existing pricing policies. Prudent and practical changes in pricing policies should be considered, both short-run and long-run. Both monthly service fees and entry fees should be evaluated in detail. Review in particular:

1. **Baseline pricing involving monthly service fees and, if applicable, entry fees.**

2. **Your approach to dealing with acuity/cost creep in at least three areas:**

    - Assisted living
    - Alzheimer's
    - Assistance-in-living services delivered to residents within independent living

    Evaluate the potential for acuity/cost creep:

    - Quantify the magnitude of acuity/cost creep
    - Evaluate tiered or a la carte pricing strategies
    - Investigate acuity/cost creep identification/monitoring systems, procedures, and cost recovery systems

3. **Review annual cost inflation vs. service fee increases.**

    Evaluate your community's pricing policy vs. reality:

    - Cost escalation
    - Price increase trends and philosophy

4. **Compare your community to the competition:**

    - Conduct product, price, and value analysis
    - Compute a price (dollars) per square foot value analysis for each unit type
        - Monthly service fee per s.f.
        - Entry fee per s.f.

Expected outcomes ***- Your finalized pricing recommendations should be consistent with your financial/operations analysis results. Modified pricing should also reflect how to actually deliver/implement the identified improvements.***

VII. Implement practical changes.

1. **Develop a *long list* and *short list* of recommended changes – setting tangible milestones for execution. Group these changes into time frames. Some typical time frames for change:**
   - Immediate
   - Next 90 days
   - Next nine months
   - Next 12 to 24 months
   - On an attrition/turn-over basis
     - Employee
     - Resident
   - Other
2. **Document the key results of this analysis along with tangible and specific action items and expected outcomes. Provide realistic schedule milestones.**

Expected outcomes ***– Figure 29-1 summarizes the upside potential for recovering the likely cost of an operations analysis. That example can also be used as an approach to computing the favorable impact of operating expense reductions.***

Benchmark Sources

I have provided relevant benchmarks throughout this book. Pay particular attention to Chapters 24, 25 and 28. Here are some additional benchmark sources:

Publication	Source
The State of Seniors Housing	American Seniors Housing Association www.seniorshousing.org
CARF/CCAC	Commission on Accreditation of Rehabilitation Facilities/Continuing Care Accreditation Commission www.carf.org/aging
Fitch Ratings	Fitch Ratings Public Finance Health Care Special Report/Median Ratios for Continuing Care Retirement Communities www.fitchratings.com

What Might a Third-Party Operations Analysis Cost?

You might pay $18,000 to $25,000 for a comprehensive one-time operations analysis. That may sound like a lot of money until you look at it from an *opportunity cost* perspective.

As Figure 29-1 dramatically demonstrates, the return on investment for a comprehensive operations analysis can be very high. In this real world example, the cost of an operations analysis could permanently save several dollars per resident-day (PRD) yet have a one-time cost of only 36 cents PRD. That $0.36 PRD represents a 0.4 percent increase for one year in typical $97 PRD expenses for a CCRC. However, the savings is likely permanent – lasting long after the one year amortization of the costs.

FIGURE 29-1

RETURN ON COST (INVESTMENT) FOR IMPLEMENTING A COMPREHENSIVE OPERATIONS ANALYSIS
A Typical Real World Situation

• 180 CCRC units @ 93% occupancy	=	167 occupied units @ stabilized occupancy
• 167 units x 365 days per year	=	60,955 resident-days per year
• Possible one-time operations analysis cost [1]	=	$22,000 (approximately)
• Cost per resident-day	=	$22,000 / 60,955 resident-days = 36 cents per resident-day vs. Typical average CCRC operating expenses of at least $97 per resident-day (PRD) [2] ↓ ***Approximately 0.4% increase in PRD expenses over the next 12 months***

Note:
A typical operations analysis will very likely result in a considerably higher permanent dollar savings PRD ← ***Approximately 0.4% increase in PRD expenses over the next 12 months***

[1] Assumes use of an experienced consultant.
[2] Weighted average of independent living, assisted living, Alzheimer's, and nursing.

Moore Diversified Services, Inc.

Call to Action

Would you consider investing 36 cents PRD for one year to potentially save $1.50 to $2.00 PRD on a permanent basis? The upside potential resulting from an effective operations analysis is usually very significant. Regardless of the outcome, an operations analysis is a necessary and appropriate preventive health check-up that every sponsor and owner/operator should conduct.

CHAPTER 30

REVENUE AND OCCUPANCY ENHANCEMENT

The Upside Potential is Significant

Starting in 2005 and continuing through 2009, some very interesting trends have evolved. In 2007, valuation cap rates were at an all time low and the value of senior living properties being purchased by sophisticated institutional investors were at record highs. Many owner/operators were selling their properties at these premium prices and exiting in total, executing either sale/lease-back or sale/manage-back strategies. Construction costs for newly developed properties continue to escalate to record highs.

New senior living product supply has moderated in recent years. For example, between 1997 and 1999, an average of approximately 54,000 units per year were produced. From 2000 to 2007, new production dropped dramatically to approximately 30,000 units per year. In addition, a new product – *senior apartments* – captured over 25 percent of the new units constructed. This further reduced the new annual supply of "conventional" senior living units. These trends clearly indicate that the conventional senior living product *supply* versus *demand* balance is experiencing a favorable shift.

As we look to 2009 and beyond, institutional investors will continue to pay premium prices for some quality properties; favoring multi-property portfolios rather than individual communities. Of course, this will only happen as the economy and housing market recovers and the credit markets become more liquid. All-in new development costs will likely escalate to new highs and new construction will continue at a moderate pace. The result will likely be consistent new demand with moderate growth in new supply. This should have a favorable impact on overall occupancies – assuming we can control and respond to resident turnover. Most importantly, independent living and CCRC properties have the potential to operate in the optimum profit and cash flow zone – if we can execute a number of meaningful initiatives.

Chapter 31 illustrates how just five vacant independent living units (90 percent versus 93 percent vacancy in a 150-unit community) represents about $100,000 in lost cash annually, along with a decrease of overall community value of approximately $1.2 million.

Call to Action

Many of the chapters in this book directly or indirectly impact occupancy and revenue enhancement. Carefully review the entire table of contents; especially Section Four as you sharpen (or initially develop) your revenues, profits and cash flow enhancement plan.

SECTION FIVE

Senior Consumer

Finances

CHAPTER 31

THE OPPORTUNITY COST OF A VACANT UNIT

Using Objective Thinking To Make Tough Financial Decisions

I had an alternative subtitle for this chapter. It was, ***"How to Lose $100,000 Without Really Trying!"*** Sometimes in senior living, we fall victim to a problem I call the "original pro forma syndrome." This means that we have difficulty coming off of our original financial projections – even though our current situation clearly indicates that some of those early projections may be faulty. Frequently, we focus on the "impossible dream" of somehow getting back to that original pro forma. That's a noble objective, but let's gets real. What's often needed is some hard nosed pragmatic thinking so one can make some tough financial decisions. One approach involves "opportunity cost."

Opportunity Costs Defined

You're probably familiar with the ***opportunity cost*** concept, which has been taught in business schools for the last 70 years. Simply defined, opportunity cost is the net financial benefit lost by either avoiding or rejecting some alternative course of action. Let's put this definition into real world terms. We often forget how very expensive chronically vacant units can be to our overall operation. The solution to excessive vacancies frequently lies in some alternative strategy that requires an additional financial investment. This investment "opportunity" sometimes appears either elusive or too expensive. But by applying simple opportunity cost arithmetic, we can bring a cost-benefit comparison of necessary alternatives into very sharp, quantitative focus.

Let's look at the typical opportunity cost of a vacant independent living unit. At relatively high occupancies, most operations costs are already "sunk." For example, it is unlikely that substantially more raw food would need to be purchased for just three to five additional residents at a particular community. It is also unlikely that any additional employees would have to be added. What other operating expenses would likely increase?

Conservatively, one could assume there would be some added cost at approximately 30 percent of a typical $2,300 independent living monthly service fee or an incremental per unit cost of approximately $690 per month.[1] Therefore, the *opportunity cost* of a vacant unit is approximately $2,300 minus $690 or $1,610 per month or $19,320 per year. That is lost cash that would otherwise go right to the bottom line.

---

[1] This monthly service fee is typical for an *existing* independent living community. A *newly* developed independent living community would likely require a higher monthly service fee.

A Practical Example

I. **Current Available Units For Occupancy**	**Approximate Actuals**
Total unit capacity of an independent living community	150 Total Units
Current occupancy @ 90%	(135)
Vacant Units	**15 Vacant Units**

II. Impact of Enhanced Occupancy

	Additional Units Occupied	**Total Net Opportunity Cost Recovery**	
		Monthly	**Annual**
Modest Enhancement	• 5 Units	$8,050 /mo	$96,600 /yr
	• 8	$12,880	$154,560
Achievable Enhancement	• 10	$16,100	$193,200

To be very conservative, one would expect to realize enhanced total occupancy of just 5 units or approximately $96,600 of NOI/cash flow enhancement annually.[1]

[1]Example: 5 units x $1,610 opportunity cost per unit = $8,050 per month or $96,600 per year.

So, the opportunity cost for just five vacant independent living units would be $96,600 per year. If these units are chronically vacant, this represents a permanent cash loss each and every year. What do you think, is it time to get creative with various alternatives - even if it requires some additional one-time cash investments? For a 150-unit independent living community, those five extra vacant units reflect the difference between 90 percent and 93 percent stabilized occupancy.

A one-time cash investment does not impact your ongoing rent roll. Examples of possible one-time investments for enhanced occupancy include:

1. A $750 to $1,000 move-in allowance.

2. Installing a stacked washer-dryer in the prospect's living unit – assuming plumbing is practical.

3. Other living unit permanent enhancements.

Keep in mind that – long-run – you essentially *own* living unit enhancements. They represent a permanent product enhancement for your community.

Vacancy problems affect more than cash flow. Just five vacant units diminishes your refinancing potential or overall selling/exit value of your community by approximately $1.0 million. That's because buyers and appraisers will value any net cash flow at about a 9.5 percent capitalization rate.[1]

---

[1]$96,600/.095 = $1.0 million

Figure 31-1 is one of about 30 financial sensitivity templates that our firm has developed to show our clients both the financial sensitivity and cost-benefit relationship of implementing action for their unique situation.[1] Using a live, interactive Power Point driven conference call with the client, we can move the two ***sliders*** in Figure 31-1 to emulate their unique financial situation. The vacant unit ***knob*** can also be manipulated to observe the sensitivity of various vacant unit scenarios. The ***opportunity cost*** windows at the bottom of the figure change dynamically; showing the sobering financial impacts.

The reason opportunity cost is frequently elusive is that it doesn't show up in any of your financials. It is an invisible, but extremely important, concept. In the next chapter, we'll put the opportunity cost to work as we discuss filling up studios and other "dog" units.

Call to Action

Remember: For every independent living unit occupied above break-even occupancy, about 70 percent of those incremental monthly service fees collected go right to your bottom line. Stay focused on the real opportunity cost of sub-par occupancy. In the example in this chapter, the cash cost is about $97,000 per year which decreases the value of your community by approximately $1.0 million.

[1]For more information on the availability of these templates, visit www.m-d-s.com.

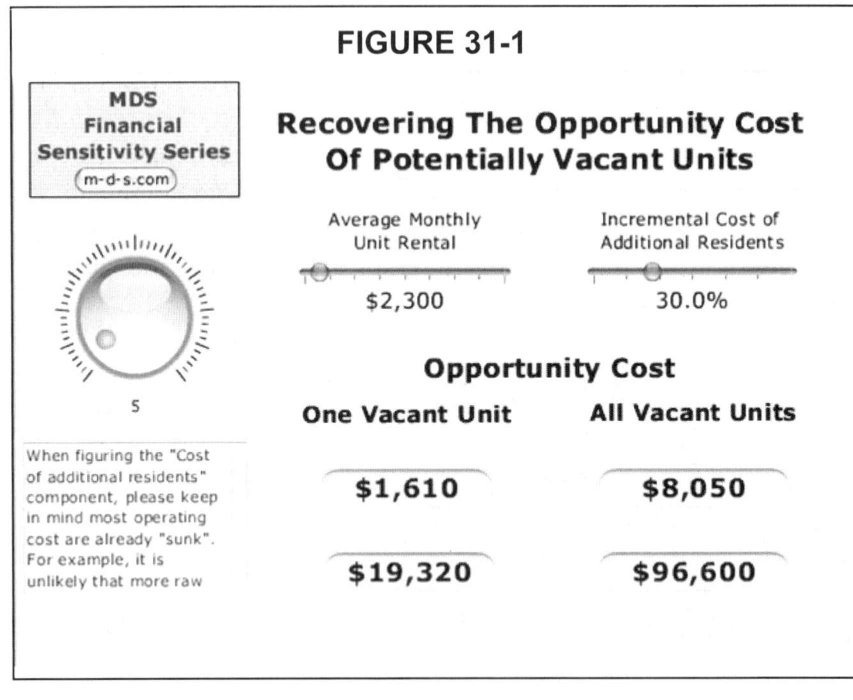
FIGURE 31-1
MDS
Financial
Sensitivity Series
m-d-s.com
Recovering The Opportunity Cost
Of Potentially Vacant Units
Average Monthly
Unit Rental
$2,300
Incremental Cost of
Additional Residents
30.0%
5
Opportunity Cost
One Vacant Unit
All Vacant Units
$1,610
$8,050
$19,320
$96,600
When figuring the "Cost of additional residents" component, please keep in mind most operating cost are already "sunk". For example, it is unlikely that more raw

CHAPTER 32

PROJECT MANAGEMENT STRATEGIES AND FEES

The Changing Dynamics Between Ownership and Management

What's New in 2009 and Beyond

The senior housing industry is experiencing some dramatic structural changes in two major areas; 1) ownership and 2) management. Consolidation of ownership is intensifying through acquisition and divestiture. Public companies are addressing off-balance sheet strategies with new levels of desired transparency. The industry is evolving into a sophisticated "hybrid" business model adopting key elements, strategies and financial benchmarks of both the commercial real estate and hospitality sectors.

A number of trends are becoming clearer regarding the maturing and increasingly sophisticated management company sector of the senior housing industry. A summary of some of the major changes include the following:

1. The complexity of the management function is increasing. Individual management contracts and entire management companies are now being recognized as having to deal with a very complex, sophisticated senior housing business model.

2. The property ownership and management company business mix is changing. Public companies and others are entering into sale/manage-back or sale/lease-back relationships with REITS, institutional investors and other financial joint venture partners. Owner/operator motivations include cashing in on some of their appreciated equity and, if a public company, getting the real estate off their books to enhance earnings per share.

3. Third-party management contract pricing strategies are changing. Management contract pricing for third-party owners is evolving from a price sensitive commodity to one where there is increased recognition of the need for a sophisticated, experienced management company that can enhance and sustain property value. Seeking out the management company with the lowest management fees is no longer the primary or exclusive competitive issue for many sponsors and owners/operators.

4. Contract terms and conditions are becoming more progressive. Management companies are negotiating enhanced financial incentives for delivering superior upside performance. More proactive expense pass-throughs and longer contract terms are being aggressively pursued by quality management companies.

5. Management company or individual contract valuation is still an elusive concept. Quantitative valuations of individual management contracts or entire management companies still lack the ability to apply generally recognized metrics, benchmarks or valuation formulas.

Senior Housing Management Is Becoming Much More Complex

The management of senior housing communities is now recognized as a complex, sophisticated business rather than a simple internal department or third-party "real estate property" management contract. The reasons for this sharpened distinction are numerous:

1. Management contract pricing is no longer considered a simple, price sensitive, competitive commodity.

2. There is growing recognition and appreciation that the management function really represents a complex business model. This complex business model includes, at least, the following elements of management and operations:

- Real estate/physical plant
- Dietary
- Health care
- Resident satisfaction
- Transportation
- Security
- Financial administration
- Asset management
- Risk management
- Human resources
- Information Technology (IT)

3. Increasing complexities of other management functions now include:

- Expanded and more complex licensing.
- Increased state regulations for certain types of senior housing properties.
- The need to deliver and manage more sophisticated direct care to high acuity residents.
- Expanded focus on purpose-built design and appropriate programmatic content for special care units including memory impairment and Alzheimer's/ dementia care.
- Increased involvement in administering ancillaries such as home health, hospice, pharmaceuticals and durable medical equipment.

4. Owners are requiring increased management sophistication. REITs, institutional investors and financial joint venture partners are not directly involved in the daily operations of a management company that is executing either a sale/manage-back or sale/lease-back relationship. However, REITs and joint venture partners are still very concerned about the quality and experience of the management company. That is because the performance of the management company could impact the income statement and the future ability to service the lease or debt service payments. Some REITs and joint venture partners are requiring subordination of the management fee to a defined and acceptable lease payment or debt service coverage ratio loan covenant.

5. The term of management contracts is increasing. It is now becoming common for certain management contracts to have an initial five year term with five year renewable options. Some of these renewable option terms extend out as far as twenty years, there are, of course, contractual clauses that could involve breaking the contract "for-cause" – a contractually defined violation of the contract. The majority owner may also choose to eventually sell the property to a third-party who might want to bring in their own management team. This is possible with appropriate contract terms and conditions. There are specific IRS requirements and criteria involving management contracts with tax-exempt not-for-profit senior living communities.

Pricing Strategies Are Changing

1. Senior housing community pricing and community financial operations models are becoming increasingly sophisticated. Some examples:

- The magnitude of upfront fees is increasing – some entry fees are now exceeding $500,000.
- Fee simple sales of retirement units as condominiums or co-operative ownership are becoming a relatively common pricing strategy.
- Tiered pricing in assisted living requires increased management sophistication; developing acuity/time measurement systems and expanding the details of reporting and billing initiatives.

2. Life care programs are expanding in both the for-profit and not-for-profit industry sectors. Many companies are now effectively involved in the complex health care insurance business – with a self contained and limited actuarial risk pool.

3. Public companies and others are using sale/lease-back, sale/manage-back and other creative joint venture strategies to get their physical plant assets off their balance sheets to enhance earnings per share. This shifting business mix from owned to managed or leased communities means that much more emphasis will be placed on expected performance outcomes of individual management contracts and management company portfolios.

The management of senior housing communities is now recognized as a significant business endeavor requiring a depth of experience and resources. As one industry leader stated, ***"We are no longer simply managing the operations of senior housing – we are now managing the complex business of senior housing."***

Consistent and effective management is one of the most important and critical elements driving the success of both new and existing senior housing communities. Some owners have a captive internal management operation. Others are changing their core business model by selling their tangible real estate assets at premium prices and evolving into sizeable management companies. Still others are retaining ownership and carefully evaluating how to best execute the management function of their senior housing community in the future. It is a classic "make or buy" decision taught in leading business schools for the last 50 years. Traditionally, it's been a strategic decision with two options:

1. **Build a strong permanent internal management resource.**

or . . .

2. **Outsource to a qualified third-party management company.**

However, a recent trend has created an important third decision option: ***"Should I sell my single property or portfolio and totally cash out, or should I sell my real estate, but stay involved and enjoy an income stream by entering into either a sale/manage-back or a sale/lease-back contract?"*** This important trend is addressed later in this chapter.

Go Internal or Outsource?

The option to internally manage or engage an external third-party management company appears to be a relatively easy decision in the short-run. But the long-run view introduces a number of variables suggesting that the management decision is far more complex. Clearly, the long-run view of satisfying community or portfolio management needs is critical to the future success of both senior housing communities and professional management companies. One thing *is* certain – senior housing communities need a defined, structured and sophisticated management function.

The possible selection of an external management company should be viewed as a beneficial, value-added strategy – both short-run and long-run. When evaluating the pros and cons of going internal versus entering into a third-party management contract, many issues must be considered. The two key issues that come to mind as potential disadvantages of engaging outside expertise are: 1) losing direct control and 2) incurring more costs through the payment of additional management fees. But this important decision must also focus on the top five community management needs to be satisfied.

Top Five Senior Housing Community Management Needs

A quality management company must address at least five key needs by providing extensive industry knowledge, experience and a comparable database. These top five needs are:

1. Systems, Policies and Procedures – Having sophisticated, yet practical, and cost-effective systems, procedures, and controls.

2. Deliver Economies of Scale – Realizing the potential for creating significant ongoing economies of scale that deliver substantial financial benefits to each individual community.

3. Staying on the Leading Edge – Sustaining the ability to stay on the leading edge of the state-of-the-art in an ever-changing complex industry.

4. Providing Operating Strategies – Executing cost-effective, consistent and focused market positioning, sales and marketing initiatives and operations strategies.

5. Implement Risk Management – Having leading edge risk management knowledge, experience and systems.

These and other objective criteria should really drive the critical community management decision of internal staffing versus supporting a rationale for outsourcing to a qualified third-party organization.

Each contractual relationship between a third-party manager and owner can have numerous variations. However, all of them should be based on sound business fundamentals. Many owners have sharpened their own internal management operations by establishing the same operating standards and expected performance outcomes that they would require of a third-party management company.

If one is planning a new, start-up community and has limited industry experience, lenders or underwriters may require the retention of a nationally recognized third-party management company. These financial risk takers obviously want the current owners to be successful, but they must always be assured that the best management and operational strategies are being deployed to avoid financial distress or potential foreclosure.

The Concept of Pass-Through Costs

For newcomers to the senior housing industry, there are frequently some serious misconceptions and misunderstandings regarding the specific services actually provided by management companies in exchange for collecting their fees. For example, the third-party management company will typically hire certain personnel and incur other costs at the community – *on behalf of the owner* – and based on the owner's prior approval. That means these costs are passed through to the community's normal operating expense budget and are not covered as part of earning the typical management fee. This cost pass-through approach is common throughout the industry. In some cases, many or all of the community's staff may be employees of the management company with their costs being passed on to the owner. For many owners, this is a preferred option.

Frequently accounting, accounts payable/receivable, payroll and information technology are services provided at the management company's Central Office to directly benefit a specific community. These costs are typically passed on to the community, in addition to the management fee.

The Top Ten Typical Management Services Provided

As in any other purchasing or outsourcing decision, it is best to receive competitive inputs from several quality management companies with established credentials and industry experience. Owner/operators must carefully evaluate a number of important services that are typically included in comprehensive management contracts and fee relationships. Some of these services include, but are certainly not limited to, the following:[1]

1. **General Management Services:**
   - Provide operations oversight and expertise
   - Supervise daily operations
   - Implement policies and procedures
   - Establish qualitative and quantitative performance objectives
   - Implement pre-opening "countdown" tasks and strategies
   - Develop and implement licensure and regulatory compliance program

[1]A number of these services may have an additional initial set-up fee and some may have equitable on-going execution and implementation charges.

2. **Sales and Marketing Initiatives:**
   - Select and install sophisticated, but efficient, lead tracking systems
   - Coordinate marketing collateral development
   - Develop a strategic sales and marketing plan and budget
   - Manage/supervise all operations and activities
   - Provide status reporting; weekly, monthly, quarterly, and annually
   - Deliver defined performance results to agreed-to budgets and forecasts
   - Conduct periodic competitive analyses

3. **Provide Operating Systems, Policies and Procedures:**
   - Develop
   - Install
   - Execute
   - Maintain

   } Accounting systems/software, policy and procedures manual, residency agreements, employee manual, external agency compliance reporting, etc.

4. **Staffing/Human Resources:**
   - Develop job descriptions
   - Recommend compensation and benefit plans
   - Recruit and interview candidates
   - Hire and fire
   - Train
   - Supervise
   - Implement payroll

5. **Overall Financial Management and Controls:**
    - Establish
    - Maintain
    - Monitor
    - Report
    - Prepare billings/collect receivables; disburse payables
6. **Budgets and Financial Management/Controls:**
    - Prepare annual budget
    - Obtain owner review and approval
    - Prepare capital budgeting and expenditure plan
7. **Develop and Prepare Monthly Financial Statements:**
    - Report monthly
    - Compare actuals vs. budget
    - Issue variance reports
    - Balance sheets
    - Income statements
    - Cash flow statements
    - General ledgers
    - Loan covenant summaries
8. **Resident Care:**
    - Develop overall care plan
    - Create resident assessment criteria

- Define/maintain appropriate standards of care
- Monitor and comply with all state and local regulations
- Define and monitor resident expected outcomes
- Monitor and respond to acuity/cost creep

9. Risk Management:

- Recommend adequate insurance coverage
- Keep appropriate insurance coverage in force
- Monitor and minimize current and future insurance/risk management costs

10. Capital Expenditures:

- Develop and execute short run capital expenditure (Cap X) program
- Design and execute a 5-year revolving capital expenditure plan and budget

These are the types of services typically provided by the management company for a defined management fee. The management company may also incur significant other approved costs that are passed on to the owner. Keep in mind that individual management contract terms and conditions can vary over a wide spectrum. Most management agreements also contain a concise list of owner responsibilities.

Effective third-party management involves a two tier seamless process; the significant resources of the management company's *home office* must be delivered and effectively integrated with the necessary initiatives taking place at the owner's *seniors living community*.

How Are Management Fees Typically Assessed?

Management fee compensation can be related to four possible milestones during the life cycle of a typical seniors housing community. The fee relationships described below deal with monthly service fee type pricing of *market rate rentals*. Special *upfront entry fee* situations are addressed later in this chapter:

1. Services Provided Pre-Opening or Before Certificate of Occupancy (CO) – Management companies have many initial tasks to perform during the critical period prior to the opening of a new senior housing community. Compensation for mature communities is normally established as a percent of gross income. However, during this period, compensation that would be derived solely as a percent of limited or no initial income is not practical or appropriate. Typically, a fixed minimum base fee is charged for services rendered. That minimum fee could be in the range of $5,000 to $10,000 per month or higher. In some contracts the fee is as high as $20,000 per month. Generally, compensation would depend on the specific role of the manager during design, construction and pre-opening activities (not including any separate developer fee type services). Pre-opening marketing is usually a very important management function. A number of circumstances could influence this initial fee (size of project, complexity of the community, degree of difficulty, specific roles of the management company, etc.).

2. Services During Initial Fill-Up – The fixed minimum base fee charged prior to Certificate of Occupancy would still apply. However, now a management fee structured as a percent of gross income is also phasing in as a new compensation factor. As occupancy grows, so does total revenue and earned management fees. A typical compensation arrangement during fill-up might be

$7,000 to $10,000 per month or 5 percent of gross income; whichever is greater.

3. Fees After Reaching Stabilized Occupancy – Basic management fee terms and conditions are typically discussed and negotiated by assuming a relatively mature community operating at or near stabilized occupancy. The typical compensation formula is to earn management fees as a percent of total income realized.[1] Typical compensation ranges between approximately 4 to 7 percent of gross income. Sometimes this total fee represents a composite of direct management fees, performance incentive fees, asset management fees (discussed later) and corporate fees.

Figure 32-1 is a summary of current industry benchmarks. This negotiated compensation factor is usually a function of project size, degree of difficulty, tasks to be performed and the expected outcomes from the management company. Some variations to this common compensation approach include a fixed monthly fee versus a percent of gross income. This is especially true when complying with IRS 501(c)(3) tax-exempt charter requirements. Sometimes, a lender may require that the management fee be subordinated to available cash flow after debt service. In a third-party management relationship the manager may still recover subordinated management fees from the owner.

[1]Gross income is a term frequently used in management contracts. The term is intended to mean any effective operating revenue directly realized from operating the community.

The 2009 Edition of the American Seniors Housing Association's comprehensive annual industry survey ***"The State of Seniors Housing"*** published the following base management fee benchmarks:

FIGURE 32-1
MANAGEMENT FEES AS A PERCENTAGE OF TOTAL REVENUE BY COMMUNITY TYPE

	Lower Quartile	Median	Upper Quartile
• Independent Living	5.0%	5.0%	6.0%
• Assisted Living	5.0%	5.0%	6.0%
• CCRC	2.5%	3.6%	4.5%
• **ALL COMMUNITIES**	**4.9%**	**5.0%**	**6.0%**

Source: The State of Seniors Housing 2009

4. Entry Fee Compensation – Projects involving upfront, one-time entry fees offer a range of compensation for "selling" the unit, initially, and for the re-sale of a vacated unit. The incentive fees observed in the industry range from 2 to 6 percent of the entry fee value. In some cases, a higher compensation percentage is used for initial (fill-up) entry fee sales versus the re-selling of entry fees for previously vacated units.

Special Incentive Fee Compensation

Special incentive fee compensation to management companies is becoming more common. Incentives are usually focused on superior performance in two time frames in a community's life cycle:

- Achieving rapid initial fill-up (exceeding financial pro forma projections)

- Realizing exceptional levels of stabilized performance (occupancy, net operating income and cash flow)

The traditional benchmark management fee of approximately 5 percent for stabilized operations is frequently enhanced when a community consistently achieves mutually agreed-upon defined superior performance levels. There are typically six operating performance incentive levels that can be considered:

1. Incentives for *Rapid Initial Fill-Up* – The initial fill-up period is very expensive and can result in significant negative cash flow from operations. There is so much cash at stake that owner/operators are willing to pay significant incentives to a management company that can take them through the critical launch period at a rapid pace. For example, a CCRC project containing 180 independent living units might have a target to reach 93 percent occupancy in 28 months after opening. This reflects an average net absorption (including turnover) of just under 6 units per month. A rapid fill-up incentive compensation schedule might look like what is summarized on the following page.

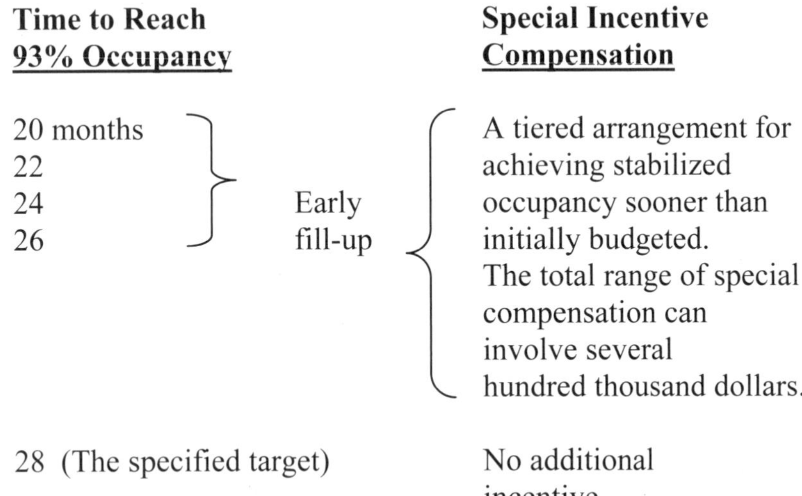

Time to Reach 93% Occupancy		**Special Incentive Compensation**
20 months 22 24 26	Early fill-up	A tiered arrangement for achieving stabilized occupancy sooner than initially budgeted. The total range of special compensation can involve several hundred thousand dollars.
28 (The specified target)		No additional incentive compensation

That special incentive may look like a lot of money until one evaluates the total *reduction* in negative cash flow and overall cash savings to the sponsor or owner-operator. Sometimes this incentive fee is not included in the management agreement, but as part of a third-party development agreement.

2. Exceptional Levels of Stabilized Performance – This performance level is usually defined and incentivized by one of four possible criteria:

- Stabilized occupancy levels above target thresholds – usually above 95 percent
- Extraordinary operating profit; Net Operating Income (NOI) or EBITDA (Earnings Before Interest, Taxes, Depreciation and Amortization)

- Cash flow after debt service is higher than projected
- Key actuals exceeding budgeted performance for a specific time period

There are certain incentive compensation limits that are tax code driven. These typically involve management relationships with not-for-profits.

3. Consistently Operating at Very High Stabilized Occupancy Levels – Some occupancy incentive arrangements increase management fees accordingly:

Achieved Occupancy	**Typical Incentivized Management Fees (Percent of Total/Gross Revenue)**
95.0% to 95.9%	5.5%
96.0% to 96.9%	6.0%
97.0% to 97.9%	6.5%
98.0% to 98.9%	7.0%

4. ***Exceeding Defined Operating Levels:*** **Net Operating Income (NOI) or EBITDA** – Operating profit and cash flow incentives are usually implemented as a share of additional incremental dollar benefits realized – above a mutually agreed-upon target level. The incentive splits for the management company typically range between 20 to 30 percent of the total incremental cash benefits.

5. ***Exceeding Specific Cash Flow*** **After Debt Service Thresholds** – Some sponsors and owner/operators prefer to apply incentives at the ultimate bottom line; as a percent of cash flow after all normal cash obligations are paid.

6. ***"Back-End" Holding Period Incentive Fee*** – A "back-end" incentive for exceeding a defined Internal Rate of Return (IRR) or other performance thresholds that are evaluated at a defined ending point of a specified holding period.

These performance thresholds can be a discrete level or a variable based on budgeted vs. actual performance that can change with time/maturity of the community. Usually only one of the six performance incentive plans is chosen to avoid duplication or compounding incentives. Certain not-for-profit related tax restrictions may apply.

Asset Management Fees

The rationale for an asset management fee is that an organization not only manages the community, but also has broader responsibilities for maintaining the integrity of the asset, such as:

- Insuring that all debt covenants are maintained and reported
- Paying the debt service in a timely manner
- Having comprehensive interaction with lenders/bond counsel, etc.

Some might argue that this is the normal role of a manager, while others are addressing this as a special compensation issue. While still rare, this fee is typically one percent of gross income. In some cases, this asset management compensation is consolidated within the basic management fee.

Who Pays What Expenses?

This issue of expenses is frequently misunderstood when owner/operators initially explore a third-party management contract. There are three basic expense categories to define and consider:

1. Expenses Included Within Management Company Fee – What does the management company provide as part of earning their basic fee? Some typical management services were discussed earlier.

2. Management Company Expense Reimbursement – What allowable direct expenses are passed on to the owner by the management company? Some typical management company expense reimbursement could include items such as travel, lodging, meals, long distance telephone, express delivery and other out-of-pocket expenses. Some contracts have an agreed-to annual expense cap.

The Administrator or Executive Director is frequently an employee of the management company. Sometimes all of the staff are employed by the management company. These costs are passed on to the owner and are not part of the base management fee. There is also the concept of other pass-through costs discussed earlier in this chapter.

3. Owner/Operator Expenses – Resources procured and expenses incurred (with prior approval) that are normally passed on to the owner.

Penalty for Sub-Par Performance

Some contracts have penalty and termination clauses for unacceptable performance below a specified minimum operating threshold. Two examples are:

- ***Occupancy*** falling below 90 percent and staying below that threshold for a period exceeding approximately 3 to 6 months.
- ***Net Operating Income*** falling below a defined threshold for a period exceeding approximately 3 to 6 months. In some contracts, the dollar impact of the shortfall is quantified and the manager must recover this deficit in order to benefit from future incentive compensation.

The management company has a contractual obligation to cure a sub-par performance problem or be subject to termination.

Termination

There are typically three categories of termination:

1. ***Without Cause*** – By Agreement
2. ***For Cause*** – Either owner or management company violates specific terms of the agreement
3. ***Upon Sale of the Property*** – New owner wants to use their own management resources or select a new manager

These important termination issues must be well defined in the executed Management Agreement – including termination compensation (if any) along with specific formulas for determining such compensation.

Termination Penalty Clauses and Compensation

Third-party management company compensation may be due for termination without cause or upon sale of the property. There are two common compensation approaches:

1. ***Severance Compensation*** in an amount equal to the number of months remaining in the current contract multiplied by the then-current monthly management fee.

2. ***A Present Value of the Severance*** formula mentioned above is used to determine final payment. This considers the time value of money and discounts the net compensation that would have been due in future months. Managers frequently have a purchase option or right of first purchase offer.

Sometimes a *"lost profits"* concept is applied wherein future gross management fees are reduced by imputing the management company operating expenses that would have been incurred to perform the ongoing management function. Alternatively, the present value of those net fees might be applied.

Term-Length of Contract

Third-party management contracts typically have initial terms that encompass three to five years; most with well-defined renewal options. Some contracts involve equity ownership/participation by the management company. In those circumstances, the term can be up to 20 years; most with defined termination options. There are some special IRS rules that apply to compensation and contract length when a for-profit management company is managing a not-for-profit community. Most contracts have the right of both the manager or the owner to terminate the contract under defined *without cause* termination options.

Management Company Pitfalls

In spite of their obvious strengths and advantages, some apparently sound third-party management companies fail to deliver full potential to their clients. There are typically five potential weaknesses that must be avoided in any selection decision:

1. The lack of consistent, ongoing involvement and oversight by the same key, experienced individuals who initially sold the contractual relationship.
2. Inadequate support from the management company's home office.
3. Inconsistent quality of contract services and sub-par performance of on-site personnel permanently assigned to the community.
4. The inability to effectively communicate and work with owners, sponsors, and boards of directors.
5. Unacceptable performance outcomes; ineffective sales and marketing results and/or excessive operating costs.

Concise contract terms combined with consistent monitoring and progress reporting systems can serve as effective early warning signals.

The Changing Role of the Management Company Concept

Large portfolio owner/operators and individual owners are selling their properties (the real estate) while retaining and executing the management function as a stand-alone future business model. These purchases by non-operating institutional investors (REITs, pension funds, equity investors, etc.) are injecting large amounts of new capital into senior housing. This is allowing owners to cash out at essentially 100 percent of value while staying involved in the management process and enjoying a substantial management fee income. In sale/lease-back arrangements, the seller can also benefit from favorable operating margins and net cash flow.

Two Basic Exit Strategies for Owners[1]

It is very important to understand the fundamental differences between two concepts that involve managing, but not owning, a seniors housing property. They are the *sale/lease-back* and *sale/manage-back* concepts:

1. Sale/Lease-Back – Senior housing property/real estate is sold to a non-operating third-party; pension fund, Real Estate Investment Trust (REIT), institutional equity investor and sometimes an individual buyer/owner. The seller frequently enters into a "triple net" lease to continue to operate the property. Triple net means the *lessee* – not the new *owner* – has both the benefits and burdens of ownership during the lease term. More specifically, the lessee is essentially responsible for all property expenses including property taxes, maintenance and repairs, utilities and insurance, just as if he or she still owned the property. In addition, the lessee pays a fixed base monthly lease fee. Finally, the lessee is typically entitled to all excess cash flow after the payment of the rent and expenses at the property.

---

[1]Be sure to *"know when to hold 'em and know when to fold 'em"* by reviewing *exit strategies* in Chapter 49.

Typical lease terms today include:

- Lessor buys the property; usually at a very attractive capitalization rate to the seller – net of any underlying debt on the property.
  - For a quality independent living project, the valuation cap rate in the 2009 time frame is typically in the 8 to 9 percent range.
  - Assisted living cap rate would be 1.0 to 2.0 percent higher.
- Lessee (the seller) essentially gets full value (net of underlying debt) but still gets to operate/manage the property.
- Unlike the manage-back concept (discussed next), the lessee controls the income statement; enjoying the benefits and enduring the challenges of realizing any operating profits and cash flow.
- What does all this cost the lessee? In mid 2009, lessees are commonly paying an annual lease rate of between 7 to 8 percent of the original lessor acquisition cost plus the ongoing cost of operating and fulfilling their triple net lease obligation. There are typically annual escalators of this lease fee that are the greater of 2 to 3 percent of the base lease amount per year or some mutually agreed-upon component of the Consumer Price Index (CPI). It is important to note that lease rates are market-driven and are related to many factors. They will fluctuate over time. The lease rate can be evaluated as a weighted average cost of capital; the seller/lessee's typical cost of debt and equity. Sellers generally feel that a 7 to 8 percent cost of capital is reasonable in today's debt and equity markets.

- Typical lease-back terms range from approximately 10 to 20 years involving individual or multiple extension/renewal options.
- In some instances, the lessee must provide security deposits and financial guarantees.
- Frequently, there is also a lessee purchase option at the end of the lease term or a right of first offer option if the owner puts the property up for sale.
- Sometimes, the lessee was not the previous owner, but is retained by the lessor to operate the property.

The sale/lease-back is very common today when sellers are dealing with REITs. It represents a well defined, "clean" and transparent transaction for both the buyer/owner (lessor) and seller/manager (lessee).

The lessee's financial rewards come from how well they can deliver net operating income; realizing cash flow after paying their 7 to 8 percent lease fee to the lessor and funding their triple net obligations. Simply stated they control the income statement, but the property's (real estate) financial statement impacts (depreciation, etc.) are reflected in the lessor's financials.

2. Sale/Manage-Back – While there are many similarities to the *sale/lease-back*, there are also some important differences:

- The most significant difference is the fact that the management company does not "own" the income statement. They do not directly incur the risk or reward of the income statement or balance sheet performance; these impacts belong to the owner.

However, the manager can either be incentive compensated or penalized for income statement performance.

- The management company performs defined services and oversight for a specific compensation package.

- Under the sale/manage-back concept, control of the management contract longevity can be subject to termination for a situation other than "for cause" (unacceptable performance by the manager). Management contracts typically have definitive performance terms (length of contract performance). Many of today's contracts can also be terminated if the current owner sells and the new owner wants to bring in their own management team. This can be a valid reason for early termination of a contract. Early termination penalty fees to be paid to the departing management company are also common. In the sale/manage-back situation, the management company can have a number of renewable contract terms that can extend the potential relationship as long as 20 years or more.

- The rewards to a management company have several important components. They include: 1) minimum/flat monthly fees prior to opening and during the initial fill-up of a new community, 2) typically a percentage of revenues during normal operations at stabilized occupancy, 3) a special financial incentive for *"superior performance"* typically measured either by very high stabilized occupancy or net operating income and cash flow above an agreed-to performance target.

- There can also be penalties for *sub-par performance*; including the possibility of contract termination if the problem is not corrected within a defined time period.

There are numerous variations to the basic management contract in a sale/manage-back scenario. Here are two examples:

- In some arrangements, managers agree to subordinate their fees or to fund future operating losses or negative cash flow positions after debt service for a period of time after the sale.
- Some owners that sell and manage-back sometimes still hold a 10 to 20 percent equity ownership position in the property.

In these ownership positions, the manager frequently has favorable upside financial performance incentives.

Call to Action

A subtle, but definite, industry consolidation is taking place. New money is being infused into the senior housing industry by REITs, pension funds and other large institutional investors. Both public and private companies are implementing off balance sheet strategies to raise additional capital and to sharpen their focus on optimizing long-run business models.

Detailed operating ratios, benchmarks and best practices must now be developed as a new business model evolves. Some senior housing operators are essentially becoming management companies focusing on *operations* with the *real estate* belonging to astute, but passive, investors. These investor-owners will be demanding optimum performance from management companies. In addition, management companies need to become a marketable asset with the ability to establish tangible values of both individual contracts and overall companies.

CHAPTER 33

FILLING UP STUDIOS AND OTHER "DOG" UNITS

Less is Sometimes More When Dealing With Problem Units

One of the biggest challenges in senior living today is the growing obsolescence of many physical plants developed over the past 15 to 25 years. What started out as a new stylish *Oldsmobile* building in the 1980s is now perceived as a vintage *Chevrolet* or *Pontiac* in today's marketplace.[1] I'm not talking about very desirable classics - many are just old with declining utility.

Many sponsors and owner/operators have become accustomed to the financial rewards from these older physical plants. The increasing operating expenses and ongoing debt service may require us to continue to charge *Oldsmobile* prices for what are now *Chevrolet-style* communities. But senior consumers and their families are gradually offering increasing resistance to these older, sub-par physical plants (see Chapter 18). Increased consumer discretion in the marketplace is focusing more and more on newer, state-of-the-art designs offering a superior mix of *product*, *price,* and *value*.

[1] General Motors stopped making Oldsmobiles in 2004!

In many senior living communities, it is common for a certain number of units to remain chronically vacant. These units, which have had no serious takers for a period of at least six months, are usually vacant for a simple reason – the senior consumer does not see them as demonstrating good value and, therefore, refuses to pay the listed rate. These units are typically too small, have undesirable external views, too long a walk to the dining room, or an undesirable, dated design. Whatever the problem, the solution is the same; correct physical design flaws where possible, or use selective tiered pricing – adjusting the prices of these units to reflect their realistic market value.

The "Original Pro Forma Syndrome"

Unfortunately, many sponsors and owner/operators suffer from a malady I call the "original financial pro forma syndrome." One of the symptoms of this economic malady is the dogged refusal to change prices and financial projections used in the original financial plan. Despite overwhelming evidence that some units are unrealistically priced for the competitive marketplace, those operators suffering from the original financial pro forma syndrome continue to hold out for an eventual sale at the original price.

But chronically vacant, flawed units rarely do sell for their original prices. They remain empty, depleting a community's potential revenues. Troublesome units are most easily identified as a community reaches approximately 60 to 70 percent occupancy. At this occupancy level, much of a community's core operating costs, such as staffing, medical services, and food service, etc., are essentially fixed. The costs remain approximately the same as if all the units were occupied. But these vacant units represent a significant revenue and profit shortfall.

The Opportunity Cost Concept

At relatively high occupancies, dog units can really impact your bottom line. That's because, for independent living, about 70 percent of your costs are fixed whereas only approximately 30 percent are truly variable (raw food, other consumables, perhaps some incremental staff, etc.) This means that each additional vacant unit has an "opportunity cost" equal to approximately 70 percent of the revenue that would be realized if occupied. Thus, a vacant unit in an existing community that would command an average monthly service fee of approximately $2,300 has an opportunity cost of more than $1,600 per month or $19,200 per year. If the community's pricing structure also involves the potential of lost upfront entry fees, the opportunity cost is even greater. So just six of these dog units can cause an operating income shortfall in excess of over $115,000 per year, and a decrease in the community's intrinsic value of approximately $1.2 million. And that doesn't consider the potential loss of entry fees. Chapter 31 addresses the details of opportunity costs.

The Reality of Price Concessions

Should you consider discounting continually vacant units? There's money on the table. A community's professional staff is usually the first to realize dog units and the need for possible pricing changes. Typically, they must then justify the strategy to top management or board members. Their task is to communicate three cold, hard facts: 1) the original financial pro forma was probably incorrect, 2) chronically vacant units are typically empty because of serious flaws, unrealistically higher prices, and not necessarily a sluggish marketplace, and, 3) the operator must bring price and value back in line with the marketplace if the units are to be sold.

Certainly, the impact of any price concession must be carefully evaluated. Reducing prices on selected units will reduce the *projected* revenue of the community and, in turn, affect the original pro forma. However, the positive impact of the decision in the long run usually far outweighs any negative short-term, projected outcomes.

Value Scoring Each Unit

How do you objectively deal with price adjustments? To come up with a workable formula for selective price adjustments, sponsors start by assessing the value of each living unit within the community. This can be done by developing a simple score sheet that quantifies the value characteristics of each unit type. Then, the relative values of similar unit types need to be adjusted either upward or downward, depending on their locations and unique other characteristics within the community.

Value scoring a community's living units can be very revealing. While chronically vacant units may be *overpriced*, other units may be *underpriced.* Thus, over time, what a community loses by lowering the price of one unit, may be compensated for by raising the price of another – at least on an attrition/turnover basis.

Neutralizing Resident Reaction

Owners often fear that current residents may become angry when they learn that another resident is paying less for a unit whose layout is identical to theirs. It is, therefore, wise to give full disclosure to your existing residents before implementing tiered pricing of selected units. Let your residents know that optimizing community occupancy is in their own best individual financial interests.

Point out that different units do represent different value and, therefore, must be priced differently. Then offer the lower-priced vacant units first to existing residents, allowing them at least two weeks to opt for these units before putting them on the market. You probably won't have many takers for that option.

This approach defuses controversy before it develops into a major problem. And experience shows that, while residents almost never take advantage of the lower-priced units, they appreciate having the option. If you present the information about selective tiered pricing properly, existing residents, like board members, will usually understand and support this pragmatic strategy.

The Vacant Studio Dilemma

There is a special class of a "dog unit" category that plagues many communities that are at least 10 to 15 years old. These troublesome units are frequently small studios in independent living with either limited or no kitchens. These small, austere units worked well as an acceptable, affordable product in the 80s and early 90s. Now, many of these smaller units suffer chronic vacancies for extended time periods.

Many sponsors and owner/operators are gradually coming to the conclusion that the solution to some of their chronic vacancies might be combining two small 300 s.f. studios into a single, 600 s.f. one-bedroom unit. Sounds simple, until you pencil out some lost revenue and the total cost of conversion – including transforming one studio's bathroom into a more functional kitchen. The costs of retrofit for combining two studio units can range from

$12,000 to $15,000 or more. Installing a doorway through the wall between two adjacent studios is normally not a problem unless there is a load-bearing wall or one has closet space on either side of that common wall. Modifying the kitchen and bathroom plumbing is a more complex issue.

Another common challenge is the fact that some of these studios may have a random distribution of occupancy throughout the community, which further complicates the conversion strategy. Some sponsors are dealing with this occupancy challenge by combining only those adjacent units that become vacant on an attrition basis. Others are offering one-time financial incentives to get certain residents to free up the needed adjacent unit by moving to another unit in the community. Still others are selling certain residents – who can afford it – on the advantages of upgrading their studio to the larger retrofitted unit.

A Real World Conversion Example

Let's assume you plan to combine two adjacent 300 s.f. vacant studios priced at $1,300 per month into one 600 s.f. one-bedroom unit. Recognize that the competitive marketplace revenue for the converted unit will probably not yield $2,600 per month (2 x $1,300). The competitive market rate for a 600 s.f. one-bedroom unit might be approximately $1,800 per month – representing a loss in revenue yield of $800 per month – or a net loss of about $640 per month after adjusting for lower operating expenses for single person occupancy plus the new debt service cost to pay for retrofitting the unit (see Figure 33-1).

Combining two small studio units into a one-bedroom unit will likely improve marketability and occupancy, but the resulting *theoretical* cash flow will probably be reduced by $640 per month, or $7,680 per year after appropriate revenue and expense adjustments. Before you reject this as a bad idea, take a sobering look at your realistic alternatives. You must consider the much larger opportunity cost for two chronically vacant studio units that, due to heavy fixed costs, will incur about 80 percent of their operating expenses when vacant. That's a total opportunity cost of approximately $2,080 per month or $24,960 annually ($1,300 per month x 2 x .80 = $2,080 per month). The decision to combine may well be the lesser of two evils.

For any two studios, your long-run decision boils down to this; what is the probability that you are better off reducing your *theoretical* gross potential revenue by $7,680 per year versus facing the very real possibility of continuing to lose $24,960 per year? Just about all the empirical evidence and market leading indicators point to "biting the bullet" on unit conversion. At the very least, it may be worth a limited experiment with two or four studios before launching into an extensive conversion program throughout your community.

FIGURE 33-1

LOST REVENUE "YIELD" BY COMBINING TWO SMALL INDEPENDENT LIVING STUDIO UNITS

	Monthly Impacts
I. Independent Living MSF	
•Two 300 s.f. Studio Units	
- Each at $1,300/month	$ 2,600/month
•One 600 s.f. One-Bedroom Unit	(1,800)
II. Loss of Revenue Yield	$ 800 /month
III. Adjust for Reduced Expenses (Less Meals, Etc.)	(250)
IV. Add Debt Service for $15,000 Retrofit Cost	90
V. Net Lost Revenue/Cost Impact	***$ 640/month***
	Vs.
VI. The Potential Opportunity Cost	***$2,080***

Moore Diversified Services, Inc.

A One-Bedroom Conversion?

Not only are studios becoming very undesirable, some *one-bedroom units* are being combined and converted into *two-bedroom apartments*. This one-bedroom conversion appears to be the start of an emerging trend.

Call to Action

Dog units don't fix themselves. The passage of time will not likely cure the problem. It maybe time to "bite the bullet" on making permanent improvements for the future.

CHAPTER 34

HOME EQUITY - A BENIGN BUT VALUABLE ASSET

Competing For and Tapping a Huge $1.2 Trillion Resource

***Note:* As this book goes to press, we are experiencing a serious economic recession and credit crisis that has negatively impacted home values and sales in most markets. The national economy will always experience cycles – but sound strategies will always stand the test of time.**

How would you like to have an ***interest-free loan*** of $15 to $20 million or more with an indefinite payback period? Sound too good to be true? Well, welcome to the world of refundable and non-refundable CCRC entry fees primarily funded by seniors liquidating their home equity by selling their home. Entry fee pricing is addressed in detail in Chapter 42. Oh, by the way, under current tax laws, your residents would likely also avoid a charge from your friendly IRS professional for imputed interest.

Here's the catch; most seniors are reluctant to tap into their existing savings portfolio to pay today's typical CCRC entry fees that can range from $150,000 to $400,000; some as high as $500,000+. But many are willing to trade all or part of the net cash from the sale of their home – in other words, their net home equity.

As seniors contemplate moving into retirement communities, most must address the sale of their home. On one hand, most seniors recognize their changing personal needs and the growing hassles and expense of home ownership. On the other hand, seniors also have strong emotional and almost unbreakable ties to the homes that they have lived in for as long as 40 to 50 years. This attachment is so strong that it can be a sales and marketing deal-killer.

However, when properly positioned, selling a home can be a significant marketing opportunity for senior living communities.

The Financial Stakes are High

The gross home equity potential of age 75+ seniors is estimated to be approximately $1.2 trillion. It was growing at about $72 billion per year or roughly the net worth of Bill Gates! But that was before the economic recession and credit crisis that unfolded in 2007 and 2008.

Seniors obviously consider their home a valuable asset. Astute financial planners define the home more specifically as an **illiquid, benign asset**. That's because pent-up home equity is not earning current income or helping seniors with their current finances. To many professionals and a growing number of savvy seniors, the home is both an asset and an opportunity cost. This opportunity cost concept is addressed in detail in Chapter 35.

Typical Home Equity Conversion

A senior's home equity is typically converted to a more liquid asset under two situations:

1. When the senior dies and their estate requests are implemented.
2. When the senior sells their home and opts for alternative living accommodations.

When seniors opt for other senior living accommodations, the liquidated asset can be added to their existing savings portfolio and invested to produce increased current income. This is the case, for example, when a senior moves into a market rate rental independent living community. A portion of that liquidated asset can also be used to fund required entry fees for CCRCs that offer upfront entrance fee pricing.

Home equity represents a huge asset for many seniors. Consider these startling statistics:

- **The home ownership rate** is approximately 77 percent for seniors 75 and older. Mortgages are typically paid off.
- **The median value of a senior's pent-up home equity** in 2009 was, on average, in excess of $160,000.

Home selling is currently a problem in 2009 and some home values are, at least, temporarily depressed. In this book, I'm using a conservative ***average*** home equity of $160,000. Typically, this is the market you're trying to capture.

A large percentage of age 75+ seniors, who have a current income affordability gap of about $1,000 per month, could sell their home and thereby increase their savings portfolio and increase their affordability. Many would now be able to afford to pay the full market rate monthly service fee without spend-down! Those words should be music to many seniors' ears.

Others could adopt a very prudent spend-down strategy that would be financially responsible. Of equal importance, this strategy could optimize their quality of life.

Need Versus Want

In helping seniors put this asset to work, we must address two important and sometimes apparently conflicting issues: what seniors really *want* and what they actually *need.* Seniors *want* to stay at home – pure and simple. They are attached to their cherished homes; one that is full of love and memories. Sure, it's larger than they really need and maintenance has become a bigger challenge as the years go by. But every nook and cranny of that home reminds them of a lifetime of experiences.

The Opportunity to Serve *Needs*

There is an opportunity, however, to creatively and prudently unleash the tremendous economic clout of the senior's home equity asset. We can do that while helping seniors live their remaining life with dignity and independence – and with physical and financial security. We can also assist them in leaving a financial legacy to their children – an important financial goal for many.

Further, we have the service delivery systems to help seniors either avoid or delay the steep nursing home cost spend-down ramp that has devastated many hopes and dreams over the past 30 to 40 years. Today, 70 percent of all nursing census days are associated with Medicaid residents. Many seniors did not enter the nursing home as a low income Medicaid qualified patient. But sadly, many watched their financial legacy slip away as they were forced to spend down their lifetime of savings.

Sure, asset shifting is still prevalent, but so is unnecessary and accelerated spend-down of assets. *"Preservation of assets"* and *"leaving a legacy"* are going to be the key sound bites and market positioning platforms for successful senior living and health care sponsors in the 21st century.

Seniors and their families really need practical and credible guidance to satisfy five critical objectives for situations that they face in their later stages of life. The five objectives include:

1. Expanded living and health care options.
2. Increased affordability.
3. Security and peace of mind.
4. Preservation of assets (leaving a legacy).
5. A practical, time-phased plan to accomplish all of the above.

We can help seniors accomplish this by helping them put their biggest asset - their home - to work in innovative and prudent ways. Recent changes to capital gains tax laws allow seniors to sell their current home without purchasing (or owning) another one, and still pay essentially zero capital gains tax.

With properly executed financial strategies, seniors can enjoy the following as they face the inevitable challenges of later life:

1. Increased income stream (which makes senior housing more affordable).
2. Tax avoidance.
3. Preservation of assets (leaving a legacy).
4. Estate liquidity.

There are two basic strategies that can be deployed to help seniors and their families make a decision on whether to sell one's home:

1. Liquidating home equity to increase affordability.
2. Developing prudent spend-down strategies.

Financial Sensitivity Analysis

Figure 34-1 is one of about 30 financial sensitivity templates our firm has developed to show our clients both the sensitivity and cost-benefit relationship of implementing action for <u>their</u> unique situation.[1] Using a live, interactive Power Point driven conference call with the client, we can move the two ***sliders*** to emulate their unique home sales financial situation. The savings rate and marginal tax rate ***knobs*** can also be manipulated to observe the sensitivity of various net home equity savings/investment scenarios. The ***opportunity cost*** windows at the bottom of the figure change dynamically; showing the sobering financial impacts.

[1]For more information on the availability of these templates, visit www.m-d-s.com.

FIGURE 34-1

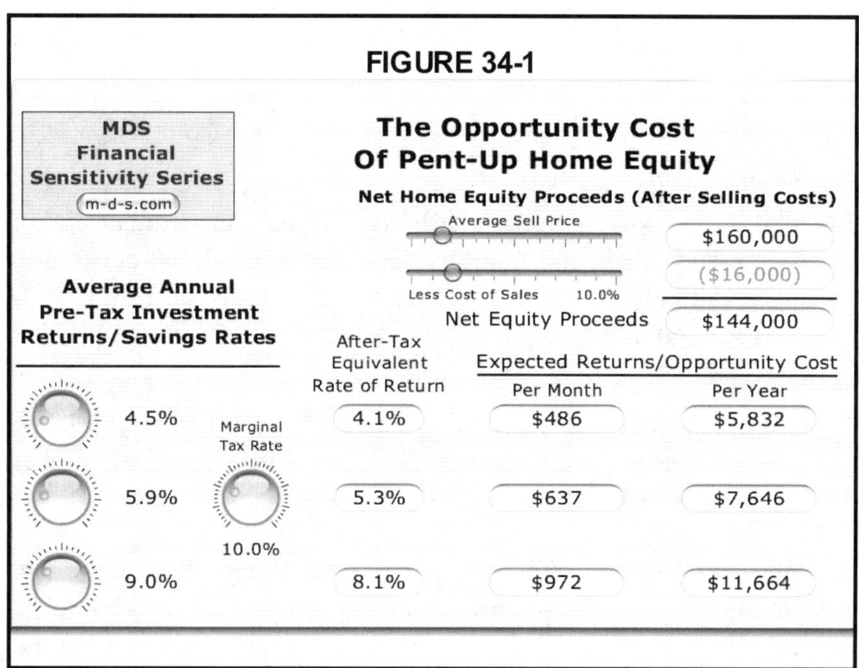

Let's look at the nuts and bolts of these strategies:

Liquidating home equity to increase affordability. Here's a typical real world scenario:

- Mrs. Barker has a current after-tax income of $31,500. She and her family make the difficult but appropriate independent living decision. The monthly service fee is $2,150.
- She sells a $160,000 home and nets $144,000, after 10 percent sales/closing costs. There is no capital gains tax impact.

- The $144,000 is added to Mrs. Barker's existing savings portfolio netting 5.3 percent or $637 per month; a $7,646 annual return ***after-tax***.
- Her annual after-tax income is increased from $31,500 to $39,145.
- She is now income qualified for the independent living market rate rental monthly service fee of $2,150 per month or $25,800 per year. The annual service fee of $25,800 represents approximately 66 percent of her current income (after home sale) of $39,145.
- Alternatively, she might opt for a CCRC charging, at least, a partially refundable entrance fee and a modestly lower monthly service fee.

Important Observation – Looking back at Figure 34-1, the after-tax income impact from investing her home sales proceeds of $637 per month actually represents about 30 percent of the required monthly service fee ($637 divided by $2,150)! Since this transaction is a *future event*, most seniors and their families don't appreciate this favorable impact during the sales and marketing encounter.

From a strategic standpoint, given the impact of aggregate home equity, you've probably increased the pool of age and income qualified prospects by 200 to 400 senior households in a typical primary market area.

Develop prudent spend-down strategies. Many seniors may not financially qualify for your community – even after the added income from their expanded savings portfolio. Some seniors may also experience financial distress after moving into your community. That's where the prudent and financially responsible spend-down strategies come into play.

Call to Action

More and more seniors are seeking financial advice from families and third-party professionals. This means that, in the future, sponsors trying to tap the $1.2 trillion asset can expect to find their pricing strategies spending more time under the microscope by senior consumers, their families, and third-party financial advisors.

Get ahead of the power curve on this important issue. Develop proactive financial strategies, market positioning, and concise answers to frequently asked questions. Then, execute a professional communications approach to the external market. Chapters 40 through 42 address proactive pricing strategies.

CHAPTER 35

IS THE SENIOR'S HOME EQUITY AN ASSET OR AN OPPORTUNITY COST?

Redouble Your Efforts to Tap This Vast Resource

Actually it is both. Age 65+ seniors have over $1 trillion in pent-up home equity. Most seniors have their home mortgage paid off. It is a valuable, but benign, asset in that it does not help the senior with their current-day finances on a cash basis. Various sources provide a range of current estimated home equity for seniors. The U.S. census reflects a median value of approximately $160,000 for *all* age groups in 2009 dollars. Other government surveys indicate home values as follows: a *median* value of $140,000 and an *average* value of $165,000 – indicating significant skewing as a function of middle to upper incomes. A home value figure of $160,000 (in 2009 dollars) was used in the analysis as indicated in Figure 35-1.

A senior's home equity is typically converted to a more liquid cash asset under two situations: 1) when they die and their estate requests are implemented or; 2) when they sell their home and opt for alternative living accommodations – such as senior living. The liquidated asset can then be invested to produce current income – such as the case when a senior moves into a market rate rental independent living community. A portion of this liquidated asset can also be used to fund required entry fees for those continuing care retirement communities (CCRCs) offering upfront pricing.

***Note*: In late 2008 and early 2009, the housing market was experiencing significant volatility. Home value benchmarks reflected in this chapter have, at least temporarily, declined 15 to 20 percent from levels experienced in early 2007.**

Home Equity Impacts on a Senior's True Cost of Living

When comparing relative costs of living, the existing benign, pent-up home equity of a senior's home is actually a cost burden. In fact, I like to call it an *opportunity cost* because the senior is losing out on an opportunity to take advantage of the income-producing potential that could be realized if the home were sold and the proceeds were invested and earning a cash return. This opportunity cost increases when we consider the ongoing real estate, utilities and the additional cost of any substantial home repairs and maintenance that could be needed (new roof, painting, landscaping, etc.). These costs are frequently overlooked when seniors estimate their current cost of living during a sales and marketing encounter.

Figure 34-1 in Chapter 34 shows that, for the average home in 2009, the cash "opportunity" for a senior liquidating his or her home equity ranged from approximately $486 to $972 per month after-tax or about $5,800 to almost $12,000 per year, depending on the assumed savings rate and the senior's marginal tax rate. This increased after-tax income can materially increase a senior's ability to afford senior living. In fact, it could represent about 20 to 40 percent of the typical senior living base monthly service fee. In senior living communities, seniors also avoid the direct cost of home repairs. Let's look at the fine line that exists between a senior who holds their home for five additional years versus selling and putting the home equity to work now. They can do this prudently and productively, while still leaving a legacy to their estate.

Hold Vs. Sell – The Issue of Home Appreciation

All this sounds great, but many seniors and their families view "cashing out" very differently. They argue against the opportunity cost theory, saying that there could be a significant financial *disadvantage* to selling and investing *today* versus holding on to a home that will surely appreciate in value over the next five years.

As Figure 35-1 shows, the financial disparity is typically not that significant. One could always speculate that a home's value would appreciate significantly. However, Figure 35-2 shows that, over a reasonable time period in most U.S. markets, relatively modest home appreciation is likely to reflect the real world situation for many seniors. Of course, there are areas of the country where, prior to the economic recession and housing crisis, double digit home value appreciation exists. Was that a "bubble" that burst and will never recover or a "trend" that, eventually, will recover to a more favorable position?

This is certainly a valid concern but, as Figure 35-1 shows, the (after-tax) disparity between selling and investing today vs. holding for an additional five years is marginal. One could always speculate and anticipate higher home value appreciation but, as Figure 35-2 demonstrates, over a reasonable time period in most markets, the hold vs. sell comparison in Figure 35-2 is likely to reflect the real world situation for many seniors.

In order to effectively communicate with seniors and their families or financial advisors, I have developed a live template.[1] I can set the template input variables to their unique situation and address a number of *what-if* questions. The results of Figure 35-1 are depicted in template format in Figure 35-3.

Call to Action

Seniors need to consider four key issues when assessing the timing of the liquidation of their pent-up home equity (i.e. selling their home). These issues include:

1. Creating a more liquid estate.
2. Generating new cash income today.
3. Possibly funding CCRC entry fee pricing.
4. Enhancing the quality of their life.

We need to do a much better job helping seniors understand these four key issues involving the timing of converting their pent-up home equity into cash.

Everyday finances are a point of concern for both senior consumers and senior living owner/operators. But each addresses the issues from different perspectives. As they analyze their financial challenges, both groups have frequently failed to properly focus on a significant common resource – home equity.

[1]For more information on the availability of these templates, visit www.m-d-s.com.

FIGURE 35-1
THE HOLD VS. SELL COMPARISON

		Scenario 'A' Sell & Invest Today	Scenario 'B' Hold for an Additional 5 Years
I.	Today's Home Value[1]	$160,000	$160,000
II.	Today's Selling Cost @ 10%[2, 5]	(16,000)	---
III.	Increase In Savings Portfolio	$144,000	$0
IV.	Future Value in 5 Years @ 6.5%:[3]		
	• Scenario 'A'	$197,292	---
	• Scenario 'B'	----	$219,214
	– Selling cost (5 years out at 10%)[2]	----	(21,921)
V.	Comparative Net Cash Position (Pre-Tax)	$197,292	$197,292
VI.	After-Tax Position	$191,797[4]	$197,292[5, 6]

The financial disparity between the hold versus sell scenarios is not significant.

[1] Composite of U.S. Census and the Federal Reserve Board 2004 Survey of Consumer Finances (escalated to 2009 dollars)
[2] Broker's fees, title company, other seller closing costs, etc.
[3] Assumes an *average* savings rate of 6.5% or an *average annual* home value appreciation of 6.5%.
[4] Pre-tax savings rate of 6.5% with a 10.0% average tax rate yielding 5.9% after-tax for a 5-year savings period.
[5] Assumes no applicable capital gains tax.
[6] Does not include any substantial home repairs and maintenance that could be required (new roof, painting, landscaping, etc.). These costs may not be covered in the normal monthly "household services" expenses seniors estimate when making the senior living move decision.

Moore Diversified Services, Inc.

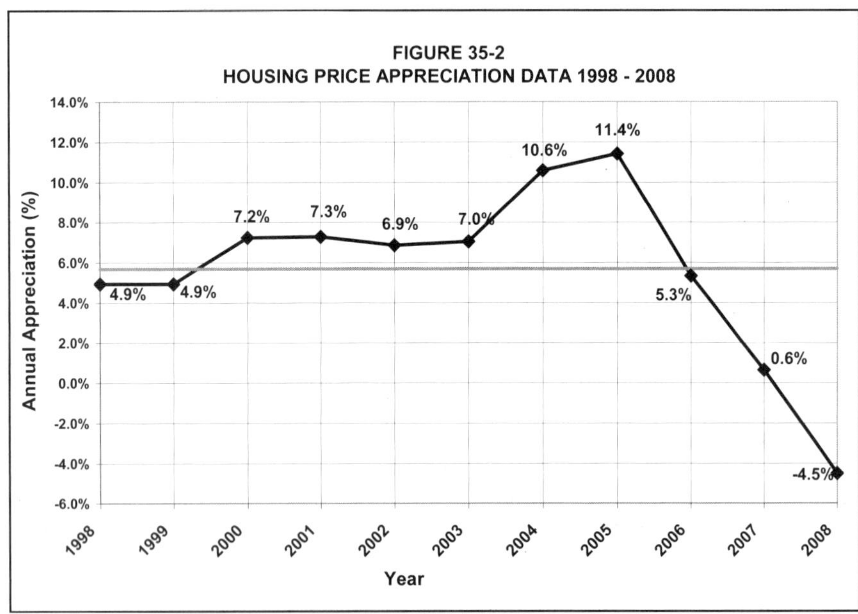

Sponsors and owner/operators must provide the leadership to direct their professional team to get this message into the marketplace in an objective and simple format. This important and valid home equity trade-off decision must become an integral part of the sales and marketing process. By the way, it makes a great new central theme for a financial planning seminar/event.

You can simplify and customize this type of analysis when helping seniors and their families better plan for the future. No longer should a senior's home equity be just a major *passive asset* to deal with when probating their estate. It should become a *working asset* while seniors live out their golden years.

FIGURE 35-3

Home Equity Analysis
The Hold or Sell Comparison

MDS Financial Sensitivity Series
m-d-s.com

Specific Individual Situational Inputs

Current Year	2009
Anticipated Holding Period In Years	5
Present Home Value	$160,000
Selling Cost As A % of Selling Price	10%
Avg Yrly Home Maint and RE Taxes	$8,000

Anticipated or Expected Per Year

Home Appreciation	Return On Investment	Income Tax Rate
6.5%	6.5%	10.0%

Scenario "A" Sell and Invest Now		Scenario "B" Hold For Additional Years
2009	Year of Sale	2014
$160,000	Home Value	$219,214
(16,000)	Selling Cost	($21,921)
$144,000	Net Proceeds	$197,292
$53,292	Compounded Return On Investment	
($5,329)	Less Income Taxes On Investment	
	Less Avg Yrly Home Maint and RE Taxes	($40,000)
$191,963	Value In 2014	$157,292
Percent Difference	22.0%	

CHAPTER 36

DO SENIORS REALLY SPEND MORE ON RETIREMENT COMMUNITIES?

A Senior Living Community Resident vs. Non-Resident Cost Of Living Comparison Shows Some Surprising Results

Breakthrough Research Findings!

The research discussed in this chapter is slightly dated, but the dramatic results and surprising conclusions are still valid.

Let's go right to the bottom line. ***My research in late 2007 confirms that the true cost of living is quite similar for an age and income-qualified senior living at home versus moving into a market rate rental independent living community.*** The findings show that, for similar types of living expenses, an age- and income-qualified senior living at home in 2007 had a monthly outlay ranging from $2,177 per month to $4,656 per month as compared to the range of independent living pricing (monthly service fees) as contained in the ***State of Seniors Housing 2007 Report.*** Those monthly service fees ranged from $1,993 to $3,429 per month with a *median* of $2,314 per month (in 2007 dollars). This comparison is illustrated in Figure 36-1.

For years, the senior living industry has been dealing with a common senior consumer misconception. While independent living monthly service fees were actually affordable to 30% to 40 percent of seniors (e.g. age 75+), many of these seniors felt that they were paying a significant premium to enjoy the benefits of a service-enriched independent living community or CCRC.

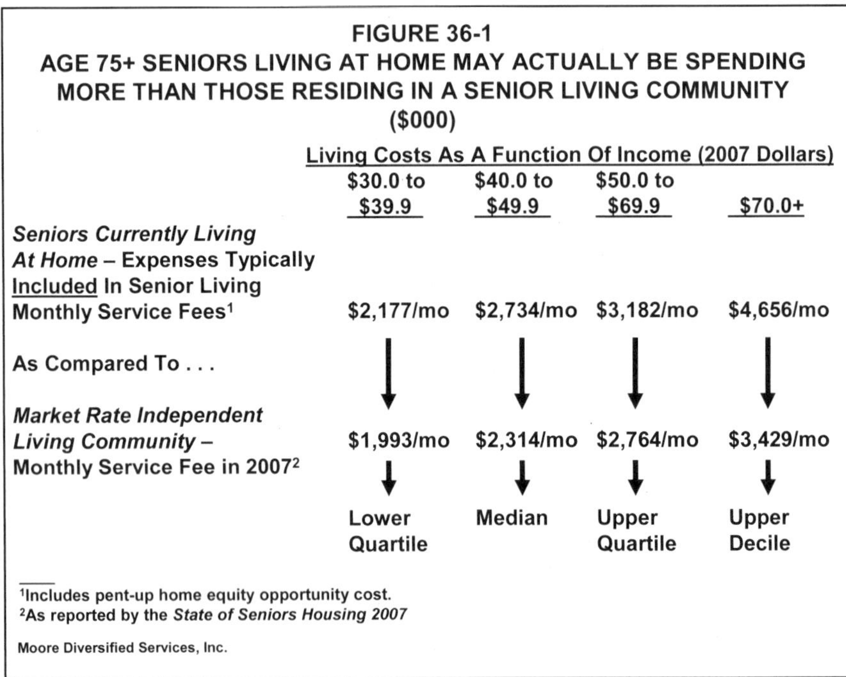

FIGURE 36-1
AGE 75+ SENIORS LIVING AT HOME MAY ACTUALLY BE SPENDING MORE THAN THOSE RESIDING IN A SENIOR LIVING COMMUNITY
($000)

	Living Costs As A Function Of Income (2007 Dollars)			
	$30.0 to $39.9	$40.0 to $49.9	$50.0 to $69.9	$70.0+
***Seniors Currently Living At Home* – Expenses Typically Included In Senior Living Monthly Service Fees[1]**	$2,177/mo	$2,734/mo	$3,182/mo	$4,656/mo
As Compared To . . .	↓	↓	↓	↓
***Market Rate Independent Living Community* – Monthly Service Fee in 2007[2]**	$1,993/mo	$2,314/mo	$2,764/mo	$3,429/mo
	↓ Lower Quartile	↓ Median	↓ Upper Quartile	↓ Upper Decile

[1]Includes pent-up home equity opportunity cost.
[2]As reported by the *State of Seniors Housing 2007*

Moore Diversified Services, Inc.

Making the misconception worse, income-qualified seniors frequently underestimate their true cost of living – at least initially. However, when some of these seniors did additional homework, many found they were spending much more living at home than they thought. The results were a more favorable and objective comparison between an income-qualified senior's current cost of living and today's prevailing independent living monthly service fees. Gradually, the industry started getting clues that this perceived cost gap might not be that significant.

However, there was no significant quantitative evidence to objectively compare these costs. In 2007, my firm was retained by the American Seniors Housing Association (ASHA) to investigate this important issue. The results backed up what we'd long suspected.

The study found – quantitatively – that the current cost of living for age- and income-qualified seniors with incomes between $30,000 and $70,000 living at home is remarkably similar to those costs for similar services offered by quality market rate rental independent living communities.

Effectively communicated, these findings should help seniors better plan for their future and will help operators address some of the most serious sales objections raised by seniors who would like to enjoy the benefits of independent living but do not feel they can afford it.

Let's restate the important findings. In most cases, an income-qualified senior's cost of living before moving into an independent living community and after are similar . . . with the true cost comparison frequently favoring senior living communities. Pent-up *home equity opportunity costs* heavily impact this comparison.

Home Equity Opportunity Cost

A senior's cost of living comparison must consider a very important issue; the *opportunity cost* of a senior's pent-up home equity. This pent-up home equity can be considered a benign, passive asset. But both consumers and owner/operators have frequently misunderstood and overlooked the current *real* opportunity cost of pent-up home equity. This important issue is addressed in detail in Chapter 35.

Specifically, this study analyzed how average household expenditures of age 75+ seniors with pre-tax incomes in the range of approximately $30,000 to $70,000 compare with typical independent living monthly service fees for the same cost of living categories. The results of this comparison are summarized in Figure 36-1. Three important expenditure/cost categories were investigated:

1. **Senior Living Community Type Costs** – The typical cost for services normally provided within a market rate senior living community's monthly service fee.
2. **Opportunity Cost of Pent-Up Home Equity** – A realistic cost of living component of seniors currently living at home.
3. **Other/Discretionary Purchases** – Expenditures seniors typically make regardless of their living arrangements.

The study focused primarily on market rate rental independent living community cost comparisons. However, many of the issues addressed would also apply to CCRC entry fee pricing and condominium and cooperative senior living communities.

The study results will help owner/operators more effectively address some of the industry's most serious sales objections. Typical sales objections of seniors are addressed throughout this book and include the following:

1. **Concerns about affordability,** depressed savings rates and the recent decline in the senior's investment portfolio.
2. **Worries about inflation** and the fear that senior living communities will jack up the monthly fees once they are residents, exceeding their current inflation experience.

3. **Perception that senior living could wipe out most of their assets** accumulated over a lifetime of making conservative financial decisions.

4. **Confusion about Medicare and Medicaid** benefits as it relates to nursing care. Hence, many seniors are unaware of the financial impact of future health care costs and the favorable benefits of CCRCs; especially those offering various forms of life care. Many CCRC life care programs pay for health care costs not covered by the Medicare and Medicaid programs.

Age 75+ Senior Spending Patterns

Age 75+ spending patterns identified in the study were based upon two frequently relied upon published resources:

- ***"Survey of Consumer Expenditures"*** – 2007 edition reporting 2005 data – This document is published every two years by the Bureau of Labor Statistics (BLS)
- ***"Household Spending"*** – Reflecting 2004 data, this is a privately published document providing expanded details that are based on unpublished BLS consumer expenditure data. The ***Household Spending*** report published by *New Strategist Publications* is in its 11th edition and greatly expands the analysis and interpretation of the summary data contained in the BLS ***Survey of Consumer Expenditures***.

These documents provided detailed quantitative support data for this analysis. The expenditure data in each of these documents was inflation-adjusted to 2007 dollars.

Actual Expenditures by Age and Income

Data on expenditures by age 75+ households are available in two major categories:

1. **Total/aggregate expenditures** of 75+ households as a function of income (refer to Figure 36-2).

2. **Detailed line item expenditures** of all 75+ households – but without specific income sorts (refer to Figure 36-3).

Note that Figure 36-2 indicates that as income increases for the *75+ households*, average annual expenditures also increase in *all* categories.

FIGURE 36-2

AGE 75+ SPENDING VS. ANNUAL INCOME

Range **of Annual Income ($000)**	***Average*** **Income Before Taxes**	***Average*** **Annual Spending** [1]	**% Increase in Expenditures as a Function of Increasing Income**
• $30.0 to 39.9	$34,500	$32,960	
			25.6%
• $40.0 to 49.9	44,540	41,400	
			16.4%
• $50.0 to 69.9	58,680	48,200	
			46.3%
• $70.0 +	113,590	70,531	

As incomes increase for 75+ households, average annual expenditures also increase.

Source: Household Spending, 11th Edition (2004 data)

[1] Refer to Figure 36-3 for typical age 75+ consumer detailed expenditure *categories*.

Moore Diversified Services, Inc.

Age 75+ expenditures are available as an average of *all* income levels as published by the Bureau of Labor Statistic's ***"Survey of Consumer Expenditures."*** This survey is conducted and published every two years.

These expenditures are summarized in Figure 36-3. In Figure 36-3, a typical age 75+ senior's cost of living has been segmented into three important categories:

1. **Goods and services that are normally provided within an independent living community's monthly service fee.**
2. **The previously discussed opportunity cost of a senior's pent-up home equity.**
3. **Other/discretionary expenditures <u>not</u> included in a typical monthly service fee.**

FIGURE 36-3
AVERAGE EXPENDITURES BY AGE 75+ HOUSEHOLDS
(In 2007 Dollars)

		Typical Expenditures for All Age 75+ Seniors (2007 Dollars)	
		Monthly	**Annually**
I.	Expenses Which are Typically Included in Senior Living Monthly Service Fees	$1,469	$17,628
II.	Pent-Up Home Equity Opportunity Cost	708	8,496
	Subtotal	$2,177	$26,124
III.	Expenses Which Are Not Included In Senior Living Monthly Service Fees	1,246	14,952
	Totals	$3,423 Monthly	$41,076 Annually

Source: Survey of Consumer Expenditures, 2005 data (published in 2007); Household Spending, Published 2006; Adjusted for 2007 dollars.

Moore Diversified Services, Inc.

Figure 36-3 reflects available data on spending patterns for *all* age 75+ seniors with *average* annual pre-tax incomes of approximately $30,000 to $40,000. Figure 36-3 and 36-4 provide average monthly expenditures for these *moderate income* seniors in 2007 dollars. It should be noted that the private pay independent living industry typically serves age 75+ consumers with generally higher pre-tax incomes ranging from $30,000 to $70,000 or higher. This means that seniors living at home that qualify for senior living communities may actually be paying more than the expenditures indicated in Figures 36-3 and 36-4. This is because age 75+ seniors have increased spending patterns as a function of income as summarized in Figure 36-2.

FIGURE 36-4
AVERAGE MONTHLY EXPENDITURES FOR *MODERATE* INCOME 75+ HOUSEHOLDS
(In 2007 Dollars)

	2007 Expenditures	Mix of Expenditures		Typical Industry Benchmark
I. Expenses normally included in an independent living community's monthly service fee	$1,469/mo	42.9%		
II. Opportunity Cost of pent-Up Home Equity	708	20.7		
Subtotal	$2,177/mo	63.6%	→	65%
III. Other/discretionary expenditures not included in a monthly service fee	1,246	36.4	→	35%
TOTAL	$3,423/mo	100.0%		100%

The overall spending patterns of age 75+ Seniors living at home is very similar to independent living costs.

Moore Diversified Services, Inc.

A spectrum of expected increased expenditures for higher income seniors was also created using available spending patterns versus income. The rationale is that, in market rate independent living, we are typically dealing with the upper 30 to 40 percent of the age 75+ income-qualified market sector. These income adjusted expenditure patterns are summarized in Figure 36-5. Note that the cost summary in Figure 36-5 includes the opportunity cost of pent-up home equity which is not a current cash burden for seniors currently living at home; but certainly factors into a new cash resource and enhanced affordability of the senior living option.

FIGURE 36-5
AGE 75+ SPENDING AS A FUNCTION OF INCOME[1]
($000)

	Living Costs As A Function Of Income (2007 Dollars)			
	$30.0 to $39.9	$40.0 to $49.9	$50.0 to $69.9	$70.0+
Expenses Typically Included In Senior Living Monthly Service Fees[1, 2]				
Subtotal	$2,177/mo	$2,734/mo	$3,182/mo	$4,656/mo
Expenses Which Are Not Included in Monthly Service Fees	1,246	1,565	1,822	2,666
TOTAL	$3,423/mo[3]	$4,299/mo[4]	$5,004/mo[4]	$7,322/mo[4]

[1] All figures in 2007 dollars.
[2] Includes pent-up home equity opportunity cost.
[3] Refer to Figure 36-3 for a cost breakdown in 2007 dollars.
[4] Senior consumer expenditures escalated for higher income seniors.

Moore Diversified Services, Inc.

Figure 36-1 shows that the spending patterns for age 75+ seniors with average annual incomes ranging from $30,000 to $70,000+ compare very favorably to the prevailing monthly fees for service-enriched, market rate independent living. Figure 36-1 also shows that the independent living cost component and the pent-up home equity opportunity cost result in an *average* non-resident monthly outlay ranging from $2,177 per month to $4,656 per month. This compares favorably with the range of independent living pricing (monthly service fees) contained in the ***2007 State of Seniors Housing Report***. Those monthly service fees ranged from $1,993 to $3,429 per month with a *median* of $2,314 per month (in 2007 dollars).

It is important to note that Figure 36-1 and 36-5 include a comparison for moderate income seniors ($30,000 to $40,000 incomes). The figures also show that, at higher incomes, this comparison with senior living cost is even more favorable and indicates that seniors living at home with $40,000+ incomes may, in fact, be spending slightly more when considering the current opportunity cost of their pent-up home equity (and home maintenance costs).

Note that in Figure 36-5, the average expenditures for those items normally included in a market rate independent living community monthly service fee range from approximately $2,177 to $4,656 per month (2007 dollars) for age 75+ seniors. Other/discretionary expenditures range from $1,246 to $2,666 per month for a total expenditure range of approximately $3,423 to $7,322 per month.

Also note, that the *mix of expenditures* is very similar and compatible with prevailing independent living community spending guidelines. Seniors are advised to spend approximately 65 percent of their available budget for independent living monthly service fees (the first category in Figure 36-5) and about 35 percent for discretionary/other expenditures (the second category). The actual ratios in Figure 36-5 are 64 percent and 36 percent.

Call to Action

The results of this study clearly show – quantitatively – that the current cost of living for age- and income-qualified seniors currently living at home is remarkably similar to those costs offered by quality independent living communities. What this means is that a typical senior's cost of living before moving into a retirement community and after are very comparable.

These findings should help seniors better plan for their future and materially assist marketing professionals in addressing some of their most serious sales objections. Seniors can not only afford to live in senior housing; many can do it with financial peace of mind while also leaving a legacy to their children or their estate. One of the key steps in breaking down these "affordability" barriers in the mind-set of seniors is to secure their understanding and acceptance of the significant opportunity cost of pent-up home equity. Once that understanding has been firmly established, seniors will be in a much better position to financially justify their decision to move to independent living.

CHAPTER 37

STRAIGHT TALK ABOUT SENIOR CONSUMER FINANCES

The Don't Ask – Don't Tell Era is Over!

Those of us in the senior housing and health care industry tend to take business and financial cycles pretty much in stride. Most of us look at a fairly broad time frame and recognize that economic cycles "come with the territory". But age 80+ seniors have a much shorter financial time horizon. And the economic trends from 2000 through early 2009 have had some very significant, and possibly irreversible, impacts on many of these seniors. This should serve as a mild wake-up call for our industry.

The Senior Consumer's Financial Dilemma

We've always recognized that seniors are concerned about their finances. Now it's time to get very specific by looking at a typical real world situation. Mrs. Barker, an 82 year old widow is entering senior living. Her family was shocked to learn that, over the past ten years, her investment portfolio experienced the equivalent of a roller coaster ride. Obviously, with more intensified cash management, Mrs. Barker's returns could have been slightly higher. But not much.

Let's look at some trends. From 2000 to 2009, the income qualified senior consumer has been hit very hard in several areas involving savings and investment returns as two of their primary sources of income (refer to Figure 37-1). For example, referring to the S&P 500 index, the years 2000 through 2002 reflected heavy losses in the equities market, while 2003 through 2006 were generally years of moderate recovery. The market peaked in early 2007 and then declined dramatically – losing over 40 percent of its value by early 2009. *(Note: As this book went to press in July, 2009, the equities markets were still experiencing significant volatility, but also realizing a modest recovery.)* Here is a summary of the senior's financial investment challenge since 2000 in terms of both the cash and equities portions of a typical income-qualified senior's savings portfolio:

- **Short-Term CD's and T-Bills** – Seniors are now realizing cash savings rates of approximately 3 to 4 percent or less (before taxes and inflation).

- **Equities** – As measured by the S&P 500 stock index, a typical income qualified senior's equity portfolio was hit with over a 40 percent decrease from 2000 through year-end 2002. Performance in the first half of 2007 indicates that a senior's typical original savings/investment portfolio in 2000 had essentially experienced breakeven recovery. This assumes that any dividends or other investment gains were taken in as income. In late 2008, the market plummeted again as indicated above. In early 2009, the market has experienced a very modest recovery.

Note that in Figure 37-1, our income-qualified senior's savings portfolio of all equity investments reflected an initial value of $500,000 early in the year 2000. To many sponsors and owner/operators that sounds very high. But, let us take a closer look at the typical composition of a senior's necessary qualifying income required for senior living as summarized in Figure 37-2.

FIGURE 37-1
THE SENIOR CONSUMER'S CURRENT FINANCIAL DILEMMA

Typical Senior's Savings Portfolio Options	Year-End Position									
	2000	2001	2002	2003	2004	2005	2006	2007	2008	YTD 5/2009
• CDs (1 Year)	6.0%	5.4%	2.3%	1.4%	1.2%	2.6%	4.5%	5.3%	4.0%	3.1%
• T-Bills (1 Year)	5.6%	2.2%	1.5%	1.3%	2.7%	4.4%	4.9%	3.3%	1.8%	0.5%
• Equities (S&P 500)										
– 500 index	-10.1%	-13.0%	-23.4%	+26.4%	+9.0%	+3.0%	+13.6%	+3.5%	-38.5%	+1.8%
– $500,000 Portfolio	$449,500	$391,065	$299,556	$378,639	$412,716	$425,098	$482,911	$499,812	$307,385	$312,918

9 Year Savings Portfolio Impact:[1, 2] ($192,615) or a 38% loss over a 9 year period.

Senior consumer finance will continue to be a huge issue in 2009 and beyond.

[1]Assumes an initial $500,000 savings portfolio in 2000. An age 75+ Senior's Social Security income averages approximately $12,600 per year while the independent living qualifying income requirement (before any spend down) is approximately $40,000. This implies a need for a savings/investment portfolio of approximately $500,000 earning a reasonable and conservative 6.5% annual return.

[2] Savings rates were depressed during the years 2001 through 2004 with a modest recovery starting in 2005, then another decline in 2009.

Two Key Financial Needs – Mrs. Barker has two primary expenditures as she moves into senior living:

1. Paying her monthly service fee.
2. Providing her some discretionary income.

Starting with the bottom line of Figure 37-2, a senior paying a typical independent living monthly service fee ranging from a low of $1,700 to a median of approximately $2,500 per month (in 2009 dollars) must have a total, after-tax qualifying income of approximately $45,000 before incurring significant spend-down of their savings portfolio. This assumes an industry spending guideline of 65 to 70 percent of their after-tax cash flow disposable income for the monthly service fee and 35 to 40 percent for other discretionary spending. For assisted living, that expenditure guideline shifts to approximately 80 / 20 percent.

The example in Figure 37-2 shows after-tax discretionary spending of $1,200 per month. That may sound like a lot of discretionary cash for a senior's lifestyle in independent living. But that pool of money quickly evaporates when you consider the ongoing cost of prescription drugs (notwithstanding the current complex Medicare Prescription Drug Program), travel, external social life and the possibility of increased monthly service fees in the future due to annual cost escalation. Seniors, like Mrs. Barker, must also look to the future possible added cost of assisted living or nursing.

There could also be a beneficial impact of medical tax deduction for Mrs. Barker. It's rather limited in independent living but could be substantial in CCRCs with life care or in assisted living and nursing.

So, in order to augment their relatively modest Social Security income to meet the minimum $45,000 after-tax qualifying income, a senior would have to have a savings or company pension portfolio of approximately $500,000 yielding an average pre-tax annual return of 6.5 percent. While this investment portfolio number seems high, many seniors have traditionally had surprisingly strong balance sheets; particularly when considering adding their liquidated home equity to their savings portfolio in order to move into independent living. However, for most seniors, that investment portfolio and their home value may have experienced a significant decline from mid/late 2008 through at least the first half of 2009.

FIGURE 37-2

COMPOSITION OF A TYPICAL SENIOR'S QUALIFYING INCOME

	Annual		Monthly	
• A 75+ Senior's Average Social Security Income[1]	$13,200	/yr	$1,100	/mo
• Interest & Dividend Income – Investment Portfolio of $500,000 Earning 6.5% Annually[2]	32,500		2,710	
TOTAL INCOME	**$45,700**		**$3,810**	
• Income Taxes Paid ***(Before the Medical Tax Deductions)***[3]	(4,570)		(380)	
AFTER-TAX INCOME SENIOR'S CASH BUDGET	**$41,130**		**$3,430**	
• Discretionary Income Budget at 35%[4]	(14,395)		(1,200)	
• Cash Available for Typical Independent Living Monthly Service Fees[4]	$26,734	/yr	$2,230	/mo

An income qualified senior needs an extensive investment/savings portfolio to supplement their Social Security Income

[1]This is the average for 2009. Many seniors have higher Social Security income and some may have additional company pension income.
[2]The investment portfolio typically includes net home equity proceeds.
[3] Significant medical tax deductions could be applicable for assisted living.
[4] Industry guidelines indicate a senior should spend approximately 65% of their after-tax (cash) disposable income for independent living monthly service fees; leaving approximately 35% for other/discretionary spending. The ratios shift to 80%/20% for assisted living.

Moore Diversified Services, Inc.

Modest Monthly Service Fee Increases Represent Real Lost Purchasing Power for Seniors

Sponsors and owner/operators consider a 3 percent to 4 percent annual fee increase as "normal and reasonable". But remember, your monthly service fee increases essentially represent a very large portion of resident's total cost of living. To them, these increases reflect a very real inflation rate and a potential loss of purchasing power. That's because they only have a very modest Cost of Living Adjustment (COLA) in their Social Security income. In fact, in 2010 there will be no COLA increase.

Note that, even with approximately $45,000 in gross pre-tax income, many seniors with a $500,000 savings portfolio would likely experience some modest spend-down if paying a monthly service fee in excess of approximately $2,200 per month. However, many seniors (especially couples) living in retirement communities actually collect higher than average Social Security payments and some have a surprisingly significant net worth.

Potential Issues and Sales Objections

Many seniors, their families and their financial advisors lack accurate information about the true cost of living in today's market rate independent living communities. This keeps many seniors who would greatly benefit from independent living from leaving their homes. Among the concerns and misconceptions that lead to some classical sales objections are the following:

1. **Affordability** – Seniors are very concerned about future affordability. Their frame of reference is heavily influenced by their lengthy tenure in their existing homes – often without a current mortgage payment. They tend to forget or don't understand the opportunity cost of their pent-up home equity.
2. **Depressed Savings Rate** – Many worry about relatively low savings rates and the changes in the value and returns from their investment portfolio from 2000 to 2009.
3. **Cost of Living** – Most seniors underestimate their current cost of living. This leads to "sticker shock" when initially considering independent living monthly service fees.
4. **Inflation** – Many seniors worry about inflation, in general, and fear that the monthly cost of independent living communities will escalate significantly.
5. **Leaving A Financial Legacy** – Finally, many seniors are focused on leaving a financial legacy to their children. That is one of their "scorecards" in life. They are concerned that opting for independent living may wipe out their assets accumulated over a lifetime of making conservative financial decisions.

The consistent results of over 900 senior consumer focus groups and numerous lost prospect surveys involving thousands of seniors reveal some surprising but consistent results. Some typical senior consumer responses include:

1. ***"Your community was just beautiful, but it was too expensive and I'm sure I could not afford it."***
2. ***"Your monthly service fee seems unrealistically high. I've never paid that much rent."***

3. ***"I liked everything I saw, but I worry that you will increase your pricing and I will outlive my assets."***

Keep in mind that these responses came from prospects that were previously determined to be *income-qualified* for market rate independent living. Leaving a financial legacy to their children is an important goal for many seniors. Prudent and appropriate financial planning indicates that many seniors can afford to move into an independent living community and still leave a legacy even if their monthly service fees are increased in the future. Still others can tolerate future rate increases by implementing a modest and prudent spend-down program while still realizing most of their estate legacy goals.

Mrs. Barker is very fortunate. She can afford today's private pay independent living. That's because Mrs. Barker also has an average home equity of approximately $160,000. Chapter 35 outlined how she can put that home liquidated home equity to work after she sells her home.

But what about the hundreds of thousands of age 80+ seniors with annual incomes below $35,000? Low savings rates, mediocre market returns and lost buying power will further complicate their financial situation.

The senior living industry is in for a serious wake-up call when we combine the recent financial trends summarized in Figure 37-1 with seniors' age-old financial concerns and classical misconceptions. Fortunately, there are a number of effective strategies to deal with these challenges. These strategies include striking a delicate balance between affordability, prudent spend-down and helping seniors leave a financial legacy.

Chapter 38 addresses innovative and appropriate financial planning initiatives, while Chapters 34 and 35 deal with innovative effective deployment of a senior's home equity resource.

Call to Action

Our understanding and sensitivity to the senior consumer financial challenges have not received proper emphasis. In large part, we've chosen to stay out of the senior consumer's personal financial planning. Their financial status has been subordinated to a *"don't ask, don't tell"* psychology. That has all changed now. We must adopt financial planning for seniors as a major product positioning platform. It must be one that is prudent and logical, involving more substance than just politically correct rhetoric or fancy sound bites.

Deepen your understanding of the real world of senior consumer finances. Using seminars open up an ethical and practical dialog with seniors and their families. Objectively state the problems, then offer practical solutions. Chapter 38 offers some innovative strategies.

CHAPTER 38

FINANCIAL PLANNING FOR SENIORS

A Necessary Financial and Estate Planning Tool for Seniors

Senior living marketing is a tricky business. There's potential failure behind every corner. One common deal killer is how our customers view the cost of senior living alternatives. Talking about financial planning would help, but many owner/operators and their sales and marketing teams either fail to recognize or are reluctant to openly discuss such important issues during critical sales encounters with prospective residents.

The Flawed Financial Mindset of Seniors

I've heard a lot of opinions in the more than 900 focus groups I've conducted. The one thing I always find is that seniors commonly have a flawed financial mindset. For example, many seniors and their families have not considered how they can put the pent-up equity value of their currently owned home to work for them in the later phases of life. Seniors certainly recognize the value of this benign asset, but fail to consider how it can significantly augment the affordability of future senior living options. Sales and marketing teams should show seniors the advantages of liquidating their home equity and prudently putting the new cash to work today (see Chapter 34). And finally, sales and marketing staff must show how seniors will still be able to leave a nest egg – a financial legacy – to their loved ones.

As I said earlier, another serious mindset flaw is how seniors view their true current cost of living. In most of my focus groups, I conduct a cost of living awareness test. Seniors consistently cannot accurately estimate their *current* monthly cost of living. They frequently forget non-recurring expenses such as real estate taxes, homeowner's insurance and home repairs. This serious misconception frequently leads to sticker shock when discussing the cost of senior living.

Deal Killing Sales Objections

Chapters 5 and 6 deal with misconceptions and sales objections. These misperceptions can stifle sales. We tend to celebrate the three percent of the market that we capture for a typical community but fail to determine why about 97 percent of our prospects get away.

These sales objections should not surprise us. We generally recognize that seniors will never forget how they were impacted by the Great Depression. But now a new breed of seniors (our prospects) has experienced a more recent financial trauma. Over the last eight years, cash returns on savings have plummeted more than 50 percent. There was a modest recovery in 2005 and 2006 with interest rates on short-term savings (CDs, two or three year T-bills, etc.) yielding about 3 to 4 percent. Surprisingly, many seniors are involved in the equities market; primarily mutual funds. During this same period, they saw their investment portfolio plummet by over 20 percent.

In late 2008 through January, 2009, the stock market experienced the sharpest decrease since the Great Depression. Since January, 2009 through July, 2009 (when this book went to press), the market has experienced a modest recovery. Still, many seniors are calling this first part of the new millennium as a "lost decade."

There is a practical solution to put this serious financial dilemma into proper perspective. Address and customize an individual senior's unique financial situation to show that senior living is, in fact, affordable. Interested? If so, I've included Figure 38-1 as one approach to a comprehensive automated senior living financial planning analysis. The actual analysis – the template in Figure 38-1 – contains approximately 15 supporting Excel spreadsheets. Refer to this web site for more details: www.m-d-s.com (follow the link on the home page that refers to "Financial Sensitivity Templates"). You can use the financial planning scenario I describe on the following pages.

FIGURE 38-1

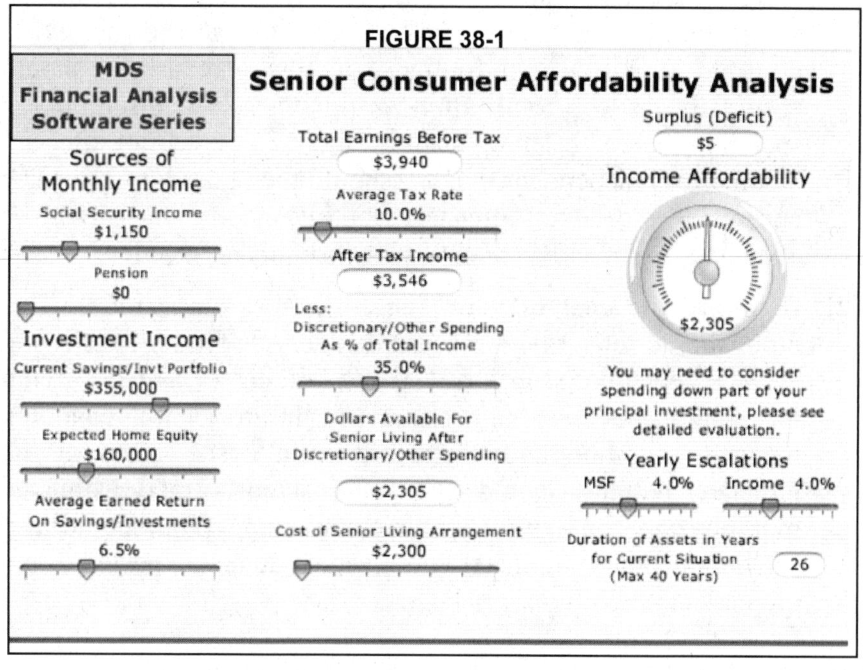

The Financial Planning Scenario

The setting should be a private sales and marketing office or conference room. The sales professional takes an age- and income-qualified senior, their family members and possibly a trust officer/financial planner through a simple, but effective, financial sensitivity template similar to the one illustrated in Figure 38-1. Use a computer screen large enough for all the participants to view. Customized inputs to this template include: [1]

1. **Tabulate the senior's available financial resources.** This includes Social Security, monthly income derived from their current investment portfolio, and any other sources of income along with an estimate of the senior's average (not marginal) tax rate. One of the outputs of this spreadsheet should accurately reflect total after-tax income. A discretionary spending income reserve – usually about 35 percent of after-tax income for independent living – should then be subtracted. The end result is the total after-tax monthly income that would be available for the independent living monthly service fee.

2. **Estimate the cost of your senior living community.** This input should reflect the base monthly service fee for each living arrangement upon entry, any tiered pricing in assisted living that might be necessary based on the resident's changing medical condition and any other extra costs. One of the template outputs should show the senior's total estimated monthly cost for living in your community. You should also provide the ability to insert your average annual expected future increases in monthly service fees.

[1]Figure 38-1 depicts a typical financial planning template used to create a senior's comprehensive customized financial plan. For more detailed financial planning software information contact Jim Moore at jimmoore@m-d-s.com.

3. **Summarize overall affordability (gap or surplus).** The template in Figure 38-1 compares a senior's total after-tax income with the community's monthly service fee and shows either a surplus or deficit. Note that the template introduces the equity value of the senior's current home based on an assumed re-sale. This estimated home value should be reduced by approximately 10 percent to account for the net available home equity cash after re-sale. This new cash resource is presumed to be added to the senior's existing savings portfolio.

4. **Analyze the consumer's affordability.** The template should provide the following information:

    - The annual interest earned on the newly liquidated home equity (invested in a safe fixed income account).

    - Social Security income, investment portfolio income and other income.

These factors then lead to total income and estimated income taxes. One end result would be the net after-tax cash available for the senior living monthly service fee. This cash resource would be compared to the actual required monthly service fee, showing either a surplus or annual spend down/shortfall.

The ultimate expected outcome would be to show the senior and family members the relative affordability of your senior living community – both now and in future years.

If the template reflects a surplus, the senior can clearly afford to live at your community and his or her financial resources could possibly *increase*. Conversely, the analysis might show the need for modest spend-down of their savings portfolio. The analysis also might show the spend-down to be at a relatively slow pace, lasting longer than the senior's expected life or residency at your community. By comparing these customized financial results with the resident's chronological age and life expectancy, family members can determine whether the estate preservation dollars are acceptable to them, thereby encouraging their loved one to accept the senior living option. Figure 38-2 outlines an approach for this financial planning discussion.

Making the Government Your Financial Partner

There is one further financial enhancement that is frequently overlooked. That is the assisted living and nursing medical tax deduction. Certain restrictions apply but, in many cases, the *full* monthly service fee for assisted living and nursing not covered by Medicare, retirement health care benefits or private insurance can be a tax deductible medical expense for the senior and, in some cases, the family. [1]

Any financial analysis you conduct should always include words of caution such as ***"The information and observations contained in this analysis may be subject to varied interpretations by professionals. Each consumer and their families should seek independent advice and counsel. Always obtain independent, second opinions on this important matter."***

[1] Refer to ***"Assisted Living Strategies for Changing Markets".*** Available at www.westridgepublishing.com .

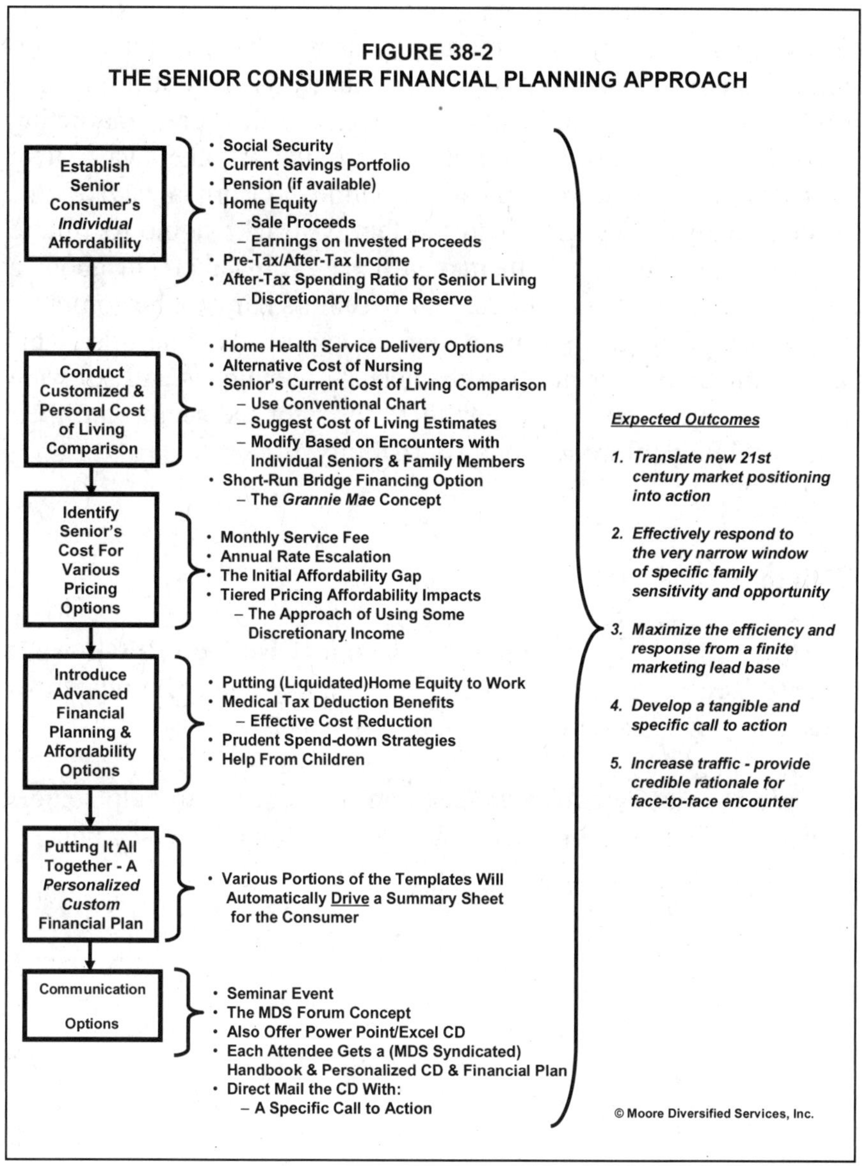
FIGURE 38-2
THE SENIOR CONSUMER FINANCIAL PLANNING APPROACH
Establish Senior Consumer's *Individual* Affordability
• Social Security
• Current Savings Portfolio
• Pension (if available)
• Home Equity
– Sale Proceeds
– Earnings on Invested Proceeds
• Pre-Tax/After-Tax Income
• After-Tax Spending Ratio for Senior Living
– Discretionary Income Reserve
Conduct Customized & Personal Cost of Living Comparison
• Home Health Service Delivery Options
• Alternative Cost of Nursing
• Senior's Current Cost of Living Comparison
– Use Conventional Chart
– Suggest Cost of Living Estimates
– Modify Based on Encounters with Individual Seniors & Family Members
• Short-Run Bridge Financing Option
– The *Grannie Mae* Concept
Identify Senior's Cost For Various Pricing Options
• Monthly Service Fee
• Annual Rate Escalation
• The Initial Affordability Gap
• Tiered Pricing Affordability Impacts
– The Approach of Using Some Discretionary Income
Introduce Advanced Financial Planning & Affordability Options
• Putting (Liquidated)Home Equity to Work
• Medical Tax Deduction Benefits
– Effective Cost Reduction
• Prudent Spend-down Strategies
• Help From Children
Putting It All Together - A *Personalized Custom* Financial Plan
• Various Portions of the Templates Will Automatically Drive a Summary Sheet for the Consumer
Communication Options
• Seminar Event
• The MDS Forum Concept
• Also Offer Power Point/Excel CD
• Each Attendee Gets a (MDS Syndicated) Handbook & Personalized CD & Financial Plan
• Direct Mail the CD With:
– A Specific Call to Action
Expected Outcomes
1. Translate new 21st century market positioning into action
2. Effectively respond to the very narrow window of specific family sensitivity and opportunity
3. Maximize the efficiency and response from a finite marketing lead base
4. Develop a tangible and specific call to action
5. Increase traffic - provide credible rationale for face-to-face encounter
© Moore Diversified Services, Inc.

Sound complicated and "blue sky"? It's not. Using this analysis, the senior and their family should have a much better understanding of whether your community is truly affordable – both now and in the future. Astute sales and marketing professionals are always looking to provide a "take-away" item and a legitimate follow-up/call to action. Burn a CD of this custom analysis and give it to the family to take home for future review. Of course, tell them you'll be calling them in about a week to answer any questions. Many seniors may not be computer savvy, so also give them a hard copy of the analysis. This important analysis is not rocket science – techniques and software are emerging to reset an accurate mindset for the senior and their family while reinforcing your affordability.

Call to Action

Regarding a senior's finances, **the don't ask – don't tell era is over!** You've got to deal with the senior's flawed mindset and misconceptions leading to deal killing sales objections.

We have an opportunity – and an obligation – to help seniors and their families properly plan for the future. The concepts covered in this chapter really work.

CHAPTER 39

SENIOR LIVING AFFORDABILITY STRATEGIES

A Practical Reality or Impossible Dream?

The first rule of sales is to know your customer. The goal of this chapter is to make you familiar with three economic classes of seniors. To sell to seniors, one needs to understand these economic classes of seniors. They are:

- The ***"Entitlement Group"*** – incomes under $12,000
- The ***"Gap Income Group"*** – $12,000 to $30,000
- The ***"Market Rate (Private Pay) Group***" – more than $30,000

As you learn about each of these three groups, consider the opportunities that each presents.

I. The *"Entitlement Group"* – Incomes Under $12,000

Seniors with incomes under $12,000 per year typically qualify for various government entitlement programs, such as the HUD 202 and Section 8 senior housing, which offer low monthly rent. But keep in mind that the original concept of the HUD 202 or Section 8 programs assumed seniors would live *independently* (preparing their own meals, for example). It was initially presumed seniors would not need assistance with typical activities of daily living. But many of these programs started over 25 years ago. Thanks to improved health care, among other advances, the number of low income seniors who have aged in place and now need assisted living has skyrocketed beyond the initial projections of a quarter-century ago. Sadly, there are no consistently-funded entitlement programs to pay for these additional services. Approximately 19 percent of the country's age 75+ households are currently members of the "Entitlement Group".

II. The *"Gap Income Group"* – $12,000 to $30,000

The greatest unmet need in senior housing today is the lack of affordable services and living options aimed at serving seniors with incomes that are moderate, but not low enough to qualify for subsidies or government entitlements. Nor can these moderate-income seniors afford to fully "private pay" for senior living. Labeled the *"Gap Income Group"*, this sector of the senior market has annual incomes between $12,000 and $30,000. These seniors currently represent about 35 percent of all U.S. households over age 75 (refer to Figure 39-1).

III. The "Market Rate (Private Pay) Group" – $30,000+

Many seniors with incomes in excess of $30,000 qualify for *"market rate"* senior living. That means they can afford to pay prevailing rates beginning at the lower end of today's senior living private pay pricing spectrum. The "market rate" group currently represents about 47 percent of the nation's age 75+ seniors.

The Gap Group Economic Squeeze

Figure 39-1 illustrates how the Gap Income Group is caught in an economic squeeze between the other two economic classes of seniors – the very low income group who qualify for entitlements, and the income-qualified market rate group who can afford private pay. Trapped between these two economic classes, the Gap Income Group is significantly underserved and represents *very* large numbers. A shocking 35 percent, or approximately 4.1 million, age 75+ households fall into this "trapped" category. Figure 39-2 depicts this economic conundrum. Note these are 2009 demographic projections.

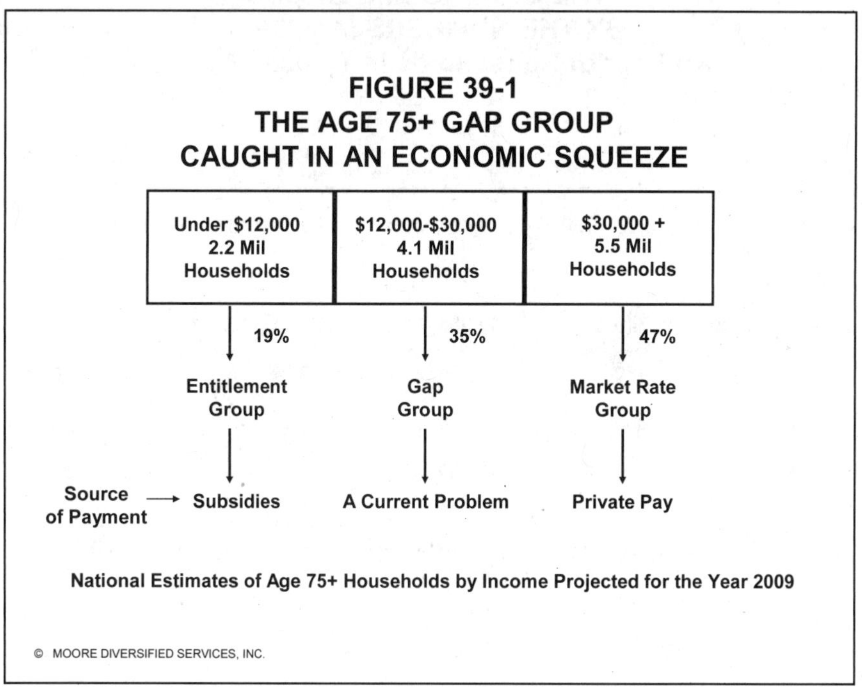

Affordability Gap

As Figure 39-3 dramatically demonstrates, the Gap Income Group cannot afford the monthly service fees needed to live in independent or assisted living. These monthly fees typically range from $1,600 to $2,900 for independent living, and approximately $2,200 to $4,000+ for various levels of assisted living. In some cases, Gap Income Group seniors can only afford half that amount. Some progress is being made with Medicaid Waiver programs for assisted living and moderate income tax-credit senior apartments.

FIGURE 39-2
THE GAP INCOME GROUP
BY THE NUMBERS (Age 75+)
(Number of Households in Typical Markets)

	Under $12,000		**$12,000 - $30,000**		$30,000 - $45,000		$45,000 +	
	No.	%	**No.**	**%**	No.	%	No.	%
Total U.S.	2,204,692	19%	**4,096,406**	**35%**	1,476,540	13%	4,016,328	34%
Atlanta	20,905	21	**31,330**	**31**	16,950	17	30,895	31
Boston	35,740	20	**60,950**	**34**	28,830	16	56,180	31
Dallas	24,430	19	**39,700**	**31**	22,715	18	39,590	31
Denver	10,050	16	**19,770**	**31**	12,425	19	22,610	35
Phoenix	19,220	30	**43,590**	**33**	25,915	19	44,577	33

Figures for typical metropolitan areas in 2009

Source: Claritas
MDS Analysis

FIGURE 39-3
AFFORDABILITY OF THE GAP INCOME GROUP
Typical Primary Market Area

Gross Pre-tax Income	Ability to Pay/ Affordable Service Fee[1] Independent Living	Assisted Living
$12,000-$14,999	$ 585-$ 730	$ 720-$ 900
15,000- 19,999	730- 975	900- 1,200
20,000- 24,999	975- 1,220	1,200- 1,500
25,000- 29,999	1,220- 1,350	1,500- 1,800
Typical Required MSF	$1,600-$2,900[2]	$2,200-$4,000+

Actual pre-spend-down affordability levels of the age 75+ *Gap Income Group* fall <u>well</u> <u>below</u> typical senior living *private pay* pricing requirements.

[1]Assumes a 10% *average* tax bracket and a senior's spending criteria of 65% and 80% of disposable income (after-tax) for independent living and assisted living monthly service fees, respectively – with no spend-down or help from family members.
[2]The lower monthly service fee might be associated with older properties that are no longer state-of-the-art.

Moore Diversified Services, Inc.

Without considerable spend-down or help from children, a senior's qualifying annual income would likely have to exceed $30,000 to afford independent or assisted living – and that's in after-tax dollars! Figure 39-4 presents the big picture of senior living affordability. Chapters 42 and 44 deal with spend-down, and Chapter 40 provides more details on what seniors can afford to private pay for senior living.

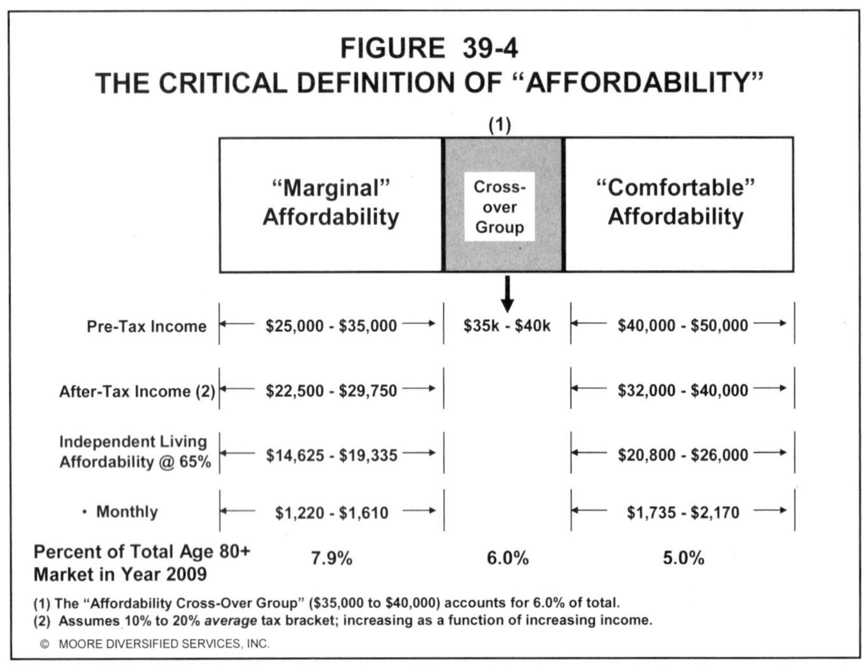

When the impact of aging-in-place intensifies and reaches crisis level, the Gap Income Group will finally be widely recognized as a huge economic and social challenge. We need creative solutions to break down the economic barriers. Financial viability will be very difficult to achieve, but if we can do it, the result will perhaps be the biggest breakthrough in serving seniors in the 21st century.

Call to Action

Keep two very important issues on your radar screen:

1. Recognize your realistic (affordable) market may be smaller than initially perceived.

2. If at all possible, consider some meaningful charitable content to help some low to moderate income seniors – especially if you're a tax-exempt not-for-profit organization.

As an industry, we'll eventually have to answer the question, ***"Do we and our government have an obligation to serve this very worthwhile group"?***

SECTION SIX

Pricing Strategies

CHAPTER 40

LEADING EDGE PRICING STRATEGIES

Market-Responsive and Financially Viable Approaches Create a Win-Win Situation

One of the big lessons learned over the past 10 years is that the senior consumer – regardless of affordability and affluence – looks at senior living pricing far differently than the owner/operator. Consumers' perception of value versus "extravagance and excessive cost" has caused many communities to flounder or, at least, seriously reconsider their pricing.

"Sticker Shock" is Not Just a Cliché

The words "sticker shock" has taken on a new meaning. Sticker shock has long been experienced by shoppers in new car showrooms and, more recently, consumers who visit senior living communities.

In focus groups and exit interviews, seniors clearly indicate that, although they say they can't afford certain communities, many really mean that, in their opinion, certain communities are too expensive or have insufficient perceived value. When it comes to senior living, not too many seniors get caught up in Alan Greenspan's highly publicized economic definition of "irrational exuberance". Most seniors are very conservative when it comes to money matters with senior living pricing – many struggle with striking a delicate balance between price, benefits, and value.

Price Vs. Value

"Forget all of the fancy words, how much does it cost to live here?" The first thing seniors want to know is the last thing astute sales counselors want to tell them. Ideally, the answer to this pricing question should have been the top priority of the development team when the senior living community was in the concept stage. The strategy is called "design-to-price". Creating a design heavily influenced by a specific and reasonable monthly fee target should be a fundamental objective in a new project's planning phase. But, all too frequently, consumer price and value are subordinate to the overriding situation-driven concern of making the initial financial pro forma work to satisfy the investors, the owner/operator, and the lenders.

Remember, profit flows from price and an acceptable price flows from the creation of legitimate value. In sales and marketing, we must always attempt to build value before discussing price with senior consumers and their families. At the end of the day, your pricing must be ***market-driven*** – not ***situation-driven.***

The Top Ten Market-Driven Pricing Attributes

Senior living pricing attributes must be market-responsive and not merely the result of recovering poorly managed, escalating costs. Figure 40-1 summarizes my top ten market-driven pricing attributes.

FIGURE 40-1

THE TOP TEN SENIOR CONSUMER MARKET-DRIVEN PRICING ATTRIBUTES[1]

1. Deliver reasonable ***affordability***
2. Make pricing ***easy to understand***
3. Provide visibility and credible policies regarding future ***cost escalation/inflation***
4. Create obvious high ***perceived value***
5. ***Ensure security*** of "investment"
6. Possibly offer ***asset appreciation*** with time
7. Optimize ***preservation*** of capital assets
8. Provide for reasonable *(estate)* ***liquidity***
9. Be ***actuarially sound***
10. Meet or beat the ***competition*** in terms of:
    - Absolute price

      and/or
    - Demonstrated perceived value

These pricing attributes should be used as a strengths and weaknesses pricing checklist. Use it to gauge the pricing success and true value of your community, as well as that of your competitors.

Moore Diversified Services, Inc.

[1] For both market rate rental and entry fee pricing.

While it is not possible to score extremely high on all these attributes, a community that scores relatively low on most of them is probably in trouble. The marketing team needs to clearly understand the significance of these attributes in order to be able to favorably position your community for affordability and value to counter common sales objections.

Four Major Pricing Problems

At age 75 or older, seniors must make some of the most difficult and important decisions of the rest of their lives. Understandably, many are looking for any way to delay many of these complex decisions. Decision reluctance and procrastination are major challenges that sales and marketing professionals must overcome.

There are four mental roadblocks that come up repeatedly as potential deal-killers. Here is my problem-solution response:

Problem #1: ***Misconceptions about senior living affordability and the senior's current cost of living.*** In formal focus groups and informal discussions with thousands of seniors, I have consistently found that seniors lack a clear understanding of their current cost of living. Sound unbelievable for depression era consumers? Seniors typically forget the cost of real estate taxes, home repairs, insurance premiums, and other bills they don't pay every month when estimating their expenses. Some even underestimate bills that they do pay each month. It's not unusual for seniors with minimum annual incomes of $35,000 to $40,000 or more to initially estimate their cost of living at between $1,000 and $1,400 a month. After some discussion and subtle probing, many revise their estimates to between $1,900 and $2,400 per month.

With these types of misconceptions, picture the sticker shock seniors experience as your sales professional proudly announces what it costs to live at your community. Many seniors think the community is overpriced and they certainly could not afford to live there even if they liked what they saw!

Solution: ***Address these misconceptions during the early stages of the sales encounter***. Most marketing brochures have a cost of living comparison sheet. These are good, but they are not enough. You first have to plant some seeds: ***"Mrs. Barker, seniors like yourself who live in their private homes tell us that their current cost of living is between $2,100 and $3,000 a month. Of course, some budgets are higher and some are lower. But have you factored in periodic expenses such as real estate taxes, insurance premiums, and other important cost of living items?"*** This non-threatening dialogue can be very effective in tactfully correcting misconceptions and laying the foundation for selling value. Chapters 5, 6, 38 and 41 are required reading for this important issue.

Problem #2: *Fear of inflation*. Many seniors worry that annual price increases in senior living communities will be arbitrary and far exceed any inflation they would experience if they stayed in their current homes.

Solution: *Make sure the customer knows that your price increases are not arbitrary.* Address increases as "normal inflation." Explain that a senior living community manager faces the same types of cost increases for food, utilities, taxes, and so on as a homeowner. Point out that a well-run community can curb inflation better than individual homeowners through mass purchasing and operating economies of scale. Tell them that the annual senior living monthly service fee cost increases have averaged about 3.5 to 4.5 percent since 1990. But, bear in mind that what might appear to be nominal inflation to you may be perceived as a serious concern for your residents. With initial service fees of $2,200 a month, a 4 percent annual increase would mean Mrs. Barker's annual outlay would increase from $2,200 per month to almost $2,600 within five years. That's an annual bump of approximately $90 per month! In 2009, average short term CDs yielded less than 4 percent per year and the Social Security Cost of Living Adjustment (COLA) was about 5 percent. There will be no COLA increase in 2010!

Problem #3: ***Recognize the desire to preserve assets and leave a legacy.*** "Asset preservation" and "leaving a legacy" are magic sound bites in price positioning to seniors. Most seniors are preoccupied with leaving a financial legacy to their children and grandchildren. And they frequently underestimate the value of their pent-up home equity, although chances are it is considerable.

Solution: ***Make this desire work for you.*** Your community's market rate rental price position should be: ***"Mrs. Barker, we think you should maintain complete control of your valuable assets and manage them as you choose."*** Make sure Mrs. Barker understands that, since she is income-qualified with respect to your monthly service fees, it is not likely that she will significantly deplete her savings portfolio. The price positioning statement should be: ***"Mrs. Barker, you can put your newly liquidated net home equity to work for you now and still be able to leave most of it to your estate."***

If your community is a CCRC that charges an entry fee, consider offering one pricing option that is highly refundable at 80 to 90 percent. Also consider a lower entry fee with declining refundability over time for those seniors with more modest assets, or for those without significant heirs or estate legacy concerns (see Chapter 42 for more details).

Problem #4: *Price-value misconceptions.* Seniors are typically far from understanding the value of the service package offered in senior living communities. As one senior told me, ***"Heavens, I've never paid that much rent before."***

Solution: *We are in a service-enriched, benefit-driven business*. We have to sell uncomplicated, honest value. But that's easier said than done. We must sell a package of bundled *benefits*, not individual *features* or price points.

The ultimate test of how well you have developed and positioned your pricing strategy is whether or not you can deliver on this promise: ***"Mrs. Barker, what if you could live here at the Gardens of Westridge for the same amount or less than your current cost of living today – and still leave most of your current estate to your children? We can provide you with the kind of living arrangements and services that we've discussed for no more than your current cost of living. And the largely refundable entry fee that you are required to pay now will be less than the net proceeds from the sale of your home. This means you can still leave most of the value of your home sales proceeds and current savings portfolio to your estate."***

Before making your pitch, make sure you can back up your claims. Residents should generally pay no more than 65 percent of their after-tax cash income for monthly independent living service fees, or about 80 percent for assisted living. The remaining cash is for other necessary and discretionary purchases not covered by the monthly service fee.

There is evolving anecdotal evidence that a number of seniors are spending larger portions of their incomes for senior living options. Some may even be spending down their assets and/or receiving financial assistance from their adult children. But, assuming normal industry standards, it takes a total annual pre-tax income of more than $40,000 to cover today's independent living monthly service fee, which typically exceeds $2,000 per month.

Price-Value Indexing

There is a way to implement a check and balance system on your finalized pricing strategies. Divide the individual base monthly service fees of each of your independent living and assisted living units by their individual livable floor areas to come up with a monthly service fee-per-square-foot value index.

Next, do the same thing for your competitors to see how you stack up. I'm not suggesting that consumers typically make senior living decisions on a specific dollars-per-square-foot basis, but our focus groups and other research clearly indicate that consumers draw, at least, subliminal impressions from the amount of space received for the money. ***"This sure looks like a lot for the money,"*** shows that space and monthly cost registers with consumers. In any event, it's good to see how you compare to your competitors.

Other Important Issues

There are other important challenges that affect pricing. For the most part, they are addressed in major chapters throughout this book. So, to develop a more complete frame of reference on pricing strategies, you need to also address these other issues:

	Refer to Details in Chapter
1. Pricing for Improvements	19
2. Home Equity Impacts	34, 35
3. The Income Statement	26, 27
4. Financial Planning for Seniors	38
5. Resident Vs. Non-Resident Cost of Living Comparisons	36
6. Community of Choice Vs. A Price-Sensitive Commodity	47, 48

The ultimate pricing challenge that spans the life of your community is to provide the market-responsive services that residents want and need while covering all of your costs and making a fair and reasonable profit. You must also be prepared to develop an effective price-value counter attack for both new and existing competitive threats.

Chapters 40 and 41 address the quantitative considerations involved in pricing along with price positioning. Chapter 42 deals specifically with the complex world of upfront entrance fees. Figure 26-1 in Chapter 26 depicts a typical independent living income statement and required pricing in 2009. As Figure 40-2 indicates, the required pricing for newly developed independent living in 2009 – given the stated assumptions – is approximately $2,650 per month. Chapter 42 addresses how that monthly service fee can be reduced with an entry fee pricing model.

FIGURE 40-2

KEY ELEMENTS OF TYPICAL INDEPENDENT LIVING PRICING

Cost to be Covered	Monthly Cost	Percent of Total Cost
• Operating Expenses @ $53 PRD[1]	$1,610/mo	58%
• Debt Service[2] Payment	$ 900	32
• Cash Flow/Equity Returns[3]	$ 265	10
Total Average Monthly Service Fee Per Unit	**$2,775/mo**	**100%**
• Less Second Person/ Miscellaneous Revenues	($ 125)	
Base Monthly Service Fee Per Unit	**$2,650/mo**	

[1] Per Resident-Day
[2] $200,000/unit @ 70% debt, 30% equity, 7.0% interest, 30 years.
[3] When combined with the profit/cash flow from *second person charges* and *other miscellaneous revenues.*

Moore Diversified Services, Inc.

Seniors are concerned about price and value, but they also know there's no free lunch. Remember, whether you are a for-profit or not-for-profit organization . . . happiness is positive cash flow <u>after</u> debt service!

Call to Action

In retrospect, was your existing community designed to optimum price? Probably not. Using 20-20 hindsight, take a look at what you would have done differently. Now, determine if you can change anything today – possibly as units turn over and are remarketed. Finally, sharpen your price vs. value market positioning and message – assume you're explaining it to your mom.

CHAPTER 41

THE PRICE IS RIGHT?

Price Positioning Is More Science Than Art

As Chapter 40 pointed out, we are in a service-enriched, benefit-driven business. Yet, we have to sell easy-to-understand, honest value. Easier said than done!

Effective senior living pricing involves striking a delicate balance between:

- Covering your ***total*** costs and profit objectives, while delivering acceptable financial ratios

and . . .

- Being affordable, competitive and consumer-driven for your market area

These objectives are at opposite ends of the price positioning spectrum, which frequently presents significant challenges. And serious, *yet avoidable,* mistakes are being made by many sponsors at both ends of the pricing trade-off spectrum.

The Service-Enriched, Value-Added Concept

Regardless of your ultimate pricing structure, remember you're in a *value-added, premium priced service delivery business*. Look at it as if it were similar to an entree listing on the dinner menu of a fine restaurant. If you were to unbundle *everything*, the menu pricing would probably drive most consumers into sticker shock! Many of us will pay the "packaged menu price" but feel "nickeled and dimed" when everything seems like an added extra. You stand a much better chance of marketplace success by creating a value package through the effective combination of an array of *benefits* (not *features*). Frequently, a *feature* does not convey utility or value to the consumer. A *benefit* more appropriately communicates something tangible for the senior consumer.

Owner/Operator Pricing Perspectives

Covering capital costs and operating expenses with appropriate pricing is a two-step process:

1. Charge enough to cover all your current basic capital costs (debt service, investor return and capital improvements) and operating expenses.
2. Provide a hedge against normal inflation of operating expenses.

But just covering these obligations is not enough. You must also realize acceptable operating profit margins, debt service coverage ratios, net cash flow, and annual internal rates of return to satisfy investors and/or to fund mission objectives.

Sounds simple, but, as we observed in Chapter 24, operating expenses can be a constantly moving target. This obviously makes it harder to establish fair, consistent pricing.

The Consumer Marketplace Pricing Perspective

The optimum senior living pricing structure for senior consumers must demonstrate at least five market-driven attributes.

Your pricing should be:

1. Easy to understand
2. Equitable
3. Perceived as good value
4. Affordable
5. Seamless (covering both shelter and services/care costs)

It should be noted that senior living pricing involves paying for a *service-enriched living arrangement*. That includes all shelter services (housekeeping, food, utilities, taxes etc.) along with a reasonable array of living unit design options (the real estate component).

Figure 41-1 summarizes the delicate balance that must be achieved when developing pricing strategies.

FIGURE 41-1
PRICING STRATEGIES MUST STRIKE A DELICATE BALANCE

Consumer **Market-Driven**	***Operator*** **Project-Driven**
1. Affordable	1. Cover operating expenses
2. High perceived value	2. Service underlying debt
3. Competitive in the marketplace	3. Provide lender safety margins
4. Provide hedge against excessive future escalation	4. Provide cash for other ventures
5. Credible and rational	5. Deliver entrepreneurial profit

Moore Diversified Services, Inc.

Communicating Your Pricing to Seniors

Striking a delicate balance between your internal financial needs and the competitive forces of the external marketplace is very important. But your pricing strategy still has a major hurdle. You have to convince the senior consumer and their family that you have a credible value-driven story to tell.

Independent Living and CCRC Pricing Options and Rationale

Senior marketing prospects and their families have a myriad of questions. Figure 41-2 provides a summary of frequently asked questions regarding entry fee and monthly service fee pricing models.

In order to effectively position and communicate your pricing to the senior consumer and their family, a carefully conceived pricing rationale must be developed. Here are some suggestions on how to explain pricing.

Explaining the monthly service fee. Attempt to respond to two senior consumer concerns (and potentially serious misconceptions):

1. **Cost of Living** - Establish the senior's true, ***current*** cost of living. Seniors frequently underestimate their true/actual cost of living (See Chapters 5, 6, and 38).

2. **Affordability** - Clarify affordability. Seniors frequently do not understand what they can realistically afford to pay. For example, a typical monthly service fee for a project might be structured and positioned accordingly:

FIGURE 41-2
FREQUENTLY ASKED QUESTIONS
(Explaining Two Common Senior Living Pricing Structures To Seniors)

	Entry Fee	Monthly Service Fee
What Does it Pays For?	A one-time cost that basically covers the "bricks and mortar" cost of your living unit and a share of the public spaces. In some cases, part of the entry fee is also considered a significant pre-paid medical cost benefit. This is considered a life care benefit.	Essentially replaces most current cost of living expenses and the cost of maintaining your current home. When entry fees are not involved, the monthly service fee also covers the cost of debt payments for financing the cost of the community.
What Sources of Money Will I Use?	Typically paid by a portion of your new cash resource, realized when you sell your home. Your existing savings portfolio principal balance could essentially remain unchanged.	Your current monthly expense budget for living at home that is paid for with your current income.
Does this Cost Increase Each Year?	No . . . In fact, your estate could get up to a 95% refund of this one-time payment. (Upon your death or move from the community).	Yes, but modestly. Service fees will increase annually, along with inflation, similar to what you experience in your current home. Expect increases of approximately 4% to 5% per year.
Are There Tax Benefits?	Yes, depending upon possible life care benefits (such as pre-paid health benefits that may be offered). A significant portion of this initial entry fee may be eligible for a one-time medical tax deduction.	Yes. Certain health-related resources such as assisted living and nursing may be subject to an annual medical tax deduction. Some restrictions may apply.

Seniors will generally understand this step-by-step pricing description and rationale. It helps lay the foundation for creating favorable value perceptions.

Moore Diversified Services, Inc.

- A weighted average fee (for all independent living units) might be $2,175 per month for an existing community and approximately $2,700 per month for a recently developed project.
- These fees are consistent with the actual current cost of living and affordability levels for approximately 35 to 40 percent of seniors age 75 and above in a typical primary market area – assuming they have home equity that, upon sale, will be added to their savings portfolio or would pay a substantial portion of the entry fee for a CCRC.
- A factor of 65 percent is universally accepted as the optimum percentage of the total ***after-tax income*** that seniors should pay for services provided in independent living. The remaining 35 percent would be allocated for discretionary spending. This spending ratio would be lower in cottages/villas due to fewer prepaid services being included in the monthly service fee.
- The senior's ideal independent living after-tax affordability threshold is therefore typically computed as follows:

$$\frac{\$2{,}700/\text{month}}{0.65} = \$4{,}154 \text{ per month or } \$49{,}845 \text{ per year } \underline{\text{after}} \text{ taxes}$$

- Assuming an average tax rate of 15 percent, the senior's ***pre-tax income*** should be approximately $58,645 <u>before</u> any required spend-down.

Sounds high? The affordable arithmetic is pretty straight forward.

Explaining the CCRC entry fee. The basic entry fee is typically equivalent to the reasonable value (all-inclusive cost) of the independent living unit as if it were purchased and owned as a fee simple home or condominium.[1] For example:

- Assume an average project entry fee is approximately \$200,000 with a resident's individual residential unit average living area of 1,050 square feet (*before* including an "undivided share" of the common/public spaces).
- The value indicator:

  $$\frac{\$200{,}000}{1{,}050 \text{ square feet}} = \$191 \text{ per square feet}$$

  (This is reasonable considering both hard and soft development and construction costs.)

The magnitude of the entry fee should, in general, be reasonably consistent with senior's average net home equity in a typical primary market area. That's because:

- Many seniors will be willing to "trade" all/some of their net home sales proceeds for the entry fee.

  However…

- Seniors are usually very reluctant to tamper with their existing savings portfolio (even if they could easily afford it)

Figure 41-3 provides a summary of various senior living pricing options.

[1] In some instances for life care CCRCs, a portion of the entry fee is also used to cover prepaid (future) health care expense obligations.

FIGURE 41-3
SUMMARY OF INDEPENDENT LIVING AND CCRC PRICING OPTIONS

Type of Pricing	Typical Market Positioning
I. **Market Rate Rental**	A fixed monthly fee that covers a wide array of services; many of which seniors also pay for when living on their own. A similar, but typically lower, monthly service fee is charged for those communities that also require either an entry fee or offer fee-simple ownership. In those cases, much of the recovery of the "real estate cost impacts" are either reduced or eliminated within the monthly service fee because of the unique pricing structure.
II. **Entry Fee** • Fully/Partially Refundable Or • Non-Refundable	Under the entry fee structure, the resident does not "own" the real estate or the living unit *fee-simple*. They essentially have a "life estate" right from the sponsor or owner/operator. The upfront fee frequently is quite similar to the total capital costs of the unit as if it were being sold as fee simple ownership (like a condominium). However, there are also situations where a portion of the entry fee is also considered pre-paid medical benefits if the owner/operator or sponsor is also offering a form of guaranteed life care. See Chapter 43 for details.
III. **Ownership**	
• Conventional Ownership • Condominium	With the ownership option, the senior may actually take "title" to their unit either in the form of conventional ownership, much like a single family home or condominium.
• Cooperative	Under the cooperative concept, the senior "owns" a defined undivided interest within the community. In most cases, the senior or their estate is responsible for selling the unit. The seller, however, must comply with previously agreed-to residency restrictions and disposition terms and conditions.

Refundable entry fees (vs. non-refundable fees) minimize tax implications to the sponsor or owner/operator. [1]

[1] Applies to for-profit organizations.

Moore Diversified Services, Inc.

Explain the type of pricing and market positioning. Figure 41-3 provides a summary of independent living and CCRC pricing options along with typical market positioning. It shows examples of how to explain your pricing to senior consumers. Figures 41-4 and 41-5 provide additional price positioning details. Use this information as guidelines to develop your detailed pricing rationale and market positioning statements.

Pricing active adult senior housing. Chapters 13 and 14 dealt with some complex issues of effective active adult pricing.

Tax implications. Senior living pricing involves a number of consumer and owner/operator tax issues. It is important to discuss these issues with a knowledgeable tax professional.

Call to Action

Revisit the delicate balance of pricing that is needed to satisfy your needs as a sponsor or owner/operator while offering competitive, market-responsive price positioning for the senior consumer. Expand – yet simplify – the story your sales and marketing team must discuss with future prospects.

FIGURE 41-4

PRICE POSITIONING FOR YOUR SENIOR LIVING COMMUNITY (Explaining Pricing to the Senior Consumer)

What Costs Are Covered

A quality, financially responsible community like ***The Gardens at Westridge*** has three basic costs to cover:

1. **Your new home.** Much like the current value of your current home, condominium or apartment. Must cover/charge for the initial cost of development and construction.
2. **Public spaces.** All residents pay an equitable share of the cost of upkeep for the luxurious public spaces in our commons building – including common space in health-related buildings.
3. **Monthly operating expenses.** This includes a wide spectrum of valuable services provided directly for you along with proper maintenance of the entire campus. Most of these services replace many of those burdens that are now part of your current primary cost of living.

In some cases, a prepaid health care benefit is also part of the financial relationship with the community.

How Residents Pay For These Costs

These costs can be covered by a single monthly service fee or a combination of two pricing mechanisms:

1. The ***monthly service fee*** covers the actual cost of providing essentially the same services you currently pay for in your home plus a number of other valuable services that you will now use and enjoy. When no entrance fee is paid, the monthly service fee also covers the cost of your new home and maintaining the common public spaces.
2. The ***entry fee*** (admission or life estate fee) covers the cost of your new home plus a share of the luxurious common spaces, health-related resources and in, some cases, pre-paid health benefits.

When you consider your current home equity applied to the entry fee and your current income/cost of living budget you'll discover what many other seniors have realized – "The Gardens at Westridge is surprisingly affordable!"

Moore Diversified Services, Inc.

FIGURE 41-5
PRICE POSITIONING FOR THE OWNERSHIP/UPFRONT FEE PRICING VS. CONVENTIONAL MONTHLY SERVICE FEES
(For Different Senior Consumer Preferences and Propensities)

Value-Enhanced Upfront Fees	Straight/Conventional Monthly Service Fees
1. Maintain the same stable existing savings portfolio the senior had prior to home sale: • Income qualified seniors can afford (and prefer) to pay slightly lower monthly service fees with *current income* – using their home sale proceeds to pay the one time upfront entry fee.	1. For seniors who would prefer to keep and invest their liquidated home equity proceeds: • Manage their own savings/ investment portfolio – expanded by their home sale proceeds.
2. For seniors who ideally desire future estate preservation and "no hassle" estate liquidity: • No home to sell by their family upon their death • Senior would have predictable legacy/estate proceeds in the form of a guaranteed refundable entry fee commitment as a contractual obligation.	2. Seniors who prefer only monthly service fees can usually afford the higher monthly fees.
3. Many seniors would feel that the value-enhanced entry fee is a good investment – with a potential tax advantage.	3. Some seniors may desire to put some of their estate/capital assets to work *now* – in various personal ways: • Gifts to children • Grandchildren education • Charitable contributions • Etc.

Owner/operators could expand the development of this price positioning – possibly offering both pricing options – after careful consideration.

Moore Diversified Services, Inc.

CHAPTER 42

CREATIVE ENTRY FEE PRICING STRATEGIES

Making the Most of Rare "Interest Free Loans"

Senior living entrance fees, where else in the world can a sponsor or owner/operator get an ***interest free*** loan – including one that may or may not ever have to be repaid? Refundable and non-refundable entry fees reflect a common senior living pricing strategy – especially for a CCRC. They are particularly useful in coping with the challenges of expensive projects in high cost markets.

Creative Use of Home Equity for Entry Fee Payments

In Chapters 34 and 35, we discussed that we've been tapping the home equity resource for over 30 years. So it is time to take a new strategic look at an old concept. Let's focus on the creative use of a senior's liquidated home equity to address the most common upfront fee concept; *refundable* and *non-refundable* entry fees.

Refundable entry fees essentially represent an interest-free loan from the senior consumer to the sponsor or owner/operator. With recent tax law changes, there is currently no threat of imputed interest by the IRS to the senior. The sponsor gets to use the senior's money interest free – until the senior either dies or moves off the sponsor's campus. Why would a senior agree to do that?

This is where acceptable past trends and future pricing strategies may be drifting apart.

In the past, it was very common for CCRC sponsors using entry fees to offer both significantly prepaid "life care" health benefits and reductions in the required independent living monthly service fee (as compared to the straight market rate rental pricing concept). Today, Type 'A' full life care is still common, but contracts that limit, qualify or eliminate *full* prepaid life care benefits are becoming even more common. These contracts are categorized as Type 'B' and Type 'C' life care, respectively. Refer to Figure 43-1 in Chapter 43 for general definitions of three basic life care contracts.

Sponsors are now trying to limit or, at least, contain their future actuarial/financial exposure. With today's CCRCs, it's imperative that upfront fees be properly positioned and effectively communicated; the senior consumer must feel that they're getting significant tangible benefits that make sense from both a short-run and long-run financial planning perspective.

Non-refundable or "traditional" entry fees have also been an acceptable upfront fee pricing alternative. It's very common for a CCRC to have two pricing plans (refundable and non-refundable) for the same type of living unit. The refundable pricing plan frequently costs at least 30 percent more than the non-refundable plan for the same unit.

In reality, the non-refundable pricing method represents a form of significant spend-down of assets for the senior. For example, a unit with a $200,000 entry fee, whose refund obligation declines at 1.5 percent for each month of residency (very common in the industry), results in the senior experiencing an effective asset spend-down of $3,000 per month ($200,000 x 0.015 = $3,000). And that's in ***addition*** to paying their monthly service fee outlay. Why would a senior agree to this concept? In the old days, it was primarily faith, trust, and possibly a pre-paid health care benefit. Today, competitive, affordable, pragmatic pricing is fast becoming a major priority with financially astute seniors and their advisors. It is important to note that the non-refundable entry fee spend-down concept is not necessarily a negative or unfair pricing concept. It is a pricing alternative; making a *typical unit* more affordable for seniors with more modest assets.

Here are four entry fee strategies to help you sharpen the focus of your entry fee price positioning:

1. ***Help seniors avoid sticker shock.*** In a very pricey market, seniors are generally more reluctant to pay relatively high, $3,500+ per month independent living service fees as compared to committing to a one-time entry fee with a lower monthly service fee. Ideally, the required entry fee pricing, on average, should be essentially be equal to or less than a senior's typical liquidated home equity in that market area. That's because many seniors are willing to convert part of their liquidated home equity to pay the one-time entry fee. Many are very reluctant to draw funds out of their existing savings portfolio.

   Upfront fees generally work best in high cost markets which also have high home equities. This strategy acts as a hedge against monthly service fee sticker shock. That's because the real estate costs of the unit and a share of the common/public spaces must be recovered through either a portion of the monthly service fee or an upfront charge. As I stated earlier, many seniors are willing to trade a significant portion of their net liquidated home equity for an entrance fee – if it's equitable and competitive.

2. ***Help seniors make value-driven trade-off decisions between leaving a financial legacy and addressing current affordability.*** Seniors want entry fee flexibility with no serious complications. For the same unit #101, one senior with children and grandchildren might want very high guaranteed entry fee *refundability* (75 percent to 90 percent) and be willing to pay a premium for this "leaving a legacy" benefit. Conversely, a senior with limited estate legacy concerns may not be as sensitive to refundability, but wants to live in unit #101 at a more affordable entry fee. This pricing differential for the same unit type is not "voodoo economics" for either the senior or the sponsor or owner/operator. It's a function of sound actuarial theory essentially involving the present value of the cash flow for each pricing plan.

3. ***Show seniors how to legally avoid taxes.*** Using liquidated home equity for entry fees delivers another significant benefit for both the consumer and the sponsor – ***legal tax avoidance.*** Today, home sale transactions are largely tax free. With the entry fee concept, the senior should be paying a lower monthly service fee. That means taking less retirement funds into taxable income for either the one-time entry fee and the recurring monthly service fee. But remember, you should get your own independent advice from your qualified tax professional, as well as advising each senior you consult with to do the same.

4. ***Develop prudent spend-down strategies.*** Some seniors eventually experience at least modest financial distress. There are practical spend-down "safety nets" where the senior can continue to live on your campus because you agree to reduce your eventual contractual entry fee refund obligation to cover their current payment shortfalls. Remember, this should be a pricing exception – not a common policy.

An increasing number of seniors are seeking financial advice from families and third-party professionals. You should recognize that seniors and their advisors will likely be spending more time putting your pricing strategies under a microscope in the future to look at value and fairness. ***Also assume that the consumer and these professionals may or may not really understand all aspects of your pricing concept.***

Entry Fee Pricing Strategies

Entry fee dynamics play a major (and sometimes complex) role in those communities deploying an entry fee pricing strategy. What follows is an outline of some entry fee pricing fundamentals that impact financial performance.

There are two distinct financial/accounting conventions that must be recognized when dealing with entry fees:

1. ***Generally Accepted Accounting Principles (GAAP):***
   - This is a very valid and appropriate accounting method; but it focuses heavily on the *non-cash* aspects of entry fees.
2. ***The real cash impacts of entry fee dynamics.***

The GAAP accounting approach to dealing with entry fees on formal financial statements involves (in part) amortizing entry fees into income from two perspectives:

1. **Non-refundable entry fees** are a form of deferred revenue and they are amortized into income over the ***remaining life of the particular resident***.
2. **Refundable entry fees** are another form of deferred revenue and they are amortized into income over the ***useful life of the campus*** (somewhat like a physical plant depreciation schedule).

Both of these amortizations are essentially *non-cash transactions*. But these *non-cash transactions* can sometimes be confused on GAAP financial statements as a portion of real (cash) income. This frequently gives the false impression of a stronger cash position than that which really exists.

The cash reality of entry fee dynamics represents a number of important financial issues:

1. **Refund Obligation** – When a resident dies or moves off the campus and the community has made a commitment to some form of refund; that disbursement is either made upon the resident leaving the campus or, more typically, the actual re-sale of that unit.
2. **Re-Sale Proceeds** – Once the re-sale takes place and the overall transaction is complete, a portion of the new cash from the re-sale of that unit is used to provide a source of funds for the refund.

3. **Gain on Re-Sale** – Since the re-sale of the former resident's unit is typically at a higher price than the original entry fee sale and the refund obligation is usually less than 100 percent, there is a resulting ***gain on re-sale***.
4. **Net Cash Gain** – This net gain on re-sale generates real cash in the reporting period when the transaction has completed.
5. **Free Cash Flow** – This is additional "free cash flow" that can and should be used for operations. It is also part of the available cash resources that are typically considered when computing two very important loan covenant and liquidity ratios:
    - Debt service coverage ratio
    - Days cash on hand

Information contained within the following figures provides some additional ideas on establishing some creative entry fee pricing strategies.

Gain On Entry Fee Re-sale – Figure 42-1 shows that your typical gain on re-sale of an entry fee can be substantial. Note that this results in significant additional annual cash flow as these sales are executed due to resident turnover. The example in Figure 42-1 is typical and realistic for many of today's CCRCs. The example shows an annual cash flow impact of approximately $1.4 million. However, this cash flow experience can be <u>very</u> volatile in any given year. As an example, let's use the $180,000 refund obligation and the gain on re-sale of $53,971 per unit shown in Figure 42-1. The potential impact of *five* unit turnovers might look like this:

• *Gain* – If <u>Sold</u> (5 x $53,971)	$ 269,855
• *Obligation* – If <u>Unsold</u> (5 x $180,000)	<u>900,000</u>
	$1,169,855

At least in the short-run you have a $1.2 million cash flow challenge!

FIGURE 42-1

THE GAIN ON RE-SALE OF AN ENTRY FEE UNIT IS VERY ATTRACTIVE

1. **Potential Gain Per Unit on $200,000 Entry Fee Re-Sale:**
   - Original entry fee of $200,000
   - Re-sale value in 4 years of $233,971 (Based on 4-year escalation assumption of 4% per year)
   - 90% refund obligation (of original entry fee sale) to senior's estate $180,000 [1] (.90 x $200,000) = Gain on a single entry fee sale of $53,971 ($233,971 - $180,000)

2. **Total Annual Gain on Sales @ 18% Annual Resident Turnover:**
   - 150 units @ 93% occupancy = 140 units @ 18% turnover = 25 re-sales per year x $53,971 average gain per entry fee re-sale = $1,349,275 per year = total gain on re-sales

3. **Typical Re-sale/Refund Terms:**
   - Upon actual *re-sale* of a resident's specific unit

     or . . .

   - Approximately 9 to 12 months, whichever comes first[2]

Some start-up communities offer higher refunds or more beneficial refund terms to the first 40 to 50 "Charter Members" as a marketing incentive for the new, start-up community.

[1] Upon death/move-out and re-sale of the unit.
[2] Some communities do not guarantee this time commitment.

Moore Diversified Services, Inc.

The Concept of Net Operating Margin – Adjusted (NOM-Adj)

This potential for substantial cash flow impacts both the not-for-profit and for-profit industry's definition of **Net Operating (Profit) Margin – Adjusted (NOM-Adj)**.

Entry fee proceeds and monthly service fees are both an integral part of a community's compensation (revenue) for services rendered.

The not-for-profit industry and major tax-exempt bond underwriters now recognize the application of this net cash gain upon re-sale of entry fees as a valid component of operating income:

1. This gain impact at the bottom line has been classified as Net Operating Margin (NOM)-Adjusted.
2. Note that the concept of NOM-Adjusted is equivalent to Net Operating Income (NOI) or earnings before interest, taxes, depreciation and amortization (EBITDA) when the net gain on entry fee cash is considered.

In essence, entry fee cash, net of refunds, is a valid and integral part of the income statement on a ***cash basis***.

Entry Fee Dynamics

Entry fee dynamics appear to be a complex situation, but it becomes somewhat fundamental when broken down into the individual issues.

Entry Fee Spend-Down – Figure 42-2 shows how the non-refundable portions of entry fees (versus time) results in effective financial spend-down to the senior consumer. It should be noted that this "spend-down" is not necessarily a strong negative. If your community is offering tangible and specific life care benefits and competitive pricing, then this reduction in entry fee pricing for declining refundability can be an equitable affordability benefit for the residents. The declining refundable "slope" represents how your community is actually "earning" the entry fees with the passage of time over a specified time period. My reference to spend-down deals primarily with how consumers and their advisors might look at the added "costs" of declining entry fee refundability. The positive benefits of non-refundable entry fees must be a major market-positioning strategy.

Figure 42-3 provides additional details on declining entry fee refundability and the concept of spend-down. Figures 42-2 and 42-3 emphasize the importance of clearly communicating to consumers and, possibly, their financial advisors. Some of your competitors may be at a financial disadvantage when compared to your well-conceived pricing strategies. For example, competitive advantages include the various entry fee pricing alternatives you might offer and how you effectively earn these fees by providing services and benefits over the life of the resident as he or she lives at your community.

The Economic Equivalent of Entry Fees – Figure 42-4 shows how to compute the *economic equivalent* impact of *entry fees* on monthly *service fees*. Simply stated, this means giving the consumer some monthly service fee (reduction) credit in exchange for their upfront payment of an entry fee as if they were otherwise earning interest on that amount of money in a CD, etc. What this means is that, if you are charging an upfront entry fee and are not offering prepaid health care benefits, you should probably consider reducing the ongoing monthly service fee by an amount that is somewhat equivalent to the kind of interest consumers would earn on that block of money. Figure 42-4 also suggests the possibility of a sponsor or owner/operator arbitrage strategy.

Tax Benefits Related to Entry Fees – The reduction in monthly service fees previously discussed results in an indirect tax benefit to the resident. With the reduced monthly service fee, they will not have to draw as much money out of their tax-deferred retirement account into taxable income. Figure 42-5 provides a simple example of this concept.

Call to Action

Take the senior consumer's interest free loan (entry fees) very seriously. Look for ways to provide unique financial benefits to the senior while recognizing the cost of capital arbitrage value to you.

FIGURE 42-2

SUMMARY OF DECLINING BALANCE/NON-REFUNDABLE ENTRY FEE "SPEND-DOWN"

$200,000 Entry Fee

Non-Refundable Rate @ 1.5% Per Month

Decreased Refund/ Effective Spend-Down	Minimum Refund Guaranteed @ 90%	80%	50%	0%
• Spend-Down Per Month	$3,000/mo	$3,000/mo	$3,000/mo	$3,000/mo
• Total Potential Spend-Down/Estate Refund	$20,000	$40,000	$100,000	$200,000
• Time to Total Spend-Down (In months)	6.7	13.3	33.3	66.7

Non-Refundable Rate @ 2.0% Per Month

Decreased Refund/ Effective Spend-Down	Minimum Refund Guaranteed @ 90%	80%	50%	0%
• Spend-Down Per Month	$4,000/mo	$4,000/mo	$4,000/mo	$4,000/mo
• Total Potential Spend-Down/Estate Refund	$20,000	$40,000	$100,000	$200,000
• Time to Total Spend-Down (In months)	5.0	10.0	25.0	50.0

The positive benefits to the senior consumer involving non-refundable entry fee "spend-down" must be clearly communicated to prospects and possibly their financial advisors.

Moore Diversified Services, Inc.

FIGURE 42-3
CONSUMER "COST" OF CONVENTIONAL ENTRY FEES WITH EXISTING COMPETITORS

	Actual Consumer (Cash) Cost/Spend-Down As a Function of Decline in Refundability			
	@ 1.5% Per Month		**@ 2.0% Per Month**	
Entry Fee	**Per Month**	**Annual**	**Per Month**	**Annual**
$100,000	$1,500 /mo	$18,000 /yr	$2,000 /mo	$24,000 /yr
125,000	1,875	22,500	2,500	30,000
150,000	2,250	27,000	3,000	36,000
175,000	2,625	31,500	3,500	42,000
200,000	**3,000**	**36,000**	**4,000**	**48,000**
250,000	3,750	45,000	5,000	60,000

With some pricing vs. benefit plans, senior consumers could be paying a heavy price when opting for some conventional, non-refundable entry fees; especially if there is no substantial pre-paid health care or substantial reduction in monthly service fees. For example:

1. The *opportunity cost* of tying up $200,000 @ 5%: **$10,000/year**
2. The annual *reduction* in their $200,000 entry fee refundability at a minimum of 1.5% per month ($3,000/mo x 12 mos.): 36,000

Total Senior Consumer *Hidden* Cost Potential[1] **$46,000/year**

While the senior consumer may be getting some health care benefits and a reduced monthly service fee (in exchange for the entry fee "investment"), it's clear there could be some significant "imbalances" in true value received. For example, a limited-but-typical life care benefit could be 60 days in health care which would be approximately a $12,000 benefit (in nursing) and approximately $6,000 per month covered by the consumer thereafter (versus approximately $36,000 per year in consumer cost) as shown in this Figure.

Some competitors may offer limited but more favorable life care benefits.

Moore Diversified Services, Inc.

[1] Sponsors and owner/operators must also clearly communicate that the cost for declining refundability on a particular unit can be up to 30% lower than 90% refundability for the same unit.

FIGURE 42-4
THE ECONOMIC EQUIVALENT CONVERSION OF SENIOR CONSUMER ENTRY FEES TO POTENTIAL MONTHLY SERVICE FEE CREDIT/REDUCTIONS[1]
(Assumes No Pre-Paid Health Care Benefit)

	Economic Equivalent MSF "Value" at Various Costs of Capital				
Entry Fee	5%	6%	7%	8%	9%
$100,000	$417 /mo	$500 /mo	$583 /mo	$667 /mo	$750 /mo
125,000	520	625	729	833	938
150,000	625	750	875	1,000	1,125
175,000	730	875	1,021	1,167	1,313
200,000	**833** [2]	**1,000**	**1,167**	**1,333**	**1,500**

A $200,000 upfront entry fee has an economic value and would otherwise earn $833 per month at a 5 percent average annual "investment value". This can be viewed from three perspectives:

1. A *reduction* (credit) in monthly service fee to the resident
2. A *cash flow "kicker"* to the sponsor – owner/operator
3. Possibly meet in the middle; a blend of perspectives #1 and #2
   - For example, give the resident a $450 per month reduction in the normal market rate rental monthly service fee

     Plus . . .

   - Sponsor or owner/operator keeps cash flow "kicker" of approximately $380 per month or $4,560 per unit per year. For 150 units at 93% occupancy, the total annual impact would be $638,400 per year in effective cash flow.

The sponsor or owner/operator benefits from "arbitrage"; the 7 percent approximate actual cost of capital vs. 5 percent cash credit to the senior consumer or retaining a portion of the 5 percent credit.

Moore Diversified Services, Inc.

[1] Assumes a Type C Life Care Plan.
[2] Example: $200,000 x .05 divided by 12 = $833/mo.

FIGURE 42-5

SENIOR'S PERSONAL INCOME TAX ISSUES/ADVANTAGES

Examples of Potential Reduction In Monthly Service Fee		Annual Personal Income Tax Savings For Various *Average* Consumer Tax Brackets		
Monthly	**Annual**	**10%**	**12%**	**15%**
$350 /mo	$4,200 /yr	$420 /yr	$500 /yr	$630 /yr
450	**5,400**	540	**650**	810
875	10,500	1,050	1,260	1,575
1,000	12,000	1,200	1,440	1,800

Concept/Example:

By paying a $200,000 entry fee (Figure 42-4); the resident's monthly service fee was reduced by $450 per month or $5,400 each year.[1] In essence, the resident is avoiding an additional after-tax income requirement of $5,400 each year. If he/she is in the 12% *average* tax bracket, they are saving $650 in taxes.

This tax savings concept is somewhat elusive. In the example above, the thinking would go like this:

1. An upfront fee of $200,000 would be a one-time payment.
2. The resident would also get a reduction in monthly service fee of $450 per month (see Figure 42-4).
   - This portion would, effectively, be "paid" in ***tax free dollars.***
   - Because, in essence, they would have to take less money ($5,400) into (taxable) income from their otherwise tax sheltered retirement fund.

Moore Diversified Services, Inc.

[1]Refer to Item #3 in Figure 42-4.

CHAPTER 43

LIFE CARE IN CCRCs

Financially Viable Promise or Actuarial Nightmare

The life care concept actually started more than 30 years ago with well intended not-for-profits attempting to execute a meaningful mission. Some of the very earliest life care definitions involved "give us all of your assets and we will take care of you for life". As time passed, that concept was not market-responsive for many seniors with growing financial sophistication.

The next phase of the life care concept involved structuring defined life care benefits (with qualifications and limitations) carefully integrated with specific entry fee refund policies. The basic concept of life care is to structure the advanced payment (the entry fee) and, in some cases, a portion of the monthly service fee to fund future life care for a population of residents at a particular community. Three basic types of life care contracts have emerged in recent years. These three contract types are summarized in Figure 43-1. Actually the three basic contract types in Figure 43-1 reflect somewhat of an oversimplification of the complexity of this important consumer benefit and sponsor owner/operator issue.

The most important thing to remember if you attempt to deal with life care is that you are basically a health care insurance organization with a rather limited risk pool. Think of your 300 residents in this insurance risk pool as compared to large scale insurance companies that typically have hundreds of thousands of policy holders in their respective risk pools.

FIGURE 43-1
CCRC LIFE CARE CONTRACT TYPES

There are three types of basic life care contracts. Names and definitions may vary by state and specific CCRC. This figure reflects general contract type definitions. Each type typically has a one-time, upfront entry fee pricing concept and a recurring monthly service fee.

Type 'A' – Extensive – This plan offers the most benefits to the seniors and represents the greatest potential financial risk to the sponsor or owner/operator. Type 'A' plans typically include:

- Housing
- Residential services and amenities
- Specific health related services (assisted living, nursing, etc.)
- Essentially no substantial increase in monthly charges (from basic independent living monthly service fees) when resident moves to assisted living or nursing except for extra meals in health care and annual inflation adjustments.

Type 'B' – Modified

- Similar services as Type 'A' contract except resident's monthly charges may increase on a fee for extra service concept, but usually at a discount from posted "street rates" for these services.[1]

Type 'C' – Fee For Service

- Similar services as Type 'A' contract, but monthly charges increase consistent with the appropriate posted "street rate" pricing for level of care/health services provided.[1]

[1] "Street rates" are defined as those rates charged to consumers from the external market who moved directly to health care and did not pay an entry fee initially to move into independent living.

Moore Diversified Services, Inc.

The life care concept presents a substantial benefit for the senior consumers in their later stages of life. In many cases, it basically caps or limits their future health care exposure. Of course, at the same time it creates financial exposure for sponsors and owner/operators.

Just like sophisticated insurance companies, there are actuarial methodologies that are used to insure that any life care plan that is actuarially sound; both now and in the future years.

The rather simple life care definitions of the three types of plans illustrated in Figure 43-1 have many variations in competitive markets. That's because sponsors and owner/operators are becoming much more sophisticated in striking a delicate balance between hedging their actuarial/financial risks while offering competitive financial benefits for the senior consumer.

Typical Real World Life Care Benefits and Refund Policies

Life care benefits and refund policies cover a very wide spectrum of options. Some typical options are summarized on the following pages.[1] These benefits and refund strategies reflect actual CCRCs; some of which are in direct competition with each other.

[1] Before finalizing a life care benefit and refund strategy, it is <u>imperative</u> that you implement a comprehensive market feasibility study (with a strong competitive analysis) and a detailed financial pro forma.

Project	Health Benefits Included in Entry Fee Pricing	Specific Refund Policy
A	Whether temporarily or on a permanent basis, a resident admitted to the personal care unit or into the medical center, *the resident continues to pay the same monthly fee when they were in independent living. There are no additional charges.*	The entrance fee is 100% refundable within the first 90 days upon withdrawal. *After 90 days, the entry fee is prorated at 2% per year for five years to 0% upon withdrawal from the community. The entry fee is only refundable upon death during the first 12 months.* It is prorated in equal amounts for the year, including partial months. *After 12 months, there is no refund upon death.*
B	*360 days of coverage per apartment (22 days per calendar quarter) for assisted living, Alzheimer's care or skilled nursing care.* The coverage can be applied to any level of care and utilized by couples for either spouse. *Residents are required to use applicable Medicare (based on bed availability), Medicare-equivalent HMO or private long-term care insurance benefits first before using continuing care benefits.*	42% or 82% refundable. *8% is payable to a long-term care administration fee.* The balance of the entrance fee declines at 2% per month until it reaches the minimum refundability level. *After they have used their benefit, residents have the ability to apply up to 50% of the refundable portion of their entrance fee toward ongoing care.*

Project	Health Benefits Included in Entry Fee Pricing	Specific Refund Policy
C	*60 days of assisted living or nursing care included in pricing.* After 60 days, resident receives 10% discount on going rates for each level of care.	Entrance fee declines to zero at 2% per month of residency and any withholding specified in the Residency Agreement. *Should a death occur during the first 25 months of residency, there will be a refund minus 4% for each full or partial month of residency.*
D	Residents receive full care and pay the same monthly fee throughout their residency.	Entrance fee is fully refundable during the first 90 days. After the first 90 days, it declines to zero at 20% per year for five years.
E	Residents receive five free days of care per year in the skilled nursing facility (up to a maximum of 15 days). After that, the residents pay a discounted rate (approximately 15% off of the street rate).	Declines to zero at 1.6% per month over a 60-month time frame.

Project	Health Benefits Included in Entry Fee Pricing	Specific Refund Policy
F	Supports the capital cost and provides reserve funds to ensure the continuation of the community. Residents have priority access to assisted living and 10 free days (not accumulative) per year in the health center as needed as well as priority access.	There is a 90-day probationary period during which the total amount of the entry fee is fully refundable upon termination of the contract. The entry fee is amortized at the rate of 1½% per month. In the event a resident requires permanent care in the health center and the entry fee has not fully amortized, then the resident will receive credit on their monthly bill of 1% per month of the entry fee until it is fully amortized.
G	Priority access to assisted living and skilled nursing with a 25% discount off of the street nursing rates.	Refundable based on straight line amortization for periods of forty or sixty months, depending on the circumstances.

Project	Health Benefits Included in Entry Fee Pricing	Specific Refund Policy
H	60 day lifetime benefit in assisted living or skilled nursing (semi-private room) and 10% off the current rate for any additional time in assisted living or nursing home. Residents in assisted living who have paid an entrance fee get the 60-day lifetime benefit for going into a semi-private nursing home room and 10% off the current rate in the nursing home after the 60 days have been used up.	If the Residency Agreement is canceled and move-out is within the first 50 months, then the refund is the entrance fee minus 2% for each full or partial month of residence and minus any withholding specified in the Residency Agreement. In the event of a resident's death during the first two years of residency, the return of the entrance fee to the estate is as follows: • Days 1-90 - 90% • Days 90-1st Yr. - 60% • During 2nd Yr. - 30%
I	Unlimited use of assisted living and skilled nursing facilities, including Alzheimer's care - at no additional fee, with the exception of two more meals.	100% refundable during first 90 days. 95% - 91st day through 1st year 90% - During 2nd year 85% - During 3rd ear 80% - During 4th year 75% - During 5th year and beyond - never less than 75% Refund is paid upon resale of the unit.

Project	Health Benefits Included in Entry Fee Pricing	Specific Refund Policy
J	Receive 30 days care in the health care center at no charge. Then have guaranteed access to health care services at a reduced rate.	Fully refundable during the first 90 days. After 90 days, declines to zero at 1.5% per month for 67 months.
K	Unlimited assisted living or health care services at no additional cost.	Fully refundable in the first 90 days - then the refundability declines to zero over a six-year time frame. In the event of death after the first 90 days, there is no refund.
L	Residents receive lifetime assurance of the availability of on-site unlimited assisted living services and skilled nursing services. These health care benefits are provided at no additional cost to the monthly service fee.	Entrance fee is fully refundable during first 90 days. After 90 days, refundability starts at 90% and declines by 1% per month for 7½ years to zero. There is also an 80% refundable plan. Upfront fees are 68% higher than the fully refundable pricing plan.

Project	Health Benefits Included in Entry Fee Pricing	Specific Refund Policy
M	Unlimited use of assisted living, skilled nursing and Alzheimer's care facilities at no additional monthly cost to the resident.	Two payment plans - 75% and 60%: 75% Plan 1st 90 days 100% 1st yr. 95% 2nd yr. 90% 3rd yr. 85% 4th yr. 80% 5th yr. & beyond 75% 60% Plan 1st 90 days 100% 1st yr. 95% 2nd yr. 90% 3rd yr. 80% 4th yr. 70% 5th yr. & beyond 60%
N	Unlimited nursing care at the same monthly fee - plus the cost of additional meals if more than one meal per day is required.	Three entrance fee plans - 0%, 50% and 95% refundable. 100% of the entrance fee will be refundable during the first five months. Then the refundable amount declines by 2% per month to the selected entrance fee plan amount.

Project	Health Benefits Included in Entry Fee Pricing	Specific Refund Policy
O	All levels of care, including acute care, physicians' and surgeons' services, skilled nursing care and personal care services, with no change in the monthly service fee. Residents are required to have Medicare coverage for both Part A and Part B.	100% refundable during first 90 days. After 90 days, the refundable amount declines by 1 2/3% per month. After 60 months, there is no refund. If there is a death after 90 days, the apartment reverts back to the community.
P	Upon acceptance by the Board of Directors, the community promises to care for its residents throughout the aging process through a contractual agreement. This continuity care contract guarantees that each resident will have a home for life. The accommodation fee is tied to the commitment of continuing care. The obligation stands regardless of whatever future medical or financial condition the resident may encounter.	The accommodation fee for independent apartment and assisted living is 100% refundable within the first 90 days and 75% refundable from 90 days to 180 days. There is no refund after 180 days.

These real world projects demonstrate the wide range of life care and refund options that exist today. Both of these important issues must strike a delicate balance between hedging financial risk and being market-responsive.

Actuarial Concerns and Issues

As mentioned earlier in this chapter, sponsors and owner/operators that are offering life care programs must recognize that they are in the health care insurance with a rather limited risk pool. There are companies that specialize in conducting actuarial studies specifically for senior living life care programs. Basically, they forecast the financial burdens and obligations out in time based on existing residents' morbidity and mortality. The primary question they attempt to answer is, ***"Will the cash flow of the community be properly realized out in time as the condition of the resident's change, with many of them requiring health care?"*** They then discount these future financial expectations back to present value (just like an employee pension fund does) to determine the surplus or deficit of this "fund".

Future Operating Expense Increases

Some sponsors and owner/operators do not realize that, with life care, their future operating expense profile can change considerably with the passage of time. That's because of the following sequence of events that typically take place with life care plans:

1. When a new community opens, most of the residents are obviously opting for independent living.
2. In order to fill the assisted living and nursing portion of the campus, it is common and appropriate to accept residents from the external market place.

3. These external marketplace residents do not pay a substantial independent living entry fee as they directly enter the health care operation on a fee-for-service basis.
4. With the passage of time, an increasing number of the original independent living residents experience health related problems that cause their permanent transfer to either assisted living or nursing.
5. When that happens and depending upon their specific life care plan, they may be paying far less for that assisted living unit or that health care bed than the so-called "street rates" typically charged to residents from the external market place.
6. What happens on a very subtle, but definite, basis is that the operating expenses of the assisted living or nursing operation continue to escalate with increasing life care residents paying less than "external" market street rates. The revenue from the health care operations starts to decline because, depending upon the specific life care plan, residents continue to pay essentially the same monthly service fee that they paid in independent living.

A good example of that would be the Type 'A' plan whereby the single resident who permanently moved from independent living to nursing would continue to pay the same rate that they paid in independent living plus the possibility of extra meal charges and annual inflation. There is, obviously, a huge differential between independent living monthly service fees and market nursing rates per patient-day.

With the passage of time, the census in the assisted living and nursing operation shifts from primarily residents from the external market paying street rates to life care residents moving from independent living to the health center. Surprisingly, a number of sponsors and owner/operators had not figured that future impact into their initial pro formas.

Couples – A Worst Case Financial Dilemma

There is a worst case situation for older senior consumers. This involves older couples either living at home or opting for many Type 'B' and Type 'C' life care contracts. The couple represents a worst case situation if one of the couple requires health care, while the other prefers to remain in their current residence (just like the situation they would face if they were still living at home). This dual living arrangement situation is a substantial new financial burden that this couple must face. With many Type 'A' life care plans, this financial exposure is reduced significantly. In a typical situation, if one spouse moves to nursing and the other remains in independent living, they still continue to pay only the independent living monthly service fee with perhaps a modest extra cost for the extra meals in health care. This is a major advantage and substantially reduces financial exposure due to declining health.

This consumer benefit, obviously, translates into the worst case situation for the sponsor and owner/operator who offers a substantial life care benefit (Type 'A'). This worst case potential financial burden for the sponsor or owner/operator typifies the need for a very substantial and credible actuarial analysis to accurately forecast the frequency of occurrence of these future expense/cash flow burdens.

There is another financial burden which a growing number of seniors are experiencing. Take the case of a widowed female who requires nursing care only temporarily (at least in her mind). She obviously wants to maintain her independent living unit because she feels she will be moving back there shortly. During the period that she retains the independent living unit, but also occupies a nursing bed, she must pay both the monthly service fee for independent living and the daily rate for nursing. This benefit coverage is typically not factored into many life care plans. This financial burden can become significant if her nursing home stay is longer than anticipated – which is a frequent occurrence.

There is a potential consumer disadvantage involving the Type 'A' life care plan. Consumers may well be paying a premium if they never have the need to access higher levels of care. But, just like purchasing long term care insurance, this is a financial planning initiative that many seniors accept comfortably.

Tax Benefits

The IRS allows for a medical tax deduction as defined in *IRS Publication 502 – Medical and Dental Expenses*. Basically, what this means is that a fairly significant portion of the initial entry fee and, in some cases, a continuing portion of the monthly service can be deducted.

The normal procedure for accessing this benefit is to receive an annual financial statement from the CCRC's finance department which indicates what percent of the initial entry fee can be legitimately deducted as a pre-paid medical expense. Keep in mind that it is a one-time event. However, the finance department may also offer a professional opinion and guidance regarding *annual* deductions of a portion of the monthly service fee for the same purpose. You must always encourage your residents to seek their own independent advice and counsel from their accountants regarding the position of management regarding taxes at a particular CCRC. There are other tax considerations which must be evaluated. These can best be articulated in your state by seeking appropriate third-party professional advice and counsel.

Call to Action

Creative life care plans are becoming more market-responsive. Obviously, to the senior consumer, it can offer a number of attractive safety nets. But you must approach this concept with extreme caution. That's because there are three trends involving today's seniors:

1. The average entry age of a new resident is increasing.
2. The average age of the existing population in a community is typically increasing.
3. Acuity levels for both assisted living and independent living residents appear to be increasing.

Since you are essentially getting into the health care insurance business, these trends can impact your potential future financial exposure.

Sophisticated senior living organizations are responding to these trends and challenges by offering modified life care contracts. These typically fall into the category of a Type 'B' life care plan. Limits are typically put on the number of days in health day, both cumulative and non-cumulative, and there may be other restrictions. Basically, sponsors and owner/operators are attempting to hedge their risks by putting a cap or a ceiling on their total financial exposure.

Properly conceived, these plans still offer significant benefits to the senior consumer. Access appropriate advice and counsel and consider these life care plans very seriously.

CHAPTER 44

BALANCING THE FINANCIAL OBJECTIVES OF BOTH SENIORS & SPONSORS

It's Time for Creative Financial Positioning

The time is now to narrow the financial gap between the desired expected outcomes for both CCRC sponsors and the senior consumer. Sponsors and owner/operators need new and sharpened market positioning that helps them sell the primary benefits they offer: *product, price and value.* But those benefits don't hit home until the senior realizes the true financial benefits of making the most difficult decision facing them for the rest of their lives. Sponsors are also seeking creative approaches to raising capital and realizing a reasonable return on investment while overcoming the senior's rational and irrational concerns about finances.

Seniors want to live out their final years with reasonable physical health, financial security and a comfortable living arrangement. They seek ambience and dignity while optimizing their independence. Many also want a living arrangement that avoids the increasing hidden costs and growing hassle of home ownership.

But what many seniors and their families fail to focus on is a sound financial plan - one that preserves their assets allowing them to leave a financial legacy. That's one of their success scorecards in life. Ideally, a sound financial plan should allow them leave a flexible, liquid estate in the *future* while offering them a *current* direct or indirect return on any up-front costs (entry fees, etc.) associated with their senior living "investment."

What the Senior Needs

A realistic definition of "affordable" senior living is elusive. To determine how much a senior can spend for senior living, we must first make two important qualifying income adjustments. Demographics provide *pre-tax income* needed for senior living, but seniors must pay for senior living in *after-tax dollars.* Ideally, seniors should not spend more than:

- 65 percent of their *after-tax disposable income* for monthly service fees for independent living.
- Approximately 80 percent for assisted living.

For seniors in independent living, the remaining 35 percent of after-tax income is used for other necessary expenses and for discretionary/lifestyle expenditures. Assisted living residents have a more limited lifestyle and discretionary spending options. Therefore, it is realistic to apply more of their after-tax income to monthly service fees. These affordability guidelines are before any consideration of spend-down of assets. Spend-down of assets is certainly a reality for many seniors.

The Price Sensitivity of Independent Living

Pricing is driven by the need to cover both capital costs and operating expenses. The sensitivity of these costs cuts both ways. At the low end of the monthly service fee pricing spectrum, it is difficult to significantly reduce capital costs enough to create true affordability. That's because a $5,000 per unit *decrease* in capital costs – using borrowed money at a 7 percent interest rate – saves residents only $350 per year, or $29 per month in interest cost. At the high end of the pricing spectrum, both capital costs and operating expenses come into play when trying to strike a balance between avoiding premium pricing and optimizing affordability, while still delivering acceptable operating profit margins.

Using a fancy term favored by economists, senior living pricing is very *inelastic.* This means that monthly service fees can't realistically drop below a specific economic floor in attempting to achieve true affordability. But moderate market price increases at the high end can lead to premium pricing and, possibly, wide swings in critical operating ratios and financial returns.

The Operator's Pricing Needs Quantified

Let's look at a typical newly developed 150-unit "market rate" independent living community:

- Operating expenses are $53 per resident-day (in 2009 dollars), or $1,610 per resident per month (at an average of 30.4 days per month).
- The total, all-in development cost is likely to be at least $200,000 per unit.
- The community is financed at 7.0 percent with 70 percent debt and 30 percent equity.

Note that all-in cost includes land, site development, bricks and mortar, and soft costs – everything to bring the project on-line and achieve a stabilized occupancy of 93 percent. Figure 23-1 in Chapter

23 summarized the typical all-in costs for a 150-unit independent living project, while Figure 26-1 in Chapter 26 showed a complete income statement.

These examples, which represent average costs in 2009 for a new, developed independent living community, require residents to pay monthly service fees of about $2,600 to $2,800. This fee covers operating expenses of $1,610 (57 percent of the fee), a debt service payment of about $1,000 (36 percent), and cash flow/entrepreneurial profit of $190 (7 percent). There is actually some additional profit realized from second person occupancy and miscellaneous income (beauty shop, extra meals, etc.) that is not included in this baseline pricing analysis.

Cracking the Affordability Nut By Reducing Pricing

So, if you'd like to offer a more affordable senior living community in your market area, you must first answer this critical question: ***Where can you realistically cut costs? And by how much?*** Let's take a closer look at capital costs and operating costs.

Capital Costs – Operating expenses are difficult to reduce, so most sponsors initially focus on capital costs. If you could reduce capital costs and the resulting debt service payments per unit by as much as *20 percent* or $40,000, you would reduce the required monthly service fees by only $230 per unit per month, or about 8 percent - from $2,800 per month to $2,570 per month. That's because debt service costs are only about 36 percent of your monthly service fee requirements. Therefore, it's not easy to achieve significant affordability by tightening the reins on just capital costs or interest rates. In fact, someone could *give* you the land and discount the cost of the building, and you still might have a significant affordability challenge!

One-time entry fee pricing models can help offset some of the capital costs that need to be recovered. However, entry fees won't significantly reduce ongoing monthly service fees.

Operating Costs – Seniors in independent living and CCRCs, regardless of their economic position, need the same basics: meal service, housekeeping, comprehensive shelter services, high quality of care and, frequently, significant assistance with activities of daily living. If seniors don't need or want these services, they would live happily in their own homes.

Whether for-profit or not-for-profit, sponsors and owners find it difficult to deliver these basic services for less than $42 to $52 per resident-day, or $1,275 to $1,580 per month for independent living. Assisted living operating costs can be as high as $90+ per resident-day. *Operating costs are the economic affordability nut that must be cracked.*

Action to Take

Forget the well-intended hype and face up to the affordability challenge with a realistic understanding of your numbers. There are at least three possible outcomes:

1. You may discover that your income-qualified market is not as deep as originally perceived.
2. Your operations can be enhanced to expand affordability.

3. If you're a not-for-profit, you might more realistically define your mission and expand your charitable content.

The challenges are significant – but the opportunities are huge.

Creating a Win-Win Financial Plan

Sponsor and consumer desired outcomes really come together when we can position our senior living options as a prudent and necessary financial planning decision. There are at least 25 senior living personal financial and investment positioning strategies. Here are six:

1. Offering hassle-free living that avoids the increasing hidden costs and growing complexities of home ownership for seniors over age 75. The key challenges these seniors face are increasing real estate taxes, complicated home maintenance and upkeep, and escalating insurance and energy costs. A common concern is the loss of future home value appreciation when opting for senior living. But this financial concern is usually more than offset by the more controlled total cost of senior living, while seniors realize the returns by investing their liquidated home equity. Chapters 34 through 38 address this important concept.

2. Hedging many of the risks of runaway health care service delivery costs by accessing reliable, high quality services on an as-needed basis within a senior living campus. This is a high value alternative to premature nursing home admissions, ineffective and costly home health services or the delaying of necessary preventive or corrective health care initiatives.

CCRCs offering various levels of guaranteed life care can deal with this consumer concern very effectively. But remember, the actuarially driven financial risks to the offering life care sponsor can be significant.

3. Recognizing that a senior's home equity is really at the core of most senior's financial planning resources. Progressive communities are showing seniors how to put their liquidated home equity to work – while preserving most of the cash value of this asset plus their current savings portfolio principal as a *future legacy* to their estate. If you charge up-front fees, you should also show a direct or indirect return on the senior's investment.

4. Structuring prudent spend-down plans may be necessary for some seniors in order to private pay for desired services that maximize independence and quality of life. Over 70 percent of the patient-days in institutionalized nursing homes are Medicaid reimbursed because many of the patients have spent down their assets at a much faster pace than is really necessary with today's senior living options. You should show seniors how to avoid unnecessary spend-down, while offering moderate income seniors reasonable approaches to prudently planned spend-down that will not leave them destitute within the period of their remaining expected life.

5. Tax shelters and financial arbitrage are not just for high rollers or sophisticated Wall Street investors. Advise seniors that, under specific conditions, they can deduct a significant portion of the monthly service fees and entrance fees paid to the community as a medical tax deduction.

Arbitrage is a fancy term sometimes used to describe realizing the benefits of the alternative cost of money. Simply stated, a for-profit sponsor might have to borrow money at 7 to 8 percent while a senior is having to accept a 2 to 3 percent investment return on a portion of their savings portfolio. Would you be willing to give the senior 4 or 5 percent *credit* for the use of some of their money? You both win. This is the essence of a new, innovative win-win pricing strategy being developed. The senior has to take less money into taxable income each year because you are crediting them with a slightly lower monthly service fee. The for-profit sponsor saves about 2 percent on the cost of the capital they would otherwise have to borrow. That can result in hundreds of thousands of dollars in additional annual cash flow. More on this in Chapter 42.

6. Creative pricing by some sponsors are showing seniors how to put their home equity to work now. As stated earlier, preserving much of their home equity proceeds and their current savings portfolio value as a legacy to their estate is a major objective for many seniors. Let's face it, a $200,000 entry fee that declines in refundability by 1.5 percent per month results in cash spend-down of $3,000 per month or $36,000 per year. That's in addition to the monthly service fee they're paying. Sure, they may be getting tangible benefits for that cost, but you've got to go the extra mile to clearly communicate those benefits. If you think you have trouble really understanding and explaining your entry fee actuarial analysis, imagine how an 80 year old senior must feel!

Finally, do you think you could consistently make good on this offer: ***"Mrs. Jones, what if you could live here at The Gardens at Westridge for the same or less than your current cost of living –***

and you can still leave most of your current savings portfolio and the proceeds from the sale of your home to your children? That's because we can provide you with the kind of flexible living arrangements and services for no more than your current cost of living."

And for communities that charge an entry fee: ***"Mrs. Jones, the largely refundable entry fee that you'll be paying will usually be no more than the net proceeds from the sale of your home. That means you can afford to live at The Gardens at Westridge and still leave most of your home sale proceeds (90 percent entry fee refund) and the principal amount of your current savings portfolio as a very important legacy to your family."***

A word of caution: Some of today's "traditional pricing" may become obsolete as our industry focuses on more resident-centered financial strategies.

Call to Action

It's time to take a new look at an old problem. Most of us try to prudently hedge future lifetime risks. We have wills, trusts and life insurance and sometimes even long-term care insurance. We try to make sure that we have enough retirement income to live a normal lifestyle. But after age 75, many seniors lifestyle is far from normal – and surprisingly little specific thought is frequently given to preserving an estate accumulated over a lifetime of conservatism. The sobering reality is that there can be a large gap between a comfortable and financially responsible retirement and the final reading of the will. Many older seniors resist the realities of planning for the future. Astute senior living sponsors can provide significant help while sharpening the favorable market positioning of their senior living community.

A senior's final years should never be seriously compromised in order to just maximize the financial aspects of their estate. We have an opportunity and an obligation to show seniors how that final phase of life can be executed as an optimum, financially responsible plan.

So, with that in mind, here's a look at a new and necessary market positioning platform.

21ST CENTURY SENIOR LIVING MARKET POSITIONING

"Considering senior living can be a prudent, practical and necessary personal financial planning imperative — just like health insurance, life insurance and estate planning."

Moore Diversified Services, Inc.

Chapters 5 through 7 deal with this important issue in more detail.

SECTION SEVEN

A Look Into

The Future

CHAPTER 45

BUILD VS. BUY

The Implications for Future Growth

Expanding senior living holdings frequently comes down to two options; build a new community or buy an existing one. It sounds like a simple decision, but in today's environment it is actually very complex.

Build Option – From a qualitative perspective, you would have the opportunity to create a new state-of-the-art senior living design, possibly pick an optimum site and probably avoid a number of situation-driven issues that could exist with the purchase of an existing property. However, the barriers to entry involving overall zoning and site approvals could stretch the development schedule and cost significantly. You could also face the unavoidable escalation in hard and soft costs for the project. And it could take up to 30 months before the realization of stabilized occupancy and optimum cash flow.

Buy Option – Buying an existing property involves the advantages of immediate cash flow and investment returns. Barriers to entry issues involving new project approvals are avoided.[1] Essentially, ***"what you see is what you get"***. The performance profile of the existing project should be obvious from a detailed review of current occupancy and financial operations and the results of other due diligence efforts.

[1]Be sure that the previous owner did not enjoy some "grandfathered" approval exceptions that you might not be allowed to inherit.

There are some challenges. Would the acquisition be yesterday's product that is not currently state-of-the-art? New or existing competitors might be offering a more market-responsive product. You could experience undetected physical plant flaws, deferred maintenance and operational problems that were not detected during your due diligence process.

Escalating senior living construction and land costs have created some very complex quantitative issues; turning the build versus buy decision into a hot debate. For example, total all-in costs (construction, development, and financing) that used to average about $120,000 to $150,000 per unit can now easily be in the $180,000 to over $200,000 per unit range.

The key financial metric for decision making purposes is usually the project's Internal Rate of Return (IRR) which basically answers the question, ***"what will be the average annual return on a cash investment over a five-year holding period with an assumed sale at the end of the fifth year?"*** This analysis typically looks at the unleveraged (debt-free) cash flows from each year's performance and the net cash flow resulting from the assumed sale. These annual cash flows are then discounted back to the present value to determine the average annual investment returns.

The IRR analysis for the buy option is relatively simple – it would compute the IRR for five full years of projected stabilized property performance. The build scenario is more complex because there would be at least two years of construction and fill up, leaving only three years of stabilized performance for a five year "holding period". You could extend your time horizon to seven years; two years of fill-up and five full years of stabilized operations.

Figure 45-1 summarizes key qualitative issues. Figure 45-2 is an MDS template/dashboard that demonstrates the evaluation of a typical real world situation that might be available in 2009 and beyond.[1] Key input variables assumed are:

- Acquisition Cost — $180,000 per unit
- Approximate All-In Cost for New Independent Living Development — $200,000 per unit

FIGURE 45-1
BUILD VS. BUY – QUALITATIVE ISSUES

	Pros	Cons
I. Build	• Deliver State-of-the-Art Design • Optimize Site Selection Alternatives • Can Avoid Situation-Driven Issues	• Up to 30 Months Before Realizing Optimum Cash Flow • Barriers to Entry May Be Significant • Risk of Growth of All-In Costs
II. Buy	• "What You See is What You Get" • Immediate Cash Flow and Investment Returns • Avoid Barriers to Entry Issues • Market-Responsiveness is Obvious/Proven • All-In Cost Defined	• Buying Yesterday's Product? • New/Emerging Competitors Might be More Market-Responsive • Premium Priced Acquisition Costs • Risk of Undetected Physical Plant or Operation Flaws

Moore Diversified Services, Inc.

[1]For more information on the availability of these templates, visit www.m-d-s.com.

FIGURE 45-2

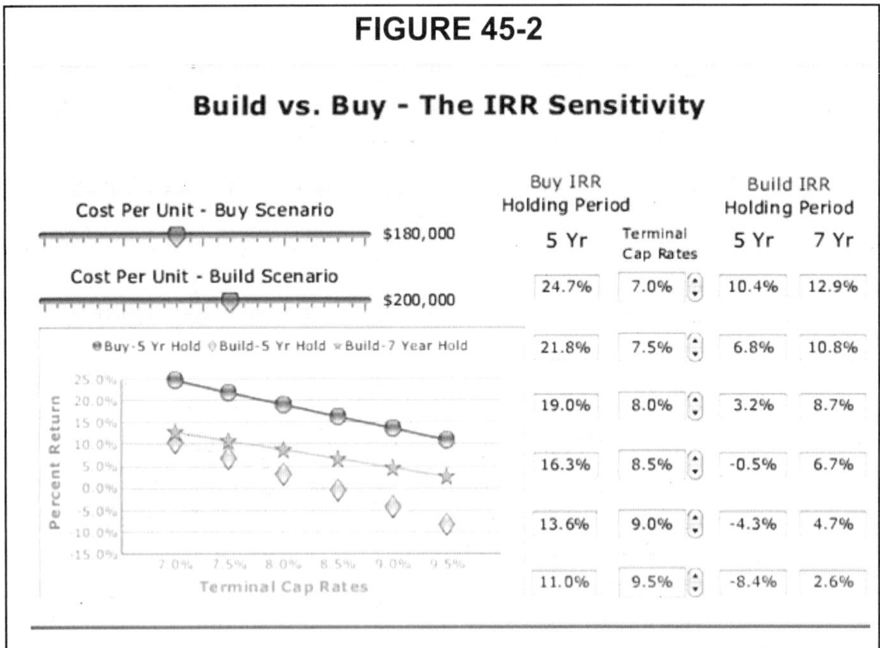

Buy IRR Holding Period 5 Yr	Terminal Cap Rates	Build IRR Holding Period 5 Yr	Build IRR Holding Period 7 Yr
24.7%	7.0%	10.4%	12.9%
21.8%	7.5%	6.8%	10.8%
19.0%	8.0%	3.2%	8.7%
16.3%	8.5%	-0.5%	6.7%
13.6%	9.0%	-4.3%	4.7%
11.0%	9.5%	-8.4%	2.6%

Call to Action

The build vs. buy decision involves careful consideration to <u>both</u> qualitative and quantitative issues. Don't rationalize or oversimplify your decision criteria.

Keep in mind that the possible percent returns illustrated in Figure 45-2 assume you have used realistic inputs when conducting your analysis. Ideally there should be a favorable spread in capitalization rates; initial *acquisition* cap rates should be 1.0 percent to 1.5 percent lower than *terminal* (assumed future sale cap rates).

CHAPTER 46

NEXT GENERATION PRODUCTS FOR SENIOR LIVING

Avoiding Market Myopia

"*Product Life Cycle*" and *"New and Improved Next Generation Products*" are common business buzzwords. Most industries place a high priority on creative change; attempting to avoid *market myopia* – a blurred vision of the future. They respond to changing consumer demographics and psychographics by frequently altering their strategies over time. Automobiles have new styling changes almost every year and a major redesign every three to four years. Clothes don't wear out – they just go out of style very quickly! New and improved food products are constantly changing – quick preparation, low fat, low carb, organic, etc.. Hotel and restaurant companies have developed multiple products offering a variety of service offerings and price points. It's true, some industries resisted market-driven change and stayed with their original business model. Railroads remained just that – railroads. 20/20 hindsight indicates they should have positioned themselves as being in the "transportation business". Traditional airlines are being hammered by no frills, low cost start-ups who deliver high value and customer satisfaction. And most are still profitable even in this current era of escalating fuel and labor costs.

In the short-run, responding to the local competition and satisfying our existing residents is obviously very important. But increased strategic focus needs to be on the changing profile of the future senior resident.

Today's 80-year-old widow was in her 30's and 40's during the Vietnam War era, her mid to late 60's during the economic boom of the mid-1990s and in her 70's when the high tech bubble burst leading to an economic recession. Chapter 4 provided an expanded background on the lifetime "birthmarks" of today's 80-year-old senior; creating a significantly different mindset today. Senior living and health care providers can no longer simply say, ***"Welcome to our community and enjoy our definition of the status quo."*** That's because tomorrow's senior living marketing opportunities no longer consist of "the usual prospects". Future residents will be more outspoken and demanding – raising the bar of expectations and outcomes – while they clearly articulate their wants and needs.

A word of caution: Don't get mislead by the current favorable opinions expressed by your *existing residents*. In some respects, they may not necessarily reflect the changing mindset of your *future resident.*

Some industry leaders are considering some new product and service innovations; they are actually addressing four important market-driven issues and potential sales objections. These are:

1. Many Seniors Complain About the Hassle of Current Homeownership and Ongoing Maintenance – They seek their definition of downsizing and are willing to explore alternative living arrangements.

2. The "I'm Not Ready Yet" Syndrome – For many seniors, this means they're not yet ready to accept service intensive independent living. They want choice and flexibility.

3. Consumer Psychographics and Value Perceptions are Changing – Senior consumers have sharpened their definition of value which typically involves product, price, choice and service options.

4. Seniors Want Financially Sound Options to Convert Their Pent-Up Home Equity – Industry leaders are sharpening their approach to better access a huge capital source of over $1.2 trillion. That's the pent-up home equity of today's seniors. Many seniors are now skeptical about making stock market investments and are currently struggling to get a 3 percent to 4 percent after-tax return on their cash or near cash savings. Meanwhile, owner/operator's current cost of debt capital is approaching a range of approximately 6 to 8 percent. Many owner/operators are increasingly offering refundable entry fees to put home equity to work while lowering monthly service fees which seniors must pay with after-tax income.

Let's look at some insights into some of the new market-driven product and pricing strategies that are being implemented. Some examples include:

1. New living unit designs are changing as today's (and tomorrow's) consumer is looking for moderately larger living units. In the past five years, assisted living units have made the transition from 350 s.f. studios to modest sized 450 s.f. to 550 s.f. one-bedroom units. In the past, independent living one-bedroom units had approximately 650 s.f. of livable area and two-bedroom units were approximately 900 s.f. Now these living areas are creeping upwards by at least 100 s.f. to 150 s.f. Room designs are being optimized with amenities such as walk-in closets and more elaborate master baths. The demand for a two-bedroom unit has changed the overall product mix from approximately 30 percent two-bedroom units to at least 60 percent for that unit type.

2. Senior apartments are a relatively new product that are responding to the "I'm not ready yet" sales objection. They look a lot like independent living except they do not offer an extensive mandatory service package such as meals and housekeeping. The public spaces are well appointed, but on a smaller scale. Over the past two years, this product has captured more than a 25 percent share of new construction while offering both low/moderate income and market rate pricing models. Refer to Chapter 15 for more details.

3. Nursing homes are entering a new era. Physical plants that have been operating with semi-private accommodations for 30 to 40 years are experiencing occupancy problems. That's because moderate acuity private pay residents are now opting for assisted living while those with high acuity care needs seek out newer, private occupancy nursing accommodations.

Some operators are offering both assisted living and nursing using integrated, yet separated, synergistic strategies. One operator that also offers adult day care calls this product a "small market CCRC".

4. Fee-Simple condominium ownership or cooperative investment offer yet another shift in the senior living product life cycle. Properly conceived "ownership" sales of living units can offer a seamless conversion of significant pent-up home equity.

Sponsors and owner/operators are always seeking innovative approaches to financing senior living projects – while being market-responsive and reasonably affordable. Two pricing techniques that have met with selective success are the selling of independent living units as condominiums or cooperatives. In the condo concept of senior housing, the senior consumer takes a fee-simple title to their unit, much like owning a single family home. With the co-op concept, the senior consumer is the owner of a stock in an undivided share of a qualified housing co-op and is treated in a manner similar to that of a fee-simple owner of a condo.

The two most common market conditions for considering the condo or co-op pricing structure are: 1) in high cost markets where sponsors and owner/operators would have to charge a relatively high upfront or monthly service fee in order to be financially viable; or 2) where these same high cost markets also yield relatively high home value appreciation and resulting net equity upon the sale of a senior's home. It is very important that the average net home equities be similar in magnitude (or greater) when compared to the required condo or co-op pricing being offered.

For the senior consumer, the co-op or condo ownership concept offers some basic tax advantages. Sponsors and consumers should always consult with their tax advisors for tax law definitions and changes. There are significant economic and psychological benefits of "ownership" for the senior who saved for years for "their piece of the rock."[1] They can now trade part of that investment for an optimum living arrangement – with the strong possibility of future appreciation of this asset.

[1]For the younger reader, this used to be the Prudential Insurance Company's primary advertising theme.

Two Primary Challenges and Concerns

While the condo and co-op pricing concept may appear to be very favorable considering the senior's long-term, asset-oriented mindset, there are two major challenges that must be overcome:

- Concerns about liquidity and future value. Many older seniors want *optimum estate liquidity* – part of the idea of getting their affairs in order.
- Others are somewhat skeptical of the probable success of a start-up community and wonder about their ability to resell their unit at an appreciated value.

These concerns are also influenced by advice provided by families, professional advisors and other fiduciaries.

Some are offering two innovative models:

- Full-service condominiums offering extensive services and a full continuum of living arrangements. The condos are owned fee-simple by the residents while the health related and other service components are owned by a third-party investor or the owner/operator.
- Condominiums with a resident services component (dining, etc.) but which do not offer on-campus assisted living, Alzheimer's or nursing. These types of services can be accessed through facilitated home care. Condominiums offer seniors hassle-free ownership and maintenance along with the potential for future appreciation in value.

CCRCs requiring upfront entry fees are escalating in price. Owner/operators are increasing the level of entry fee refundability upon resident death or move-out in response to changing consumer choice and psychographics.

These are just a sampling of innovative product offerings as senior living progresses through its life cycle. There will be many more in the future.

Implement a Flash Value Strategy

For years, I've worked with a concept called *flash value*. Flash value is a fairly obscure, but surprisingly simple, way of quantifying and thereby maximizing perceived value in the eyes of the consumer. Flash value as a quantitative index is what the consumer *thinks* an item or service costs divided by your *actual* cost.

Through consumer testing (focus groups, etc.) you can identify a menu of design characteristics or services that exhibit a positive "flash value index" of at least 2:1. This means that the consumer *thinks* the item is worth at least twice as much as your actual cost. Typical high flash value items in seniors housing include larger units, extensive high quality millwork, walk-in closets, attractive public spaces, recessed solid core living unit entry doors, incandescent vs. fluorescent lighting, wall coverings and artwork, interesting roof lines, and "breaks" in exterior elevations. The list could go on, but the ideal outcome is for senior prospects and their family to comment, ***"This place sure seems to offer a lot for the money!"***

Some of these ideas obviously work best with newly designed communities. But don't overlook the potential to implement creative change in existing communities. Remember, we have average annual resident turnover of about 32 percent in independent living and over 50 percent in assisted living.

Statistically, we are essentially recycling our independent and assisted living resident population every two to three years. The lost opportunity cost of an older vacant independent living unit being offered at $1,900 per month is approximately $1,500 per month or $18,000 per year (see Chapter 31). A 150-unit community at 90 versus 93 percent occupancy has 15 vacant units or a total annual opportunity cost of $270,000.

Call to Action

The best call to action motivation for planning for the future came from an 85-year-old senior. He told me,

"Jim, the future is not what it used to be . . . but if you can see the future, you can get there before it happens."

It's time for a creative, market-driven renaissance for many communities. Like most industries, we really need to project our thinking into the future and attempt to answer this difficult question: ***"If we knew then (2000 to 2006) what we know now (2009) . . . would my community look different?"*** The time to act is now.

CHAPTER 47

COMMUNITY OF CHOICE OR A PRICE SENSITIVE COMMODITY?

The Ultimate Market Positioning Challenge

In my consulting activities, I try to live in as many senior living communities as possible. So far I've had short stays in over 130 of them. As I was having dinner one evening with a distinguished gentleman, he said, "***You know, I was somebody once.***" The lady at the next table chimed in, ***"The management and young people who work here are just delightful -- but they really don't understand us."*** This community seemed to have all of the right services and amenities. The staff knew all the residents on a first name basis. But, there was something missing and that was a true understanding of each resident's inner emotional needs. We all recognize the importance of *demographics,* but now we must also focus on the changing *psychographics* of seniors. Chapter 4 provided expanded details on the changing mindset of today's seniors.

Changing Expectations

A new generation of seniors is gradually emerging that will expect much more from our senior living communities. Today's typical prospect is an 80-year-old senior who was born during the Great Depression and grew up in the World War II time frame. By the time of the Vietnam War and the rebellions of the 1960s, they were in their 40s. They reached mid-life in the 1970s as members of the *"The Establishment,"* and many were approaching retirement during the boom/bust cycles of the 1980s and 1990s.

Their lifespan has created a series of birthmarks, making many of today's seniors more demanding, less complacent and more pragmatic in their continuing search for self-fulfillment and their definition of value. The men will have experienced Corporate America's "gray flannel suit era" including the transition from a period of conformity to one that emphasized entrepreneurial individualism and autonomy. Females, who were primarily homemakers, joined the outside workforce in surprising numbers, making them less passive, more worldly and less likely to settle for someone else's definition of the status quo.

There is an evolving disconnect between the situation-driven focus of many sponsors and owner/operators and what it takes to be truly market-responsive for this new breed of seniors. Sponsors and owner/operators necessarily focus on covering real estate costs and operating expenses; while delivering their definition of business success, acceptable operating profit margins and cash flow after debt service. These are certainly very important financial fundamentals. But there is an equally important question to address: ***"In the future, do I want to be perceived as offering a price-sensitive commodity or a unique value-enhanced community of choice?"*** In many cases, the deciding factor is the senior consumer's definition of good value.

Seniors Do Buy Value

Throughout life, seniors have made most of their purchase decisions by balancing affordability, choice and their perception of value. After a lifetime of financial conservatism, many seniors are now in a position to focus primarily on choice and value. In fact, many have been making value choices for the better part of their lives. They don't always opt for the lowest price commodity. Many buy Buicks and Cadillacs – not Chevrolets. They dine at the nicer restaurants and buy clothes by brand names at the better department stores – not necessarily Kmart or Sears. They travel extensively.

Sophisticated product and service providers are constantly selling seniors on value and, where appropriate, quality of life. Yet, as many seniors face the biggest, most important decision of the rest of their life – senior living options – we find that we haven't done a very good job of either creating unusual value or effectively telling our value story.

The Search for Self-Fulfillment

Directly or indirectly seniors are on a constant search for self-fulfillment. This search involves five very important quality of life attributes:

1. Experiences/adventures/nostalgia.
2. Comfort/peace of mind.
3. Individual recognition.
4. Socialization and intellectual stimulation.
5. Self-expression and fulfillment.

Astute sponsors know that the real issue is not just resident satisfaction, it's quality of life leading to exceptional value. Ask yourself this question, ***"What would I want out of the last six to ten years of my life?"*** Tough question, isn't it? If you're having trouble projecting yourself into the future, ask what would you want your parents to benefit from in the later years of their life.

Challenges and Opportunities

The primary obstacles to improving the perceived value of your community will be creativity and, frequently, cost. Making major improvements in the quality of life discipline could require increased staff time and new, innovative program strategies. This will obviously increase operating expenses. But the long-run benefits realized in distinguishing a community of choice from a look-a-like price sensitive commodity can be significant. The good news is that you can actually recover most of the additional costs you incur in delivering unique value. In fact, premium pricing and cost recovery by delivering enhanced value is the essence of avoiding the price sensitivity community syndrome. Will it be easy? Certainly not. Chapter 48 addresses a ten point program for creating and selling unique senior living value.

Today's Senior is a "Distinguished Achiever"

If one were able to inventory and make use of the aggregate knowledge, experience and resources that exist with the residents in a typical senior living community, the results would be staggering. A senior's unique capabilities, intellect and inner drives that were developed over a lifetime of productive work and community contribution suddenly do not fade away as they "retire" and move into senior living communities. But sadly, in many cases, these attributes are inadvertently suppressed – never surfacing again during the autumn years of their lives.

Call to Action

Senior living communities have a tremendous opportunity (and responsibility) to provide a truly stimulating lifestyle for the senior. Remember, today's seniors are not just survivors or older Americans – they truly are our most *Distinguished Achievers!*

CHAPTER 48

CREATING A COMMUNITY OF CHOICE

Ten Steps to Avoid Becoming a "Price-Sensitive Commodity"

Chapter 47 discussed the benefits and rationale for creating a senior living *community of choice*. The less desirable alternative was to be perceived as yet another *price-sensitive commodity* – just like your competitors. A true community of choice must deliver at least three superior benefits:

1. Provide an attractive physical plant.
2. Offer flexible value-enhanced services.
3. Deliver an extraordinary quality of life experience.

In return, you should enjoy increased resident satisfaction leading to higher occupancies, optimum value-based pricing and improved financial operating margins.

Quality of Life Defined

Defining quality of life is, at best, an elusive concept. Most of us are on a constant search for self fulfillment. And residents of senior living communities have more limited options and a shorter lifespan in order to achieve this lofty objective. In Chapter 47, I indicated that I've lived briefly in over 130 independent and assisted living communities. While the typical stay is only several days, I always mingle and dine with the residents. I try to gain a deeper understanding of their real life situation. Seniors have stories to tell involving a lifetime of distinguished achievements. They want to share these accomplishments with anyone who will patiently listen. Many also have untapped artistic and intellectual talents that, properly structured, would significantly enhance their life satisfaction. Many ladies want you to sit and hold hands while some of the men want to reminisce about war and workplace battles won and lost. The staff hugs them, calls them by their first names and monitors their well-being. But as an 85-year-old lady told me at dinner one evening, ***"I just want to talk to someone from the outside world who is really interested in what I have to say".***

Ten Steps Toward Creating a Community of Choice

Providing a value-enhanced community of choice won't be easy and it can get moderately expensive; but the payoff can be significant. As a sponsor or owner/operator, you must first create unmistakable value. Here is a ten point program for starting down this difficult, but highly rewarding, path:

1. **Give your community a modest make-over**. Optimize first impressions of your community in areas such as signage, landscaping, building exteriors, rejuvenation of interior public spaces, and improvements to individual living units. The cost will vary depending upon the age of your community. The cost recovery may not be that significant. Refer to Chapter 19 for strategies to address cost recovery of campus improvements.

2. Zero-base your existing operations. A true community of choice must be able to report a secure financial foundation to its residents. Efficient operations should deliver financial ratios consistent with recognized industry benchmarks.

3. Get inside the minds of your residents. First, talk to your residents, both individually and in small groups, to get their practical ideas on how to enhance value and improve their quality of life. Next, sample some of your residents' individual backgrounds. Determine how you could make each of their *individual* lives more meaningful.

4. Walk in your residents' shoes. Project yourself into the future thirty or forty years and ask the defining question, ***"What would I really want out of life at age 80?"*** It's safe to say your answer might be, "not exactly what I find in my community today." Explore this hypothetical further by considering what would be acceptable (and necessary) changes in areas such as living arrangements, services, affordability, value, quality of life, financial peace of mind, and staff responsiveness. Use these items as a punch list to identify your community's short comings.

5. Focus more activities on your residents' individual daily life. Quality of life attributes that are really important to Seniors include; adventures, nostalgia, new experiences, individual recognition, intellectual stimulation, self expression, and the overall feeling of self-fulfillment. If each resident was your Mom, what would you do differently? How would you want her to spend her day?

6. Promote health and wellness activities. Don't overdo it with highly restrictive, structured programs. Provide them with practical advice, flexible programmatic content, and a realistic expectation of favorable outcomes. Where possible, place a high priority on supporting and enhancing individual quality of life rather than an excessively heavy focus on regimented and institutional medical routines.

7. Leverage, motivate and train human resources. After determining how to enhance quality of life on your campus, you must encourage your staff to take ownership into this changed philosophy and new initiatives.

8. Revisit structured volunteerism. It's time to revisit volunteerism. While successful volunteerism exists on some campuses, it has not worked for many others. The reasons are two fold; lack of a structured master plan and inconsistent performance on the part of non-family volunteers. The new era of volunteerism involving specific family members may well be the answer. These individuals are more committed stakeholders who have a vested interest in their loved one at the community. Using their time and talents in an organized and carefully planned manner can result in not only enhanced quality of life for their loved one, but their efforts could possibly impact the lives of many other residents. Also consider using some of your talented residents as volunteers. Helping others could well enhance their quality of life.

9. Every resident should have an advocate. Some progressive sponsors have assigned a specific staff member to act as a "personal advocate" to look after the unique needs and interests of each individual resident on an ongoing basis.

10. Develop a "You talked, we listened" market positioning strategy. Your external market positioning could be: *"The Gardens at Westridge – The Community of Choice, Anytown, USA"*. Develop a creative communications campaign with central themes focused on the first seven steps.

Figure 48-1 recaps these ten steps while Figure 48-2 identifies ten favorable objectives and expected outcomes for your residents.

FIGURE 48-1
CREATING COMMUNITIES OF CHOICE
Ten Steps To Avoid Becoming A Price-Sensitive Commodity

1. **Give your community a modest make-over.**
2. **Zero-base your existing operations.**
3. **Get inside the minds of your residents.**
4. **Walk in your resident's shoes.**
5. **Focus more activities on your residents' individual daily life.**
6. **Promote health and wellness activities.**
7. **Leverage, motivate and train human resources.**
8. **Revisit structured volunteerism.**
9. **Every resident should have an advocate.**
10. **Develop a "You talked, We listened" market positioning strategy.**

Moore Diversified Services, Inc.

FIGURE 48-2
THE OPTIMUM SENIOR LIVING EXPERIENCE
Ten Desirable Expected Outcomes For Residents

1. **Experiences/Adventure/Nostalgia**
2. **Comfort/Peace of Mind**
3. **Affordability and Financial Security**
4. **Quality and Value**
5. **Optimize Independence**
6. **Health Maintenance**
7. **Socialization**
8. **Individual Recognition**
9. **Intellectual Stimulation**
10. **Self-Expression and Fulfillment**

Moore Diversified Services, Inc.

Call to Action

For senior's, time is not simply money – it's their remaining life! As their time horizons shorten, seniors certainly think about leisure activities. But many place an even higher value on the quality of the remaining time in their lives. This should be your central focus when developing your community of choice strategy.

The senior living industry has a tremendous challenge, opportunity, and responsibility to enrich the lives of hundreds of thousands of seniors living out their final years in retirement communities. Many are experiencing the peak of their social, financial, and health challenges. The pay-off for residents will be the enhancement of their individual quality of life. And sponsors will be taking that big step toward becoming that uniquely desirable community of choice.

CHAPTER 49

PLAN YOUR FUTURE EXIT STRATEGY NOW

Recent Business Trends May Involve Selling Out

Whether flying at 39,000 feet or attending a sold-out Broadway show, everybody needs to think about a successful exit strategy. It brings peace of mind – and, occasionally, survival – especially to senior living sponsors and owner/operators. Most of us have wills, estate plans, and life insurance; all important parts of a personal exit strategy. This certainly doesn't mean we plan on exiting life any time soon, but we realize it's sensible to be ready for anything. Most sponsors and owner/operators are seasoned professionals. So the issues addressed in this chapter may appear quite basic. If so, consider them an organized punch list of things you may already know.

Most owner/operators say they don't intend to sell, they plan to ride out various business cycles and they're not about to leave the senior living industry. Not-for-profit sponsors often assure me they've been serving seniors for many years, and plan to be around for many more.

But developing a sound exit strategy doesn't necessarily mean you're actually planning to get out of the senior living business. It means you think it's prudent to evaluate your individual project or portfolio of properties to determine their true value and overall competitiveness, while identifying any potential weaknesses. Picture grooming your assets to get a very favorable response from a hypothetical buyer; it's the acid test for financial viability and the best insurance for survival, success and profitability.

Anticipate Sale Negotiations

Start by putting yourself in the shoes of a pragmatic buyer or cautious, risk averse lender. Factor in reality by answering the five questions outlined in Figure 49-1. Assume those questions or issues might come up during buyer-seller negotiations. Realistically, consider what would surface as your organization's weaknesses, potential problems or serious discrepancies? Above all, don't rationalize.

FIGURE 49-1
FIVE NEGOTIATION TABLE STRATEGIES TO ADDRESS[1]

1. **How competitive would an objective third-party perceive your campus to be in two time frames: now, and over the next five years?**
2. **If a knowledgeable observer was scoring you and your competition on scales of 1 to 10 for product, service, price, and value, how would you measure up?**
3. **If you were on the other side of the negotiating table and about to purchase your community, what concerns would you have?**
4. **As a potential buyer of your community, are there any flaws or shortcomings that would cause you to reduce your price?**
5. **Based on your answers to the first four questions, what should *you* change over the next 18 months?**

[1] For either individual communities or a consolidated portfolio.

Moore Diversified Services, Inc.

Some for-profits feel that their shortcomings are either not really that significant and they will certainly be understood and accepted in the marketplace. Not-for-profits frequently think their heritage and faith-based humanitarian goals more than compensate for any flaws in their product, price and value. Both industry sectors could be in for major wake-up calls as product life cycles shorten, consumers become more demanding and savvy competitors (with sound exit strategies) sharpen their operations and market-responsiveness. Like many maturing industries, senior living could evolve to a price-sensitive commodity.

Current market conditions in 2009 are somewhat clouded. Interest rates have moderated in recent years and capitalization rates that largely determine value dropped to their lowest levels on record in 2006 and the first half of 2007. Now they are creeping up again. Barriers to entry for new projects are high in most markets. Obtaining approvals are difficult and development costs for new competitive projects have increased dramatically. As a result, there has been a significant reduction in new development of senior living projects in the last five years. But remember these favorable conditions may change.

It's easy to fall in love with your real estate. Don't do it. Make objective business decisions for both the short-run and long-run. From a personal planning owner/operator perspective, consider these four issues: 1) your age, 2) prudent estate planning, 3) the tax impact of a sale and 4) carefully consider what you would do with the after-tax cash proceeds from a sale.

It is also possible to stay in the business but still cash in on a major portion of your valuable assets. With a *sale/manage-back* arrangement you sell your *real estate* but continue to manage the *business* while collecting a management fee of approximately 5 percent of gross revenues. With a *sale/lease-back* you continue to operate the property and also control the income statement; enjoying the cash flow after paying operating expenses and an agreed-to lease fee. Remember selling is not just for the big players. Small one-off deals are sometimes looked at differently by large sophisticated buyers. However, in 2009 and beyond, you might just be at the right place at the right time.

Properly Plan for the Future

Little things could make a big difference as our industry matures, and third parties will evaluate your operations based on how well you have executed sound fundamentals. Further refine your exit strategy planning by answering the five future planning questions outlined in Figure 49-2. There are many other issues to consider when developing an optimum exit strategy. This chapter will address three: 1) physical plant, 2) revenue enhancement and 3) expense reduction. Each of these impact Net Operating Income (NOI), the key element in the exit value equation.

FIGURE 49-2
ARE YOU PROPERLY PLANNING FOR THE FUTURE?

1. **Do you have a proactive sales and marketing program, or are you just waiting for prospective residents to show up?**
2. **Are there any emerging trends that could alter your current resident referral patterns?**
3. **How is the aging-in-place of both your residents and your physical plant likely to affect your competitiveness over the next five years?**
4. **Are you using appropriate reserve funds to improve living units and public spaces while maintaining equitable pricing?**
5. **Do you have a detailed capital investment plan; accumulating replacement reserve dollars to allow your community to remain in "like new" condition?**

Moore Diversified Services, Inc.

Keeping up with the changing market means also investing constantly in such things as advanced computer software, training and education, and capital equipment. Whether you are a self-contained, internally operated for-profit or not-for-profit organization, charge your community a management fee of approximately 5 percent of net revenues. This won't hurt your financial profile, as lenders expect to see such an assessment as a normal line item under operating expenses.

But execute investments wisely. You can't afford to spend too much or change too little. Financial guidelines can help you decide how much is too much, but use them with caution. Different communities have different accounting systems and prices will vary according to your location, target market and competition.

Avoid the Physical Plant Cap 'X' Trap

A successful exit strategy negotiation with a potential buyer could raise a serious issue that experienced CEOs know as the *Cap 'X' value discount.* Cap 'X' is a capital investment concept dealing with capital expenditures or "reserves for replacement". For a new property, this is an imputed operations expense line item of approximately $250 to $350 per unit per year. Cap 'X' is expensed and reserved for future capital investment needs of a routine, generally predictable nature (cosmetic refurbishment, etc.). But for an older property with some improperly managed, deferred maintenance, Cap 'X' could become a deal-killing issue. For that property, buyers will try to negotiate a Cap 'X' allocation/expense as high as $700 per unit per year. For a 150-unit property, that's a value reduction of over $580,000. For example, the potential buyer's work papers might look like this: 150 units times $700 versus $350 per unit per year reflects a $350 per unit difference.

The $350 per unit difference times 150 units equals $105,000 per year divided by a 9.0 percent capitalization rate ($52,500 ÷ .090) resulting in a value reduction impact of $583,333. So, you can significantly enhance your future exit position by properly managing capital improvements while avoiding deferred maintenance problems.

Revenue Enhancement

There are two major opportunities for revenue enhancement; optimizing occupancy and ensuring that you pass all proper costs on to the consumer. In some markets, maximizing occupancy (net of turnover) may be difficult to accomplish in today's markets. However, you should be evaluating everything possible and reasonable to enhance stabilized occupancy.

Expense Reduction

The big areas of potential expense reduction are dietary, direct care for assisted living and CCRC's, and liability insurance premiums. Dietary expenses for independent living typically range from approximately $15 to $19 per resident-day. Liability insurance premiums are likely to be a largely unpredictable and uncontrollable wild card for the next several years.

For CCRC's, direct care costs offer the highest level of cost reduction potential. In working through your exit strategy, address the following three questions:

1. How efficient - really - are your direct care CNAs in serving your residents?
2. How many minutes of hands-on direct care per 24-hour day are being delivered to each individual resident?
3. Assuming you are not offering guaranteed Type 'A' life care, do you have a practical system to capture those costs and pass them on to the senior consumer in the form of an accurate and equitable tiered pricing strategy?

Don't accept your first set of answers on these important questions. Check their accuracy and explore what it would take to favorably improve responses to these important issues. Just a $1 per resident-day reduction in a 180-unit CCRC's operating expenses (less than 1 percent) could increase your selling value by approximately $679,000 [1].

There are a number of other strategies that can be deployed to enhance the selling value of your community or portfolio of properties.

[1] 180 units x 365 days x 93 percent occupancy = 61,101 resident-days x $1.00 = $61,101 ÷ .090 capitalization rate = $678,900. The 9.0 percent cap rate reflects the blended product mix within a typical CCRC.

Capitalization Rate Really Determines Value

The key value indicator for your community is your net operating income. As an exit strategy, a buyer will generally look at your community as an income producing "black box". In today's market (2009), these potential buyers (or lenders) are likely to value your independent living community at the Net Operating Income (NOI) level using a capitalization rate of approximately 8.5 to 9.5 percent. This means that, in the short run, they are willing to initially realize an 8.5 to 9.5 percent cap rate. This tells you and potential buyers and lenders about how much cash they can afford to invest for these appropriate returns. The actual determination of value is much more complex, but these are the basics. Refer to Appendix C for more details on cap rates.

This simple exit strategy rule of thumb for value indicates that, for every extra dollar of annual net operating income you realize, the value of your community increases by about $10 or more. This can be accomplished by either enhancing revenues or decreasing expenses. Remember, cash flow is the "lifeblood" of your community; whether you are a for-profit having to answer to lenders and investors or a not-for-profit struggling to fund an ongoing charitable mission.

Is Selling Out a New Business Model?

In the final analysis, some owner/operators may consider the exit strategy exercise only useful for improving their operations for long-run ownership. Not necessarily. Some public companies are making the transition from having an asset intensive balance sheet to executing a hotel/hospitality industry business model. That means that their name, image and reputation - their branding - is focusing on long-term *management* with other third parties *owning* the real estate. These off-balance sheet strategies are not just for public companies. Some large scale owner/operators may cash out completely while others may sell the real estate, but remain as a manager or leasee of the core business operations. Some smaller operators are selling their real estate and managing back the operations to optimize their estate planning objectives, while maintaining an ongoing business/financial residual. Properly structured long-term management contracts or leases can make these business model exit strategies a synergistic, win-win situation for both buyer and seller.

Call to Action

There are many owner/operators who have not considered or do not realize that, all things considered, it might be appropriate to execute an exit strategy. Kenny Rogers' advice in his classic country and western song – ***"You've got to know when to hold 'em and know when the fold 'em."*** – is certainly sound advice for some senior housing sponsors and owner/operators. Sometimes your smartest move is to get out of the game. Give this careful consideration.

But, whether you plan to fold your cards soon or hold them for a very long time, having a sound exit strategy is your ace in the hole.

CHAPTER 50

PUTTING IT ALL TOGETHER

Survival, Growth, Success and Profitability in the 21st Century

It's time to focus on two frequently heard sound bites:

- ***"What happened to the good old days?"***
- ***"Senior living is not what it used to be."***

I'll add a third one to think about:

- ***"A recession is a terrible opportunity to waste!"***

Our industry is fundamentally sound, but both the external economic environment and senior living business are getting increasingly complex. In senior living, we have a multifaceted business model involving:

1. Real Estate
2. Property Management
3. Food and Beverage
4. Lodging/Hospitality
5. Social Services
6. Health Care Delivery
7. Limited Risk Pool Health Insurance Provider [1]
8. Risk Management
9. Asset Management
10. Information Technology

[1] Type 'A' life care CCRC.

Here is an outline of a six point strategic plan to put it all together:

1. Focus on organic growth. First and foremost, focus on enhancing your *existing operations*. No single strategy will likely have a higher pay-off. This will involve executing three strategies:

- Optimize stabilized occupancy
- Enhance existing financial operations – increasing revenue while possibly reducing expenses
- Consider synergistic growth on your existing campus(es) by adding new revenue producing living arrangements and/or offering synergistic ancillary services such as assistance in living into independent living and, possibly, home health services.

Strike a delicate and critical balance between implementing these strategies without impacting resident satisfaction, standards of care or quality of life.

2. Future growth can be a sound strategy. Increasing the number of revenue producing units can increase the efficiency of both your individual properties and your central office. But always ask this defining question; "***How much is enough?***" Growth for a public company must be relentless. The investment community expects additional good news every 90 days! The public companies use the fancy term, "accretive" when referring to the expected outcomes of sound financial decisions. Accretive can also mean that your future strategies and financial plans result in *positive and prudent growth;* such as increased cash flow, financially responsible expansion in resident services or an increase in your mission objectives.

3. Make market-driven not situation-driven decisions. Seniors and their families are primarily focused on product, price, value and choice. They care little about your *challenge* or *situation*; their interests are market-driven. Their frame of reference is likely to be heavily influenced by what your competitors offer. How, realistically, do you stack up?

4. Constantly ask "what if" questions. This involves conducting internal financial sensitivity analyses while keeping an eye on the external competitive market and financial situation. There will always be boom/bust business cycles that will require execution of prudent business recovery plans.

5. Everyone needs an exit strategy. This applies to you even if you plan to hold your property indefinitely. Why? The reason is simple. Your long-term holding strategy will not be successful if it doesn't consider an acceptable exit strategy.

Simply stated, an exit strategy asks the hypothetical question: ***"If I sold my community based on current market conditions, would I be pleased or disappointed by the financial results?"*** If you'd be disappointed, ask yourself an additional question: ***"What can I do in the next 12 to 18 months to improve the outcome of this hypothetical transaction?"*** The "hypothetical" exit strategy is the *acid test* for project viability.

6. Take a realistic look at the future. Finally, revisit the past with 20/20 hindsight but, equally important, look to the future with an entrepreneurial vision. This is my final call to action!

In this book, I've devoted 50 chapters to help you survive and prosper in the short-run, while properly planning for the future in the long-run. I wish you survival, growth, success and profitability in the future.

Jim Moore, 2009

APPENDICES

APPENDIX A

OVERVIEW OF MARKET AND FINANCIAL FEASIBILITY

An entire book could be devoted to just market and financial feasibility. The purpose of this appendix is to provide the outline or structure for this very important part of the project planning process.

Market and Financial Feasibility As A Closed Loop

Feasibility methodology is gradually evolving from an art to a science. But the process still requires a tremendous application of professional judgment and conventional wisdom. The days of, ***"If I build it, they will come"*** are over. Some of the classical feasibility analysis mistakes of the 1980s and 1990s were:

1. Inadequate, improper and erroneous input assumptions
2. Faulty methodology
3. Some theories or hypotheses not supported by sound empirical data
4. Insufficient competitive analysis and field investigations
5. Flawed data analysis and conclusions
6. No direct linkage between market feasibility *outputs* and financial pro forma *inputs*
7. Failure to keep up with the ever-changing market

8. Using the rationale that inflation (growth of senior households) would compensate for any mistakes or overbuilding
9. Relying on incorrect age cohorts, income levels and annual turnover projections, etc.
10. Failure to effectively address "Aging-in-Place"

Item six is one of the most critical elements of the overall planning process. As Figure A-1 illustrates, market and financial feasibility must be *closely integrated using a closed loop philosophy.* Initially, the market feasibility study *outputs* must drive the *inputs* to the financial pro forma. The pro forma, in turn, is heavily influenced by the initial design and overall development business plan. Any future changes, such as project cost increases, must be immediately transmitted back to the pro forma. If the pro forma requires increased revenues, the market feasibility study must be reworked to determine if all of these changes and their impacts are still acceptable in the marketplace.

Market Feasibility Study Outline

It is important to have a detailed, definitive work plan for market feasibility; with tangible and specific expected outcomes. The following outline can be used as a guide if you are conducting an in-house market feasibility study or preparing a Request for Proposal (RFP) for engaging a consultant.

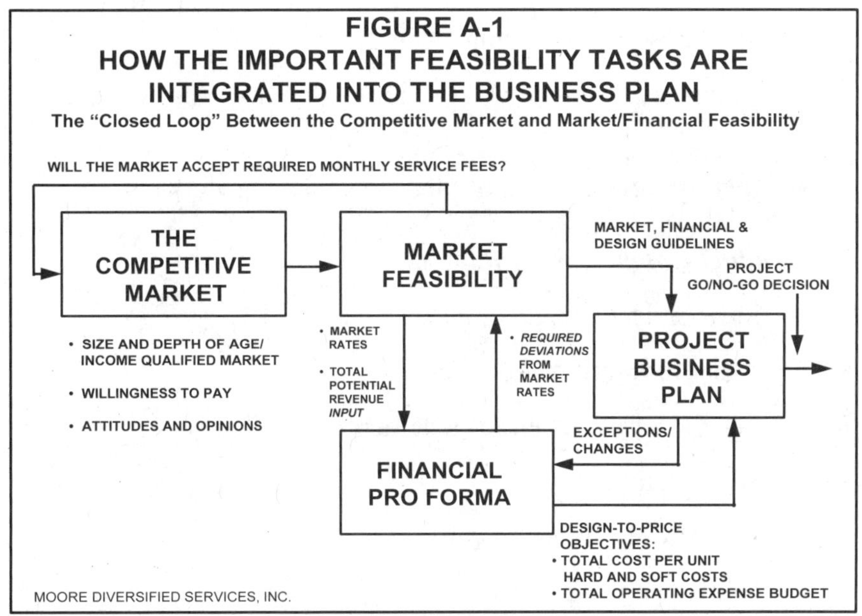

1. ***Determine Relevant Market Areas***
   - Define the primary, secondary and tertiary market areas
   - Estimate impact of population mobility trends on seniors
   - Determine impact of decision influencers (adult children)
   - Obtain resident origin profiles of competition, where available

2. ***Conduct Demographic Economic Base Study***
   - Determine total number of age & income qualified households
   - Conduct age cohort segmentation and growth projections
   - Establish senior consumer qualifying income criteria

- Determine level of incidence for need for assistance with activities of daily living (ADLs)
- Determine impact of home equity on consumer affordability
- Identify relevant and prudent forecasting safety margins

3. ***Conduct Competitive Analysis***[1]

- Independent living/congregate care/CCRC
- Assisted living/personal care
- Special care Alzheimer's/dementia facilities
- Nursing homes
- Acute care, sub-acute care
- Home health agencies
- Other senior housing products and services (senior apartments, subsidized elderly housing, etc.)
- Estimate managed care impacts – where relevant

4. ***Conduct Specific Site Analysis***

- Subject site description
- Access/egress characteristics
- Drive-by visibility/traffic counts, etc
- Surrounding development/adjacent property owners
- Potential buffers and set-backs

[1]Must include both existing and announced projects

- Appropriate zoning
- Supporting amenities, benefits and features
- Evaluate/rank alternative sites - where applicable

5. ***Estimate Overall Project Capture Rates and Market Share***
   - By age cohort
   - By qualifying income threshold criteria
   - By need for assistance with Activities of Daily Living (ADLs)
   - Primary versus secondary market area
   - Consider annual resident turnover
   - Adjust for competitive impacts (existing and planned)
   - Weighting of competition – where applicable

6. ***Conduct Unit Absorption Scenarios***
   - Estimate time to stabilized occupancy (including pre-marketing efforts)
   - Adjust for unit turnover during fill-up

7. ***Recommend Final Product Mix***
   - Unit types
   - Number of units/unit mix
   - Individual living areas/unit size
   - Pricing by unit type

- Consider special market/product segmentation:
  - Assisted living
  - Special care dementia
  - Catered living
  - Etc.
- Identify common area amenities
- Recommend services, amenities, benefits and features

Figure A-2 depicts the typical sequence to follow when evaluating your project's market feasibility.

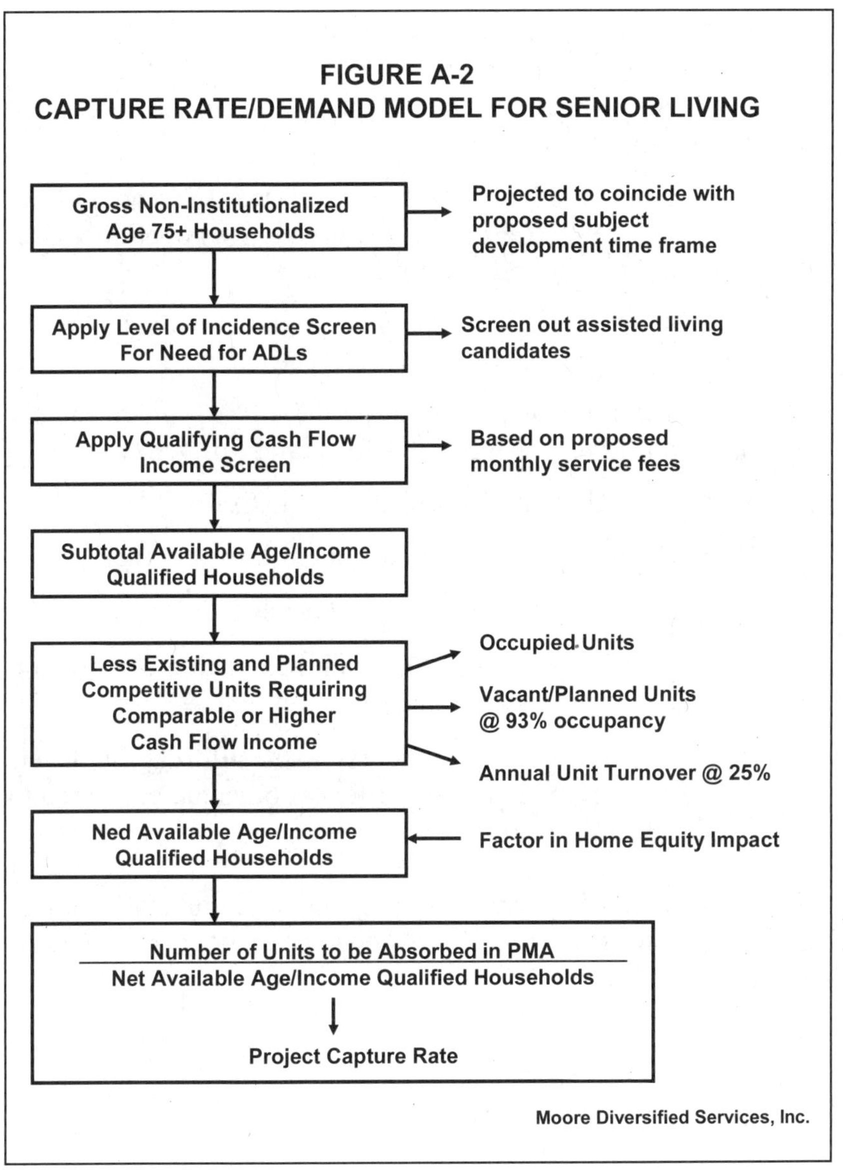
FIGURE A-2
CAPTURE RATE/DEMAND MODEL FOR SENIOR LIVING
Gross Non-Institutionalized Age 75+ Households
Projected to coincide with proposed subject development time frame
Apply Level of Incidence Screen For Need for ADLs
Screen out assisted living candidates
Apply Qualifying Cash Flow Income Screen
Based on proposed monthly service fees
Subtotal Available Age/Income Qualified Households
Less Existing and Planned Competitive Units Requiring Comparable or Higher Cash Flow Income
Occupied Units
Vacant/Planned Units @ 93% occupancy
Annual Unit Turnover @ 25%
Ned Available Age/Income Qualified Households
Factor in Home Equity Impact
Number of Units to be Absorbed in PMA
Net Available Age/Income Qualified Households
Project Capture Rate
Moore Diversified Services, Inc.

"Bottom-Line" Answers Provided by Market Feasibility

The ultimate outputs of the market feasibility study must answer the following five questions:

1. What percent of the *net* supply of the age and income qualified market (allowing for turnover, competition, etc.) must I capture in order to fill my project?
2. How is the competition doing and is there enough demand elasticity in the market for my project?
3. Is my site really as attractive as I think it is – or am I really situation-driven when I should be market-driven?
4. How fast will my project fill-up – realistically?
5. Does my final product mix meet the following criteria:
    - Responds to market wants and needs
    - Compares favorably with both the existing competition and new potential projects in the future
    - Pricing is consistent with reasonable affordability levels of my target market and offers good value compared to local competition

There is another important question which requires much more analysis: **"Will my market-responsive project concept be financially feasible?"**

Financial Feasibility/Pro Forma Outline

1. ***Develop Key Inputs to Realistic and Accurate Capital Budget***
   - Raw land cost allocation
   - Site development costs
   - Preliminary construction cost estimates
   - Contractor general conditions factor
   - Construction contingency
   - Construction interest
   - Construction time period
   - Development fees
   - Architectural and engineering fees
   - Furniture, fixtures & equipment
   - Legal and accounting fees
   - Financing costs
   - Market and financial feasibility studies
   - Initial absorption/fill-up reserve fund
   - Detailed marketing budget
   - Project contingency

2. ***Establish Total Capital/Debt Structure Requirements, Mix and Sources***
   - Equity
   - Debt
   - Other capital sources
   - Credit enhancement

3. ***Establish and Plan for Required Lender/Underwriter Criteria***
   - Debt to equity ratio
   - Debt service coverage ratio:
     - Initial
     - At stabilized occupancy
   - Debt service reserve fund
   - Cash to debt ratio
   - Average debt per unit

4. ***Set Design-to-Price Objectives***
   - Implement the closed loop concept (see Figure A-1)
   - Conduct cost containment/value engineering effort

5. ***Project Realistic Operating Expense Scenarios***
   - Actual experience (if existing community)
   - Industry data base benchmarks
   - Specific project analysis

6. ***Determine Pricing Options***
   - Flat monthly service fee
   - Monthly service fee with tiered add-on charges for increased ADLs by:
     - Levels of care/case work-up
     - Additional minutes per day for added ADLs
   - Develop preliminary menu of pricing options
   - Implement cash flow impact scenarios for various pricing options
   - Make final pricing policy recommendations

7. ***Implement Multiple Scenarios of Pricing Options Short List***
   - Based on quantitative results of previous tasks
   - Insure adequacy of:
     - Net operating income
     - Cash flow
     - Debt service coverage
   - Implement computer-driven sensitivity analysis of critical financial variables and assumptions

8. ***Estimate Total Revenues, Expenses, Net Operating Income, Debt Service, Cash Flow and Debt Service Coverage Factor***
   - During fill-up
   - At stabilized occupancy
   - 5 and 7 years in the future

9. ***Conduct Discounted Cash Flow Analysis***
   - Use appropriate capitalization and discount rates
   - Present value
   - Internal rate of return
   - Cash flow
   - Cash-on-cash return

10. ***Run a Financial Sensitivity Analysis***
    - Interest cost at +/- 1%
    - NOI sensitivity at +/- 5%
    - Fill-up rate at +/- 2 units/month

The critical questions that the completed financial pro forma should answer include, but are not necessarily limited to, the following:

1. Have I included *everything* in the capital budget that will provide adequate funds to bring my project to stabilized occupancy?

2. Are there reasonable and adequate contingencies in the pro forma?

3. Are the debt, equity and interest rate assumptions realistic?

4. Will I meet all the criteria likely to be required by lenders?

5. Have I realistically projected revenues and conservatively estimated operating expenses?

6. Will my pricing strategy cover not only my current costs; but also my best estimate of future costs – including potential cost creep?

7. Is the overall project financially prudent; delivering appropriate financial safety margins and entrepreneurial returns – after all expenses and debt service payments have been covered?

The final critical question to ask is, ***"Have I updated my market and financial feasibility study to accurately reflect all of the changes that have taken place during the planning and development process?"***

APPENDIX B

MORTGAGE LOAN CONSTANTS

A loan constant is an easy way to estimate your total debt service payment for a senior living community. The loan constant provides *one number or multiplier* that takes into consideration *three key characteristics* of an installment loan:

1. Principal payment
2. Interest payment
3. Amortization (term) of loan

Example:

Referring to Figure B-1, what is the debt payment per unit for an independent living community where the average total (all-in) cost per unit is $190,000; with 75 percent debt ($142,500), 25 percent equity ($47,500) @ 7 percent interest for 30 years?

Referring to Figure B-1:

$142,500 x .0798 = $11,371 per unit per year
Or
$ 948 per month

The annual debt service for a total of 150 units is shown as:

$11,371 per unit x 150 units = $1.7 million

You can use the debt constant table in Figure B-1 to quickly and easily calculate your total debt (mortgage) payments for various combinations of loan characteristics.

FIGURE B-1
MORTGAGE LOAN DEBT CONSTANTS

	MORTGAGE TERM[1]			
Interest Rate	**20 Years**	**25 Years**	**30 Years**	**40 Years**
5.00%	7.92%	7.02%	6.44%	5.79%
5.50%	8.25%	7.37%	6.81%	6.19%
6.00%	8.60%	7.73%	7.19%	6.60%
6.50%	8.95%	8.10%	7.58%	7.03%
7.00%	9.30%	8.48%	7.98%	7.46%
7.50%	9.67%	8.87%	8.39%	7.90%
8.00%	10.04%	9.26%	8.81%	8.34%
8.50%	10.41%	9.66%	9.23%	8.80%
9.00%	10.80%	10.07%	9.66%	9.26%
9.50%	11.19%	10.48%	10.09%	9.72%
10.00%	11.58%	10.90%	10.53%	10.19%
10.50%	11.98%	11.33%	10.98%	10.66%
11.00%	12.39%	11.76%	11.43%	11.14%

Moore Diversified Services, Inc.

[1] Based on monthly loan amortization.

APPENDIX C

THE CAPITALIZATION RATE CONCEPT

For some experienced operators, the concept of capitalization rates is very familiar and useful. For others, it may be a very foreign technical term. But, like the loan constants discussed in Appendix B, capitalization rates can play a useful role in your strategic planning and in financial communications with lenders, investors, buyers and sellers.

As used in this book, ***the capitalization rate ("cap rate") is typically the annual debt-free (unleveraged) <u>cash return</u> that prudent and experienced investors would expect to realize from a specific cash investment.*** That's typically the Net Operating Income (NOI) margin or EBITDAR (Earnings Before Interest, Taxes, Depreciation, Amortization and Rent). Currently cap rates for assisted living typically range from 10.0 to 11.0 percent and 8.5 to 9.5 percent for independent living. A 9.0 percent *typical* independent living cap rate is frequently used throughout this book.

Some Examples

Independent Living Community Potential Sale Value – If an investor expects a 9.0 percent return, what might he or she be willing to invest for a community delivering a stabilized occupancy NOI of $2,000,000 in order to yield that 9.0 percent return?

$$\frac{\$2{,}000{,}000}{0.09} = \$22.2 \text{ million}$$

In a similar manner, you can evaluate the incremental *imputed* increase (or decrease) in your project's value for any situation that would impact net operating income (NOI).

Example:

A ***capital investment*** of \$50,000 is expected to save \$12,000 per year in operating expenses; increasing NOI by a similar amount. How will your intrinsic project value be impacted (increased) at a 9.0 percent cap rate?

$$\frac{\$12{,}000}{0.09} = \$133{,}333$$

This means that the one-time \$50,000 capital investment that saves \$12,000 in annual operating expenses has increased the intrinsic value of your community by approximately \$133,333.

Cap rates are used throughout this book to quantify the dollar impact or financial sensitivity on value for certain strategies such as operating expense changes (increase or decrease), capital investment expected outcomes, and changes in revenue that impact NOI. Keep in mind that cap rates for various senior living products can vary as a function of changing market conditions.

INDEX

<u>Note</u>: In addition to this index, this book has a very definitive Table of Contents by subject matter. Consider using the Table of Contents as an expanded index.